Undead Labor

Undead Labor

Capitalism's Zombie Worker

David Bering-Porter

University of Minnesota Press
Minneapolis
London

Chapter 2 was previously published as "Analogy in Ruins: Populism, Transgression, and the Zombie," *Culture Machine* 19 (2020), available at https://culturemachine.net/.

Published by the University of Minnesota Press
111 Third Avenue South, Suite 290
Minneapolis, MN 55401-2520
http://www.upress.umn.edu

ISBN 978-1-5179-1784-5 (hc)
ISBN 978-1-5179-1785-2 (pb)

A Cataloging-in-Publication record for this book is available from the Library of Congress.

Printed on acid-free paper

Contents

Introduction
CAN'T STOP, WON'T STOP, OR THE ZOMBIE'S ENDLESS LABOR

Zombies have never been observed to sleep or rest under any circumstances.

—Max Brooks, *The Zombie Survival Guide*

IT MIGHT SEEM STRANGE to think about a sleeping zombie, but the truth remains: Zombies never sleep, and they never stop. This relentlessness is one reason the zombie seems alarming and frightening, and it is also why this monster has become such a lasting terror in our cultural imagination. Fast or slow, zombies propel themselves forward with a single-minded determination and a ceaseless drive to move and consume. The most archetypal depictions of the zombie from films like *Night of the Living Dead* and television shows like *The Walking Dead* show it as a slow and shambling monster, easily avoided in small numbers. What makes the zombie a threat is that it will follow you without self-awareness or self-regard; it keeps coming and coming, and while eventually you will need to rest or sleep, the zombie will not.

Zombies can't stop and they won't stop, and that is terrifying. More than that, there is something to this play on words, this turn of phrase, that is genuinely significant: The phrase "can't stop, won't stop" has been circulating in the discourse of rap and hip hop for over thirty years, where it has signified resilience and determination in hip hop lyrics. The phrase was codified in the genre when Young Gunz released their debut single by that name in 2003, although the meaning was likely inspired in the early days of hip hop when the Sugarhill Gang's song "Rapper's Delight" appeared in

1979, which repeatedly featured the refrain "and you don't stop . . ." Since then, it has been picked up by such luminaries in the scene as King Combs, Usher, and The Lox, to name only a few. It is the name of at least one hip hop duo and the title of one of the best histories of the hip hop generation, written by Jeff Chang.[1] The phrase "can't stop, won't stop" signifies a kind of guiding principle for a culture of hustling, laboring from the margins, and doing so by whatever means necessary. The phrase seems to call back and privilege a version of the Protestant work ethic (and the spirit of capitalism, in Max Weber's terms) championed in Black culture, but certainly not limited to Black culture, much like hip hop itself. It is a version of a work ethic that belies an underlying and fundamental precarity. You hustle because you must. You work hard, often twice as hard, because there is no other option if you want to survive, let alone thrive, in a system that traditionally marginalizes and excludes those not already born into the hierarchy of privilege that has been structured by histories of race and class.

"Can't stop, won't stop" is a phrase, a mantra, a kind of performative speech act, meant to situate the speaker in a position of agency. Generally, it is spoken as a way of signifying the speaker's drive, their grit, their determination and commitment to success. The phrase is meant to convey a feeling and an impression of being unstoppable. Certainly, this is the way it is used and deployed by Young Gunz, and in hip hop and Black culture more broadly. But there is also a way in which this phrase—"can't stop, won't stop"—signifies something darker and more literal: an unwillingness and inability to stop because of the consequences. You can't stop and you won't stop because if you do, whatever is chasing you will catch up. You will slip beneath the waves and drown, swallowed up or left behind by a political and economic system that does not care about you or value you except for your ability to be productive in one form or another. As an ethos, the phrase "can't stop, won't stop" has spread from the discourse of hip hop into an experience of contemporary culture and contemporary capitalism more broadly. The culture of hustling has expanded into the mainstream, evidenced by the rise of the gig economy, a cultural ethos of overwork, and excesses in expectations of production across the economic and political board. Even fields that were traditionally secure now feel increasingly precarious due to an overburdening of work and debt. The phrase has become a mantra for all of us.

More than that, the phrase "can't stop, won't stop" seems to have become a tagline for capitalism today. We can't stop and won't stop in the face of a highly contagious global pandemic. We can't stop and won't stop polluting the environment and mass-producing greenhouse gases even as we see the concrete and immediate consequences of global climate change and the deleterious effects on global health and longevity. We can't stop and won't stop the mass incarceration of people of color and Indigenous people at disproportionate rates and the utilization of their labor without proper compensation. We can't stop and won't stop an epidemic of gun violence in the United States, along with police violence, violence against queer and trans communities, and the control and legislation of women's bodies. The list goes on. As the Marxist literary critic Fredric Jameson once said, "It is easier to imagine the end of the world than to imagine the end of capitalism."[2] All of this, I believe, has something to do with the zombie and with what I have come to understand as *undead labor,* a concept I develop over the course of this book.

This book grows out of the fundamental notions of living and dead labor that Karl Marx used to understand the dynamics of labor and work, and it takes the subsequent generation of value under capitalism as central to my analysis. Undead labor is a mode of production and a form of life, rooted in excess, that reveals how any imposed limit or indication of finitude is anathema to capital. The fantasy at the heart of capitalism is the dream of limitless expansion and endless growth; a vision of unlimited life, able to produce and reproduce without impediment and without end, unfettered even by that ultimate limitation: death. Out of the shadow of this capitalist delirium, in which the very notion of death has been foreclosed, is born a form of life without death and an ideal of production without limit. The embodiment of undead labor is not some idealized captain of industry or self-actualized worker, bringing their labor to the marketplace without impediment. Instead, what we find is a version of what appears anytime an impossible ideal is imposed as a demand on a body that is necessarily constrained by the limits of the possible: a contradiction, a psychosis, and/or a monster, which in this case takes the form of the zombie. The zombie, and undead labor more broadly, haunt capitalism from its early incarnations in the slave plantations of the colonial period to its more recent iterations as a world-ending virus or plague in the neoliberal (or biopolitical) era. Understood in the context of undead labor, the phrase "can't stop, won't stop" starts to seem like a line from a horror movie—an inability to stop even in the face of imminent catastrophe, like a car with its brake lines cut.

To point out that the zombie can't stop and won't stop—or, conversely, to consider "can't stop, won't stop" in relation to the zombie—is to effectively turn the phrase on its head; to take away its connotations of agency and ambition and to think of it, instead, as a pathology. What does it mean to think about the zombie as the kind of monster that cannot stop and will not stop, that cannot rest and is condemned to move and work endlessly and in perpetuity? What if we were to consider the zombie's inability to stop as a symptom of a larger problem? The zombie serves as a diagram of a pathological contradiction within capitalism that appears within the extensive mythology that surrounds it. The zombie has shadowed this modern political economy across its evolution from its origins into the present moment. I would ask the reader to take seriously the phrase "can't stop, won't stop" as one intimately connected to the zombie and to join me in the exploration of undead labor that takes place in this book. This is an attempt to diagnose and understand undead labor as a problem, one that brings with it questions of race, labor, and the production of value, and how they have shaped the zombie as the monster we know today in its many incarnations across histories, genres, and platforms. This reading of undead labor, through the figure of the zombie, sheds light on the conditions not just of the dead but also of the living, and reflects our own conditions of both life and labor through the demands placed on us as bodies and as subjects by capitalism.

This book explores the problem of undead labor through a series of case studies, each of which engages with questions of race, labor, and value in different ways that help define a complex concept. The zombie serves as a primary example, though not exclusively, and this is really a story of undead labor rather than a book about zombies, even if the zombie acts as a main protagonist. When we think of the zombie, we typically imagine something we might see in the long-running television program *The Walking Dead* (2010–22): a shambling body in a state of decay with vacant, dead eyes and skin rotting away to reveal the flesh and sinew beneath. It is likely cannibalistic or cephalophagic, driven by a singular drive to consume the flesh of the living. A more classical view might look more like the monster in black-and-white from George A. Romero's genre-defining film *Night of the Living Dead* (1968), in which the decay and gore is toned down but still visceral and rotting, relentlessly pursuing the living. A more recent iteration might look like the zombies from the hit Netflix Korean high school drama *All of Us Are Dead* from 2022, which follows bodies that contort and whose bones crack and snap with the force of their infection, and the violence of their transformation from the living to the undead.

These vivid examples and images stick with us and hold our attention as we thrill, laugh, and sometimes cry along with the sometimes slow, sometimes frenetic movements of these bodies on screen and their living antagonists. But each of these images, each iteration of the zombie, comes later in the longer story of the zombie and of undead labor that this book seeks to excavate. This story begins in Haiti, in what was then the French colony of Saint Domingue, sometime between 1659 and 1804, when the Western half of the island of Hispaniola was under French control. Rumors of the zombie circulated in and around the approximately eight thousand sugar plantations that served as the colony's raison d'être at the time, which was the crown jewel in France's colonial empire, sometimes called "the pearl of the Antilles"; and "on the eve of the Haitian Revolution, Saint Domingue was the most lucrative colony on earth."[3] The zombies at the time looked much like the enslaved people who were brought to live and die on the island, impoverished and ragged, so weary they seemed catatonic, although the zombie was said to have had a vacant stare that marked them as distinct from the living.

This is the zombie discussed in the first chapter, "'A Mechanical Semblance of Life': Toward a Theory of Undead Labor," which outlines the central argument of the book by developing a theory of undead labor, defined as value production extracted from living bodies pushed beyond their structural limits. To frame these ideas, this chapter looks to early examples of the zombie from travelogues and ethnographic literature, drawing on the writings of William

Seabrook and Zora Neale Hurston, each of whom gives an account of an encounter with "real" zombies in Haiti in the early twentieth century. Using the zombie as the prime example, this chapter situates this central concept within discourses of living and dead labor from Marx, as well as notions of racial capitalism and theories of value from thinkers such as Cedric J. Robinson and Vincent Brown.

This chapter develops a theory of undeadness intimately tied to questions of race, commodity production, and the reproduction of labor power in the form of living bodies. Understanding the zombie's origins in the history of Haiti and transatlantic slavery more broadly, this chapter situates these important discussions of slavery in relation to the plantation as a key site of undead labor, where the individual human subject was instrumentalized and abstracted into a state removed from both life and death, into a mythic, liminal zone of undeadness. Integral to this understanding of undeadness and undead labor is a close and contrasting reading of Michel Foucault's theories of exclusion and enclosure as technologies of power, alongside a historical reading of the foreclosure of death that appears in the work of Philippe Ariès, a contemporary of Foucault who takes up the exclusion of death quite explicitly in his writing on death in modernity. Taken together, Foucault and Ariès help to frame the significance of undeadness in a detailed reading of history, economy, and ontology that will serve as the theoretical keystone to this book.

Zombies evolve and transform over the course of their century-long history within the popular imagination. The first chapter explores the roots of the zombie, and undead labor, in the colonial plantation, laying a foundation on which to consider other, more recent iterations of undead labor as a form of life and a mode of production that shadows capitalism, even today. Undead labor begins with the excessive demands made on life and labor under the conditions of chattel slavery, but it evolves over time, just as capital does. Marx famously imagined that political economy itself belonged to an evolutionary trajectory, where examples of primitive accumulation like chattel slavery eventually (and for Marx, necessarily) give way to a capitalist mode of production. He imagined that the barbarity of primitive accumulations like slavery is eventually replaced with newer, more efficient systems of production and exchange, although writers such as Edward Baptist offer compelling evidence to the contrary.[4] Regardless, it is worth considering the tensions within Marx's own account of the purchase and exchange of labor power under capitalism.

In a much-cited passage of *Capital*, Marx imagines the meeting of two equal parties, one with labor power to sell and the other in the market to buy. This exchange takes place in the open market, subject to the guidelines and protections of the public sphere, but after the contract is made binding, the situation changes and the balance of power shifts. Marx says, "Let us therefore, in company with the owner of money and the owner of labour-power, leave this noisy sphere, where everything takes place on the surface and in full view of everyone, and follow them into the hidden abode of production, on whose threshold there hangs the notice, 'no admittance except on business.' Here we shall see, not only how capital produces, but how capital itself is produced."[5] The birthplace of capital is not, as one might imagine, in the public eye of the marketplace but is, instead, in this "hidden abode of production," which is a scene of labor. This passage is important because it grounds the birth of capital in living labor. It may have been bought and paid for by the owner of wealth, but labor is still responsible for creating capital, the birthplace of value. Speaking to the same passage from Marx, the Marxist feminist political theorist Kathi Weeks points out that "by changing the site of the analysis from a market-based exchange to a wage-based production, the labor-process itself—that is, the activity of labor and the social relations that shape, direct, and manage it—will be revealed as the locus of capitalist valorization."[6] Thus, even when wages and recompense enter the picture, the excessive demands of capital are actually synonymous with the demands made on living labor and its productive potential. When those demands made on living labor exceed the structural and necessary capacities of the laboring body—for example, when the demand to labor continually stretches past the threshold of life into something beyond, pushing the physical to the metaphysical—undead labor is born and emerges.

Weeks continues this line of thinking when she points out that work is one of the most common sites of domination and exploitation in contemporary society. Generally, it is argued that wages compensate the worker for their labor power, but even Marx was aware that in the "hidden abode of production," behind the closed doors of labor itself, something troubling remained. Weeks argues that "Marx too would seem to be quite clear that the problem with work cannot be reduced to the terms of its recompense, but rather extends into the very heart of the wage relation and the labor process it commands. That is why he insists on describing the program of raising wages as only '*better payment for the slave.*'"[7] There is something rotten at the heart of the labor relation under capitalism, even wage labor, and Marx is aware of it. It is the contention of this book that the history of undead labor, as well as the history of the zombie, help to clarify this trouble by showing the excessive demands of capital, which finds its roots not in wage labor but in slavery and the symbolic transformations of the human subject into something abstracted, objectified, and degraded or reduced—something *less* than human.

From its inception, the zombie has worked as an analogy for slavery and racial capitalism, but starting in the 1960s, the zombie's function as an analogy went into hypertrophy. In the second chapter—"Analogies of Undeadness: Populism, Transgression, and the Zombie"—we see the zombie become a metaphor for everything. Ranging from "zombie economics" to "zombie technology," from "zombie cars" to "zombie liberalism," the zombie has become a voracious force of analogy that appears across a variety of platforms, fields, and cultural locations, always crossing the discursive boundaries that delimit those networks of meaning. Just as the zombie tends to wear down and burst through whatever boundaries (windows, walls, doors) it encounters on screen, so, too, does the zombie transgress the formal and generic boundaries it encounters in discourse. At the level of form, content, and genre, the zombie proliferates, and the zombie analogy appears everywhere, serving as a stand-in for nearly anything. This chapter explores the zombie as analogy to better understand the dynamics of contagion, understood as the proliferation of sameness, looking to what the zombie can tell us about populism, overproduction, and media in the twenty-first century.

As a central case study, this chapter explores a recent version of the zombie narrative as it appears in the film *World War Z* (Marc Forster, 2013), which stages the zombie as a pandemic, a crisis on a world scale, and the cause of a breakdown of the nation-state and the global order. Depictions of the zombie in *World War Z* reveal changes in the monster in both form and content. At the level of narrative, the zombie appears as a monster of the masses and the population, functioning as a disease that spreads rapidly through violent contact. Yet, at the level of form, the digital special effects used to generate the mass dynamics of the zombies on screen reveal another set of connections to repetition, sameness, and stochastic processes in the film, providing an important perspective on how recent iterations of the zombie still demonstrate undead labor. Since the mid-twentieth century, the zombie has been a metaphor for the masses, and through an exploration of the semiotic mechanisms of analogy, this chapter refines a vision of the zombie as a populist monster that reflects the complex relations of populism to the population in the contemporary discourses of biopolitics and capitalism.

Chapter 2 explores the symbolic potency of undead labor and the excessive force of the zombie as a metaphor of viral infection and production, and in doing so opens up questions about contagion, proliferation, and sameness within the symbolic order. One of the central themes running through this book is that undead labor is founded on a symbolic foreclosure of death. Put another way, the foundation of undead labor is rooted in capitalism's demand that life exceed its own structural limitations and, in turn, this notion of life, unfettered and not limited by death, becomes the ideal to which capitalism aspires. This dream or fantasy of unlimited life and production is a kind of capitalist delirium existing at the heart of modern political economy, and evidence for this exists even within contemporary discourses of economic theory, which argue that a never-ending increase in gross domestic product is necessary for a healthy economy.[8]

Like any system of fantasy or delusion, the capitalist dream of endless growth and expansion shifts and changes depending on conditions and feedback from the world outside. For example, as fields like physics and environmental science continue to contradict the feasibility of unlimited expansion, suggesting that infinite growth is impossible in a finite system with finite resources (along with an array of supporting evidence from the world around us), capitalism turns inward, focusing instead on endogenous resources within the human subject in an attempt to get closer to the dreamed-of source of value. These changes begin in the 1960s with a shift in economic discourse and thinking that reimagines the population as "human capital," a notion popularized by the Chicago School economist Gary Becker, which attempts to account for the skills, knowledge, and information contained within any given populace as a valid investment for capital.

Becker argues for a "different kind of capital," suggesting that in addition to traditional ideas of capital as money in the bank, shares in a corporation, a warehouse full of commodities, or the factories and assembly lines that produced them, it is important to understand that "schooling, a computer training course, expenditures in medical care, and lectures on the virtues of punctuality and honesty are capital too," even going so far as to suggest that "it is fully in keeping with the capital concept as traditionally defined to say that expenditures on education, training, medical care, etc., are investments in capital."[9] The notion of human capital places special emphasis on education and training, with the understanding that these investments have the potential to yield exponential gains in the form of innovation. This has also led to a blithe confidence in mainstream business and economic discourse that innovation, generally in the form of technological development, will save us and make possible the dreams of an ever-expanding economic system.[10]

While this new category of "human capital" initially seems like a more refined economic theory, one that takes into account the significance and value of culture through the production of knowledge in science, psychology, and even the arts and humanities, it is important to remember that this concept still relies on a conception of the human as a raw material for a larger system of production. It is, no doubt, more genteel to render the value of the human in terms of the products of their minds rather than the work of their hands, but in either case, that "hidden abode of production" described by Marx is still the site where capital is created, merely updated to the service economy of the information age. Human capital continues a long tradition of rendering the human as the sole container of value, and in this way the phrase bears uncomfortable echoes of slavery, when the human being was also rendered as a commodity. Even though it emphasizes a more abstract value from the human body than just labor power, the fact remains that the theory of human capital continues the tradition of reinventing the human as a raw material to be consumed and as new territory for expansion—both of which rely on the fantasy of infinite production and the foreclosure of death.

Undeadness is what remains when death is removed from the equation of life and labor. In his profound insights into the intimate network of relations between life, labor, and death, Jean Baudrillard argued for a "challenge to death" that takes place in contemporary political economies. Baudrillard makes the provocative assertion that labor power is actually instituted on death, meaning the conversion of living matter into an abstraction of quantity and symbolic value.[11] As he points out, "A man must die to become labour power. He converts this death into a wage. But the economic violence capital inflicted on him in the equivalence of the wage and labour power is nothing next to the symbolic violence inflicted on him by his definition as a productive force."[12] In other words, what Baudrillard is suggesting is that both a symbolic and economic violence is inflicted on the human when it is redefined as the site, container, and raw material of labor and production. At first it might seem that Baudrillard is aligning capitalism with death, and this is true insofar as equivalence relies on replacing the concrete object with an abstraction or symbolic version. For example, Baudrillard argues that "the equivalence of wages and labour power presupposes the death of the worker, while that of any commodity and any other presupposes the symbolic extermination of objects."[13] Yet this relationship to death is vexed, since here death does not signify any kind of limit to life or physical existence—put another way, it does not stand for finitude in the ways that I have been using the term. Rather, it signifies the transformation of living matter into a symbolic abstraction, which Baudrillard describes as a "mutual neutralisation of life and death in sur-vival, or death *deferred*."[14]

What Baudrillard describes here as a state that is neither alive nor dead, but rather a "sur-vival," playing on the etymology of the term as something that literally means being "on top of" or "in addition to" life, is a kind of excessive or surplus life. This aligns neatly with what I have described in this book as a state of undeadness, in which only life remains once death is symbolically removed or foreclosed from the system. Indeed, Baudrillard even finds a similar point of origin for this nexus of life, death, and labor in the figure of the slave. While it is clear that Baudrillard has in mind the conditions of slavery from the classical period in Rome and ancient

Greece, in which slaves were taken, or "conserved," as a spoil of war in order to be put to work as a resource or an instrument of the household, we can update this significant insight to include the form of chattel slavery that took place in the transatlantic slave trade during the colonial period. Integrating this notion of racial capitalism into this line of thinking, it seems even more significant that for Baudrillard, "labour therefore everywhere draws its inspiration from deferred death."[15] This description of a death, deferred in favor of labor, lends itself to the story of the zombie, and to the theory of undead labor more broadly.

Chapters 1 and 2 of this book deal, in different ways, with this trajectory of labor power from slavery to the symbolic, in which undead labor is founded on excessive demands placed on living bodies pushed beyond the structural and ontological boundaries of life and death. Chapter 1 explores the history of undead labor in terms of slavery and racial capitalism, while chapter 2 takes up the symbolic proliferation that Baudrillard predicts when he describes the end of production in favor of a mode of simulation. The birth of human capital as an idea paves the way toward a reinvestment in the human body, in what has been described by Kaushik Sunder Rajan as "biocapital," as well as the digital revolution, which imagines that knowledge, skill, and digital technology will allow for the endless growth capitalism craves. These two paths—the biological and the digital—are the subject of the next two chapters of this book.

In the third chapter—"Unlimited Life: Capitalist Delirium and Excessive Growth in HeLa and *The Blob*"—undead labor is thought through in a somewhat different context, emphasizing a place of too much life, rather than a return to life through death. Drawing on ideas from biopolitics and Afropessimism, this chapter explores the uncanny vitality at the heart of undeadness. Approaching the foreclosure of death outlined in the first chapter from a different perspective, it looks to the uncanny excesses of life and the matter of the body as it is mediated by race, labor, and value. Illustrating this kind of excessive life, this chapter explores the case of Henrietta Lacks, the African American woman whose cervical cancer was the point of origin for the "immortal" HeLa cell line, and unpacks this example as a key site of undead labor, becoming a twentieth-century example of how the productive and reproductive capacities of the Black body continue to be valorized.

The HeLa cell line is an embodied demonstration of the excessive, cancerous mode of production that has grown out of late capitalism and shows the complex ways in which life and labor intersect with race, science, and technology and lead toward a crisis of overproduction. Providing context and contrast to the HeLa cell line, this chapter looks toward other sites revealing popular fears and anxieties of overproduction and reproduction run amok, finding an important touchstone in the mid-century cult-classic monster movie *The Blob* (Irvin S. Yeaworth, 1958). The eponymous Blob provides another rich example of the horror of life, a life that cannot be killed, but instead grows and devours without limit. This chapter brings in ideas from Hortense Spillers, Alexander Weheliye, and others who attempt to think through the Black body as the site of a symbolic demand for excessive production that follows the technological use of race first discussed in chapter 1. Cancer, capitalism, HeLa, and the Blob are each exemplary of a vision of life without death and speak to the capitalist delirium that threatens both life and death as we know them.

The final chapter of this book—"Putting the Dead to Work: Artificial Intelligence and Undead Labor"—explores the way that digital technologies like machine learning and artificial intelligence are providing another avenue for capital's drive to overcome death as a limit to growth and production. At the *Dalí Lives (via Artificial Intelligence)* exhibition at the Dalí Museum in St. Petersburg, Florida, museumgoers can encounter a version of Salvador Dalí himself. This digital construct has been created by training artificial intelligence on the many writings and media appearances of the eccentric artist, made while he was still alive, which serve as the raw material for the reanimation of those images to effectively re-create Dalí in speech, appearance, and mannerism. It is a digital construct programmed to greet visitors to the museum. This digital reanimation of Salvador Dalí uses the indexical traces embedded in photographs, cinema, radio, and television as the corporeal remains that are then utilized in the creation of a digital zombie, brought to life and put to work in a digital milieu. This chapter explores the effects and implications of undead labor in the digital afterlife, looking to case studies like the *Dalí Lives* exhibition and other instances of "undead" AI, such as the Replika app, a chatbot and "artificial friend" whose history also involves memorializing and reviving the dead into a semblance of life. Using the framework of undead labor developed throughout this book, the final chapter asks how artificial intelligence brings about new possibilities for zombification and undead labor in the digital age.

The question of a digital zombie, emerging from the media archives that we leave behind—archives that are now more fully fleshed out than ever in the age of digital technology and social media—leads to further considerations of what is to be done with the media traces that remain when we die. In an age of surveillance capitalism, discussed in chapter 4, more and more of our lives are subject to capture and use by the platforms, digital systems, and corporate entities that we interact with daily, yet the question of what will happen to the growing archives of dead users' data is entirely open. The informational traces of the dead are a growing resource in this era, in which tens of thousands of users die on major social media platforms like Facebook every day. Given that capitalism hates to waste a body that could be used to generate value, the possibility that new forms of the digital undead are being created and deployed grows every year.

Throughout the various iterations explored in this book, undead labor remains a mode of production and a form of life rooted in excess, the fantasy of unlimited life and endless productivity. How, then, to end a project that explores the refusal of endings? We know that the zombie was born out of slavery, a deferral of death in favor of labor. Since that time, the zombie has been a remarkably generative monster. It has proliferated on screen and across genres, and it has reproduced itself within discourse and fantasy as a potent metaphor and a contagious allegory. The zombie has remained with us since its inception and has been a lasting presence in our cultural imagination because the conditions that gave rise to the zombie in the first place—crises of race, labor, and value under capitalism—have never disappeared but shifted and evolved over time. Is it time for a reimagining of the zombie? And can the zombie become anything more than a symbol of degradation and exploitation—a monster that cannot stop?

In the last two decades, several outliers to the zombie genre have emerged. Certainly, most of the zombie's representations on screen would be immediately recognizable as a common image from the popular imagination, though some new developments have begun to appear. The film *The Girl with All the Gifts* (Colm McCarthy, 2016) takes a provocative turn in its depiction of the classic zombie apocalypse. Based on a 2013 book of the same name by M. R. Carey, *The Girl with All the Gifts* frames the zombie outbreak in terms of a parasitic fungal infection, echoing similar themes in the prestige video game series *The Last of Us.* The parasitic fungus takes over the brain and body of the human host, transforming it into a "hungry," whose only goal is to spread the infection through contact with bodily fluids. Generically, the film owes much to dystopian zombie outbreak films like *28 Days Later* (Danny Boyle, 2002) and *World War Z* (Marc Forster, 2013), both of which depict fast-moving, violent bodies who are infected with a pathogen that renders them zombies.

The Girl with All the Gifts differs from these generic cousins by showing a next generation of children born partly immune to the zombifying fungus: They still react with compulsive violence to the presence of new potential hosts (i.e., uninfected humans), but unlike the first generation of the infected, they exhibit intelligence and free will. The film follows Melanie, a young Black girl who was born infected, and slowly reveals more and more about this new generation born with a more symbiotic relationship to the zombifying fungus.[16] The film begins at a highly regimented military facility, then moves into the "wilds" of a fallen London, populated almost entirely by the infected who stand still and dormant, waiting for some stimulus to provoke them into action. As the film goes from one setting to another, we gather two important insights. First, that civilization as we know it is effectively over, as shown by the reclamation of the city by nature and the lack of any significant governmental or military presence or contact—the city is shown as entirely populated by the zombies. Second, we learn that Melanie is not an isolated case. The beginning of the film shows Melanie with other children like her, carefully contained and studied, but when we see more of the city we are introduced to "wild" children, who have also come to survive in a new kind of life.

The film is explicit in framing the passing of the old world into the new, culminating in a conversation between Melanie and Dr. Caldwell, who has been keeping Melanie alive because she believes Melanie holds the key to a vaccine against the fungal infection. Caldwell has argued that the human behavior of infected children like Melanie (complex thinking, affection, etc.) comes down to "exquisite mimicry of observed behaviors," meaning that the next generation is not truly alive or sentient, but merely mimicking those behaviors to better infect new hosts. At the end of the film, after traveling with Melanie and observing her, Caldwell admits that she was wrong and that Melanie and the other children like her are in fact living, sentient beings. This is an important revelation for the film because it cements the idea that Melanie and her kindred are a new kind of life, distinct from the initially zombified hosts, who live in symbiotic relation with the fungus in what appears to be a mutually beneficial arrangement. Melanie responds to Caldwell, "Then why should it be us who die for you?" before abandoning the old world for something new.

The Girl with All the Gifts presents a provocative and compelling new take on the zombie narrative, suggesting a new phase in the zombie's evolution by playing with the notion of evolution itself. The next generation of the infected, like Melanie, have inherited a new world, emptied of humanity and free to create their own future. In this way, the film shares similar themes with Richard Matheson's 1954 novel *I Am Legend*, which imagines a world overtaken by vampires. At the end of the novel, the protagonist learns that the vampires he has been hunting have grown into their own culture and civilization, and he is the monster that kills them when they are sleeping.[17] Yet, the question remains: Do films like *The Girl with All the Gifts* really represent a newer, more positive, or even radical picture of the zombie?

One of the central contentions of this book has been that the zombie represents a problem *of* and *in* capitalism, from colonialism to neoliberalism. To reimagine the zombie, now, as a figure of a newly revitalized world, does a disservice to both zombies and to these new stories themselves. The monsters that appear in *The Girl with All the Gifts* are certainly zombielike in form, both in the film and the larger narrative that contains them, but insofar as they are genuinely alive—and, perhaps more important, represent a new form of life altogether—they are removed from the zombie as I define it here. This is not to take away from a film like *The Girl with All the Gifts*, but rather to argue for letting new monsters emerge, perhaps related to zombies but understood on their own terms. The story of new life after an apocalyptic pandemic is both timely and worth thinking through as something distinct from older monsters, with their symbolic baggage, and the film gives us new monsters for the present moment, reflecting ideas from Afropessimism and from discourse on the Anthropocene. Not every infected body needs to be a zombie.

The other objection to this line of thinking is the assumption that giving new life to the zombie is a good thing. Hidden within this way of thinking is the idea that the zombie can be redeemed as a figure, saving it from its own abjection and transforming it by giving it new purpose. It could be argued that rethinking the zombie in this way tends to obscure the traumas of the monster's origin in slavery and degradation, a symbolic fate worse than death, an important symptom of capitalism's ongoing problems even today. But it is also important to consider that new iterations and changes will inevitably take place in the mythology of the zombie, and it is not the aim of this argument to condemn or resist them. Yet, one wonders what motivates us to redeem or radicalize the zombie as a figure, especially when the path of its redemption is more work. New labors for a new era, but labor nonetheless.

Perversely, this seems to continue the very tradition of excessive demands for labor that have structured the zombie's existence from the plantation onward, albeit for a better cause. At the heart of the arguments presented here about undead labor and the story of the zombie as a central figure in the history of modernity and capitalism is an understanding that the demands for labor and value that have been made on the zombie are too much, and so rather than giving it yet more labor to enact, perhaps it is best to allow the zombie to do the one thing it has never been permitted: to stop and rest. To die, finally. In the face of undead labor and capitalism's delirium of unlimited growth and endless production, we ought, instead, to consider the possibilities of endings, finitude, and even death. The zombie is the monster that labors and endures beyond the limits of life into a state of undeadness, rendering life and death equivalent within capitalism's monstrous system of abstraction and signaling the privileging of life above all other values to the detriment of the living; it is the monster that can't stop and won't stop. Let us instead reconsider stopping and its importance in the face of a relentless mode of production, and let these old bones rest.

1

"A Mechanical Semblance of Life"

TOWARD A THEORY OF UNDEAD LABOR

The *zombie,* they say, is a soulless human corpse, still dead, but taken from the grave and endowed by sorcery with a mechanical semblance of life—it is a dead body which is made to walk and act and move as if it were alive.

—William Seabrook, *The Magic Island*

THE ZOMBIE EMERGED from the plantations of Haiti in the eighteenth century. It reflected the life of the slave, a fate worse than death, where even death did not free them from slavery, and developed as an amalgam of African, European, and Indigenous cultures in the Americas. Zombies are uniquely modern monsters that appeared during capitalism's rapid expansion and have endured from the colonial period to the neoliberal present. Myths of the zombie tell an encoded story of capitalism's real attempt to overcome the limits of life, and even death, in the process of extracting surplus value from bodies in new ways. This project develops a theory of *undead labor,* defined as value extracted from life pushed beyond its limits, through the story of the zombie as a shadow of modern capitalism. Taking the zombie as its central object, this chapter finds at the heart of capital a desire to push past the natural boundaries of life and to overcome all limitation up to and including death, creating a condition of "undeadness," which promises a new kind of body with a limitless potential for the extraction of value.

The zombie makes for an unwieldy central figure for this project because it comes in many forms and is fundamentally transgressive—driven to cross whatever boundaries and limitations it encounters, an impulse that takes place at the level of form and content, in both the real and the abstract. We know from countless movies and media representations how the zombie is prone to bursting through doors, windows, and walls, invading the safe, intimate spaces of the home and body, the boundaries of which the zombie crosses with probing hands and mouths. This impulse also takes place at the level of form, as zombies move across the generic boundaries of film and media with the same drive as it transgresses bodily boundaries. At its core, the zombie also transgresses even such fundamental and ontological boundaries as life and death, the real and the symbolic, the fictional and the actual, since the zombie exists simultaneously as a prolific trope and popular movie monster, but one that is rooted in real cultural and religious traditions. There have been real zombies. They may not be undead in the usual sense, but they certainly exist at the liminal edges of life. In Haiti, such zombies are made at the intersection of poison and belief, as the anthropologist Wade Davis has written about at length.[1] The study of undead labor and zombies in this chapter attempts to balance instances of actual zombies with the abstract and symbolic consequences of these events and the beliefs that shape them. This porous line between the actual and the mythic should, however, be understood as a necessary ambiguity that reflects the complexity of undead labor, which emerges at the nexus of race, labor, value, mysticism, history, and economy.

Through a series of extended meditations on labor, slavery, analogy, vitality, and reanimation, this project tracks the history of the zombie as a history of racial capital rooted in undeadness and excessive life, undertaking a genealogy of the zombie that contributes to the discourses of racialized labor and its ongoing place in modern life from the plantation to twenty-first-century political economies. This is a story about labor but also about death and its symbolic foreclosure within modernity. I will argue that the condition of "undeadness" at the heart of this project is not about death at all but, rather, the dream of a limitless and infinitely malleable form of life: of taking life's capacities for growth and destruction and turning them against the living. Perhaps more important, it shows how these capacities figure prominently within the capitalist imaginary. I take up the zombie in this project not to save or redeem the zombie, and I do not seek to find its hidden, revolutionary potential. I do not believe there is any redemption in the zombie or for the zombie. Instead, this is an argument in favor of death—for finitude in a hegemony that favors the infinite.

"Dead Men Working"

In what is arguably the first zombie account to reach a widespread American audience, William Seabrook gave a lurid account of his meeting with real zombies during his trip to Haiti in the late 1920s.[2] This encounter did not, as one might expect, take place in a cemetery or some rural and isolated part of the island. Instead, Seabrook saw his first zombie laboring in the setting of a modern sugar plantation run by Hasco, or the Haitian-American sugar company. Seabrook describes the scene thus: "An immense factory plant, dominated by a huge chimney, with clanging machinery, steam whistles, freight cars. It is like a chunk of Hoboken. It lies in the eastern suburbs of Port-au-Prince, and beyond it stretch the cane fields of the Cul-de-Sac. Hasco makes rum when the sugar market is off, pays low wages, twenty or thirty cents a day, and gives steady work. It is modern big business, and it sounds like it, looks it, smells it."[3] Seabrook was clearly expecting a less developed, less modern setting for his first encounter with a zombie. He was in Haiti to write about voodoo, and he thought the zombie would be an incidental part of the story—one more local superstition to explore in the larger project of writing a travelogue of Haiti and an occult ethnography of its traditions. But it was here on a modern sugar plantation—"a chunk of Hoboken"—that he saw a zombie face to face.

The setting is important for several reasons. First, it ties the zombie to a site of labor. The sugarcane fields surrounding the Hasco processing plant had changed little since the colonial period, and during Seabrook's travels Haiti was under US occupation. President Woodrow Wilson deployed the military to Haiti to maintain stability for companies like Hasco, and it is worth noting that the period in which Seabrook encountered zombies echoed both scenes of colonial occupation and slave labor that have deep resonances in the island's history. Following from this, the second reason the setting is so important to Seabrook's account of the zombie is that these zombies were essentially slaves. They were bodies, supposedly raised from the dead and put to work for the financial benefit of their master. In this case, it is unlikely that Hasco was directly responsible for the zombies working in the fields. More likely, the zombie labor was the result of some enterprising Haitian who created, or purchased, the zombies from a *bocor* or sorcerer, who would have raised them from the grave.

This odd juxtaposition between the supernatural and the industrial in Seabrook's account of zombies is important. The echoes of slavery and colonialism are deeply resonant in the scene, but Seabrook's meeting with zombies outside Hasco also signals an important and ongoing connection between the zombie and technology, a connection that emerges from the milieu of the plantation. The zombie takes the logic of enslavement to its logical extreme: a living subject reduced to pure instrumentality, rendered into a state that is neither living nor dead but *undead*—an ontological category that reflects the strange status of the slave as a being that is simultaneously living and socially dead.[4] Following this line of thinking, Elizabeth Dillon argues that the slave plantations of the Caribbean were a site where new techniques of instrumentalizing life and labor originated in ways later defined as biopolitical and where the dehumanization of the slave occurred through a systematic array of practices. Dillon describes this "zombie biopolitics," writing that "rather than view social death as a state of being or an identity, then, I suggest it might be understood as a technology—one that colonialism (and neocolonialism) deploys, albeit one that does not ever precisely succeed in its contradictory aims of eradicating social life while sustaining bare labor."[5] Dillon puts forward the notion of "bare labor" as a way to understand the rendering of human life into commodity form, making it purely instrumental and voiding it of its place as a fulfilling and sustaining element within a more holistic understanding of human life. She goes on to point out that "the effort to forcibly manage the distribution of life through the technology of social death constitutes an originary biopolitics that took shape in the 'laboratory' of the plantation."[6] Building on Patterson's understanding of slavery as social death, Dillon goes further, suggesting that some conception of death in the social and symbolic orders is essential to the very idea of slavery and that many of the techniques and practices developed to manage the enslaved were designed precisely for this purpose. More on this to come. For now, what is important is that Seabrook's encounter with zombies understands them technologically in two senses: first, the instrumentality of the zombie's body and labor, second, the zombie as a figure excluded from the symbolic and social life of its former communities, functioning only as a pure instrument, the logic of the slave taken to its extreme.

Another reason Hasco is significant in this early literary representation of the zombie is that it stages a tension between the industrial and the supernatural, the role of superstition in Haiti, carrying connotations of primitivism and the occult, contrasted with the decidedly modern world of the factory plantation. Seabrook's travelogue was likely the first zombie representation to circulate widely beyond Haiti. The zombie was an idea, and a monster, that found especially rich soil in the popular imagination of the United States, where it continued to resonate with both colonialism and industrialism. The zombie's popularity was almost certainly due to the exoticism of Seabrook's book and the easy otherness of Haiti, on which could be projected the fears that grew much closer to home. Indeed, far from being far removed from the modern world, the zombie appears at its very heart, an uncomfortable reminder that the enslavement of Black bodies was essential to modernity, not an accidental feature or unfortunate byproduct. Finally, this account of the zombie places it at the crossroads of the real and the symbolic. The zombie, as a figure and a monster, is deeply overdetermined and spills over from the mythic into the real world repeatedly, in both this book and the narratives in which the zombie appears across media platforms. This figural excess becomes one of the defining characteristics of the zombie, crossing borders across culture, media, history, economics, and religion. Unlike traditional supernatural beings such as ghosts or vampires, the zombie is not created by lingering obsession or excessive attachment to the living world. Rather, the zombie is a supernatural monster created for economic and industrial purposes. The zombie is made to work, and its connections to race, labor, and economy run deep.

Ever the modern skeptic, Seabrook described his initial meeting with the zombies this way: "My first impression of the three supposed *zombies*, who continued dumbly at work, was that there was something about them unnatural and strange. They were plodding like brutes, like automatons. Without stooping down, I could not fully see their faces, which were bent expressionless over their work." Seabrook's language here is instructive, using "automaton" and "brute" to describe vacant bodies while alluding to connotations of race and technology. This emphasis on materiality highlights the lack of mind, spirit, or subjectivity in these laboring bodies. Like machines, these figures lacked soul or will, obeying only their keepers' commands. This impression was underscored by Seabrook's description of the zombie's eyes: "The eyes were the worst. It was not my imagination. They were in truth like the eyes of a dead man, not blind, but staring, unfocused, unseeing. The whole face, for that matter, was bad enough. It was vacant, as if there were nothing behind it." After this encounter, Seabrook speculates that the zombie's truth lies between magic and science, suggesting that these real zombies must involve drugs and suspended animation alongside the island's myths and legends. Seabrook ends his chapter on zombies by pointing out that a provision exists in the Haitian penal code that levies the charge of murder against anyone who might administer a poison or other substance to a person, creating a state of likeness to death, and "if, after the administering of such substances, the person has been buried, the act shall be considered murder no matter what result follows."[7] The zombie was a partial truth, a mysterious object between symbol, myth, and reality—a nexus of fears condensed into a single type of body.

Seabrook's description is in line with another famous account of zombies in the Caribbean, published by Zora Neale Hurston almost a decade after Seabrook in 1938 in her book *Tell My Horse: Voodoo and Life in Haiti and Jamaica.* Hurston described an encounter with Felicia Felix-Mentor, a woman who had been turned into a zombie. Hurston, a meticulous ethnographer, provided rare photographic evidence of a real zombie. Her account supports much of what Seabrook wrote, portraying the zombie as a real, symbolic object created by poison and magic within the Haitian public imagination. Hurston's meeting with Felix-Mentor, who had by then been placed in a psychiatric hospital, resembles Seabrook's own encounter with zombies but reveals another layer of significance. She described her first impressions of Felix-Mentor in the following way: "She hovered against the fence in a sort of defensive position. The moment she sensed our approach, she broke off a limb of a shrub and began to use it to dust and clean the ground and the fence and the table which bore her food. She huddled the cloth around her head more closely and showed every sign of fear and expectation of abuse and violence."[8] This tragic account contributes some important perspective to Seabrook. Felix-Mentor's gestures revealed both the history of labor—the imperative to be useful and invisible—and the trauma etched into her body.

Like Seabrook, Hurston was shocked by what she saw in Felix-Mentor's face, describing it thus: "That blank face with the dead eyes. The eyelids were white all around the eyes as if they had been burned with acid. . . . There was nothing you could say to her or get from her except by looking at her, and the sight of this wreckage was too much to endure for long." Hurston describes the zombie as a multiplicity or constellation of myths and significations, pointing out that it represents a "group of fears" that manifests differently in different parts of the population, depending on other (typically class-related) factors. To become a zombie was to go "from an educated, intelligent being to an unthinking, unknowing beast," who would not know family or friends even if they saw them.[9] Across ethnographies and anthropological accounts of the zombie, one thing is clear: becoming a zombie is a fate far worse than death, stripped of spirit and subjectivity in ways harsher than slavery since being made a zombie meant being robbed of all powers of resistance. To be made a zombie was to be brought back to life as pure instrument. It was the slave perfected, unencumbered by will, memory, or hope. The zombie is monstrous because it embodies the intimate relation between labor and trauma generated by the culture and conditions that created it.

Reading Seabrook and Hurston together, they show that the modern factory, though seemingly incongruous, is an appropriate place to encounter the zombie, but this connection is both significant and appropriate, echoing the zombie's origins on the slave plantations of colonial Haiti, where it was a monstrous incarnation of the horrors of slavery itself. The zombies that Seabrook met in the sugarcane fields near the Port-au-Prince Hasco plant were workers, instruments of cheap labor that were less than human, put to work through a monstrous process of enslavement. What distinguishes the zombie from the slave is not its relationship to labor—indeed, the early version of the zombie performs labor identical to slave labor carried out since the colonial period on the island, but rather its relationship to an excessive form of life and labor that overcomes the limits of death. The zombie is a body returned to life, but unlike Lazarus, the zombie's life is not fully returned to it. Rather, it exists in a half life, or better, a state of *undeadness*, since what distinguishes the zombie's form of life is that it is animate but not quite alive or dead. Considered in this way, the horror of the zombie is not that it is dead—especially since these early zombies were not the rotting corpses we would see in later media representations—but rather that it is marked by an excessive life, one that is too much and out of place. The horror of the zombie's "mechanical semblance of life" mirrors the life of the enslaved, whose body was valuable to the enslaver but whose subjectivity impeded the total and totalizing use of the body as an instrument. This clarifies why the zombie was a monster unique to the slave plantation and enslaved society, since becoming a zombie meant facing a fate worse than death, because death no longer offered escape from bondage.

This view of the zombie as a ravaged reflection of the living slave, rendered into the half life of a commodity, is supported by a wealth of recent scholarship that seeks to clarify these new conditions of existence brought about by the transatlantic trade in African bodies and subjects. Death was, of course, everywhere because of the horrors of the Middle Passage, but the unique conditions that produced not just the dead but the undead came into being through the world-spanning slave trade. The experience of the Middle Passage cemented this transformation through various processes that removed the subject from the context of normal life, as Stephanie Smallwood writes when she points out that "on the ship at sea the logic of commodification reached its nadir. It was here, on the ocean crossing, that the practice of commodification most effectively muted the agency of the African subjects and thereby produced their desired object: an African body fully alienated and available for exploitation in the American marketplace."[10] Smallwood's statement speaks directly to the existential and economic conditions of the African subject as slave, but more important, to the transformation in which the Black body was entirely reimagined according to a logic of commodification. Here, the body is rethought as a set of abstractions and capacities, to be measured according to parameters of value and potential productivity.

Jennifer Morgan describes this as a new emphasis on "numeracy" in Atlantic cultures. She argues that numeracy, the mathematical counterpart to literacy, was an important development in the Atlantic world, rendering bodies into numbers and reimagining the human as commodity. Morgan argues that "numeracy—fluency in the concepts of trade and exchange, as well as attention to demographics—was just one of many new modes of thinking that accompanied the origins of the Atlantic world." These "new modes of thinking"—tactics for creating and extracting value from the human body—laid the conceptual groundwork for the zombie as a monster tied to labor, existing as a mere semblance of life. Morgan uses language in her discussion of numeracy, and its accompanying shift toward accounting, that foreshadows the zombie, as when she describes demography as a "deadening enumeration of the slave trader's account book and the slave owner's plantation inventory."[11] As Morgan's account makes clear, the process of enumeration has a deadening effect, rendering her removed from vitality—neither quite living nor quite dead, but undead. A body that has passed through the veil of objecthood through a combination of commodification and death, thus made less than a full subject. The zombie is a body whose life is not their own but subject to outside forces of objectification, instrumentalization, and exchange.

With this strange relationship to life and death in mind, I suggest that the important insights into what Vincent Brown has described as the "mortuary politics" of the colonial Caribbean continue to structure the zombie in later incarnations as well.[12] As Brown points out, "Death and its meanings have historically been central to social order and tension. People have derived profound social meaning from the beliefs and practices associated with death, and they have employed those meanings—charged with cosmic importance—in struggles towards particular ends."[13] Brown's formulation of mortuary politics is useful here since it simultaneously provides insight into the reasons why the zombie emerged in the slave societies of the Caribbean and, at the same time, sheds light onto the stakes of its appearance. The mortuary politics of the zombie speak to the conditions that produced it as a uniquely embodied monster—monstrous in being reduced to pure body, an instrument neither alive nor dead. One important feature of mortuary rituals is the way they give symbolic closure in the face of the brute fact of death, yet as Seabrook and Hurston show, chattel slavery changes these mortuary politics, blurring the boundaries between subject and object, the living and the dead, particularly in the context of the plantation. The zombie, like ghosts, vampires, and other undead monsters, undoes this closure, leaving open the passage between life and death. But through its relationship to colonialism, race, and slave labor, the zombie does something unique: Like the living body, the zombie labors and generates value for its creator or owner. Its status as both alive and dead captures the logic of slavery, taken to a logical extreme. The zombie's status as an undead body—dead yet working—enables labor beyond exhaustion, reduced to an organic machine yet endowed with uncanny vitality, enough to generate value—a unique combination I am defining as *undead labor.*

Undead labor is a mode of production at the heart of capitalism, extracting excess value from bodies pushed beyond their structural limits and speaking to a fantasy of value taken beyond the processes of production and reproduction—in short, through labor. But what precisely does it mean to suggest that undead labor is a mode of production that was created from the crucible of the plantation and the practices of chattel slavery more broadly? Karl Marx and Friedrich Engels define a mode of production as something that "must not be considered simply as being the reproduction of the physical experience of the individuals. Rather it is a definite form of activity of these individuals, a definite form of expressing their life, a definite *mode of life* on their part. As individuals express their life, so they are. What they are, therefore, coincides with their production, both *what* they produce and with *how* they produce. Hence what individuals are depends on the material conditions of their production."[14] What this important passage shows is how Marx and Engels theorize life itself as something derived from the conditions that produce it. Labor is an activity and an expression of the conditions that gave rise to the living body. Thus a mode of production becomes the defining characteristic through which we can understand what a life is and how it works, a notion of life that is understood here both as biography as well as its existence as a physical and biological system.

With this definition in mind, we can say that undead labor is a mode of production generated within the conditions of modern slavery embedded within colonial capitalism that is derived not simply from the living labor of the slave, but from the uncanny vitality of the zombie, which takes the reduced and degraded form of life made possible by the conditions of slavery and extends those into a symbolic, even mythic form that is imbricated with the real conditions of the slave. To paraphrase the Marxist philosopher Louis Althusser, the zombie represents the imaginary relationship of slaves to their real conditions of existence.[15] The zombie's uncanny vitality is a form of life that *returns*, making uncanny the body it formerly inhabited, and in so doing does not simply open a passage between life and death but becomes a form of life that symbolically forecloses death itself.

To understand the full significance of this statement—that death itself would or could be symbolically foreclosed as a symptom of the zombie's rise as a mythic figure that exists at the nexus of race, labor, and slavery—it is important to clarify the ways that death has always posed a fundamental problem for capitalism. To support this bold claim, I suggest that slavery was not incidental to the development of modern capitalism but essential to it. This important line of argumentation has become a significant feature of scholarship in Black studies and intersecting disciplines. Writing on the specific conditions of slavery within the United States, Edward Baptist points out that "the idea that the commodification and suffering and forced labor of African Americans is what made the United States powerful and rich is not an idea that people necessarily are happy to hear. Yet it is the truth."[16] Baptist writes this as a preemptory rebuttal to a common way of thinking in both history and economics that suggests slavery was a "backward" or premodern system of production destined to pass into history as newer, industrialized labor came to take its place. As he points out, this serves two purposes. First, it frames slavery as something almost accidental—a minor embarrassment in the grand sweep of modernity—rather than functioning as an essential feature of the modern world; it was a claim suggesting that "slavery . . . had little long-term influence on the rise of the United States during the nineteenth century, a period in which the nation went from being a minor European trading partner to becoming the world's largest economy," a narrative that Baptist is quick to point out is "one of the central stories of American history."[17] Baptist is not alone in making this argument, which has been pointed out by leading thinkers of capitalism, slavery, and African American culture ranging from W. E. B. Du Bois to Eric Williams to Cedric Robinson, who speaks succinctly to the matter: "'The institution of American slave labor could not be effectively conceptualized as a thing in and of itself. Rather, it was a particular historical development for world capitalism that expropriated the labor of African workers as primitive accumulation. American slavery was a *subsystem* of world capitalism."[18] C. L. R. James points out that "the history of the West Indies is governed by two factors, the sugar plantation and Negro slavery. . . . Wherever the sugar plantation and slavery existed, they imposed a pattern. It is an original pattern, not European, not African, not part of the American main, not native in any conceivable sense of the word, but West Indian, *sui generis,* with no parallel anywhere else."[19] Baptist also tells us that slavery was central to American empire, with his unique contribution to this story centering around practices and techniques developed to manage the slave body and plantation. These new techniques, which aimed at maximizing the productivity of bodies and actions at the expense of their humanity, foreshadow a through line of practices relating to labor under a capitalist system, suggesting that "new kinds of labor" and new kinds of violence were developed in tandem and enacted together in these spaces.[20]

Slavery was changing through new techniques and practices designed to increase enslaved production. Baptist points out that between 1811 and 1860, there was a "total productivity increase of 361 percent" on the cotton plantations in the United States. This remarkable increase in production took place through new techniques and technologies of power imposed on enslaved lives and bodies. Baptist employs the notion of "left-handed power," borrowed from Christian theology, which he describes as the "art of secret resistance" that was used by the disempowered, enslaved, and marginalized in many sites of labor, both on the plantation and off. Left-handed power—covert tactics used when no direct avenue for challenging power was available—ranged from lying, delaying, and playing dumb to breaking tools, poisoning food, and escaping to freedom. Baptist describes these tactics for several reasons. First, to underscore that acts of resistance were commonplace on the part of the enslaved, who sought consistently to resist their exploitation and find ways to escape their bondage. Second, and more significantly, these acts of resistance formed part of a feedback system producing new methods of counterresistance that extracted ever greater value from enslaved labor. Baptist argues, "Something profoundly new was happening. Enslavers were finding ways to turn the left hand against the enslaved. Entrepreneurs redirected left-handed power by measuring work, implementing continuous surveillance of labor, and calibrating time and torture. All of this repeatedly accomplished the enslaver's ongoing goal of forcing enslaved people to invent, over and over, ways to make their own labor more efficient and profitable for their owners." These techniques took the form of "pushing systems," modular task structures of labor, and an accelerating pace, all calculated according to ratios of violence and productivity to maximize bodily output.[21] Baptist's line of thinking supports Morgan's understanding of the new "numeracy" that undergirded the Atlantic world, and adds to it by showing that both life and labor were made subject to these new forms of abstraction taking shape as the simultaneous commodification and measurement of the body and its many capacities. These new techniques, like the pushing systems described by Baptist, were quite deadly and came with an associated, and expected, decrease in the life expectancy of the enslaved. Bodies pushed past their limits led to death, with mortality reduced to nothing but production constraint.

As both Baptist and Brown show, death became a significant limiting factor for the plantation as an engine of colonial capitalism. Staggering death rates on the slave plantation and its surroundings caused a steady, unending demand for labor in the form of millions of new bodies. While the enslaved Black population died in far greater numbers, whites also died at remarkable rates in the Caribbean colonies. Speaking specifically of Jamaica, Brown notes, "In the first half of the eighteenth century nearly 50,000 European migrants were needed to increase the white population by only 5,000 or so. Through the middle decades of the eighteenth century, immigrants could not expect to survive for more than thirteen years." And while the enslaved Africans had no choice but to come to the plantations of the Caribbean and the Atlantic world, white populations from the colonizing powers also came, and died, for their chance to have some piece of the immense wealth being generated. "In the transatlantic experience . . . death and wealth and power were inextricably entangled," notes Brown succinctly.[22] The systems of slave labor and plantations worked to instrumentalize life across the board, although racial categories and divisions helped to maintain the colonial order of things, and thus death became a problem for capital. Given the plantation's brutality and death toll, it might seem counterintuitive to suggest that death posed an obstacle to capitalism rather than a byproduct. Yet, despite its cheapness, the instrumentality of life engendered by the system of chattel slavery within the larger logic of capitalism, living labor is nonetheless at the heart of the system, and death was a significant limit to the potential productivity of the plantation and to capitalism more broadly. This, in turn, necessitated new developments that would displace and foreclose death, symbolically, if not in actuality, revealing at the core of capital itself a dream of unlimited life, productivity, and value.

Death was a problem for capitalism, and this difficulty manifested through the actions of capitalists, plantation owners, and enslavers, who tried to account for it by mastering it through abstraction. From the slave's perspective, this unusual relation between life and death inverted the values of both terms: Life became the source of suffering, while death became a means of resistance and escape from a system that instrumentalized life itself. A minor but instructive example of this appears in Jacques Tourneur's 1943 film *I Walked with a Zombie*, which shows how these basic ontological values are turned inside out—not only by the appearance of the undead in the form of the titular zombies, but in the customs of the Black descendants of slaves still living and working in the sugar plantations of the fictional Caribbean island of Saint Sebastian.

Tourneur's film is an example of the early zombie movie, more drama than horror, which is deeply invested in the zombie as a Caribbean monster, clearly drawing on ideas from both Hurston and Seabrook. It follows a nurse who moves to the island to take care of the ailing wife of a sugar plantation owner. Sugar is the island's sole economic engine, run by the same family since the colonial era and slavery. The film is striking—especially for a film from the 1940s—for its sympathetic perspective on the plight of the slaves and their descendants, the Black residents of the island who still work in the cane fields and on the plantation. The viewer is introduced to the island through the eyes of a nurse, who is blind to the many marks of suffering that remain, most notably the figurehead from one of the original slave ships that populated the island, which now stands in the central courtyard family compound, which is now colloquially dubbed *ti misery* (translated as "little misery" in the local patois)—a depiction of Saint Sebastian, pierced with arrows. The figurehead is both literally and figuratively at the center of the island for which it is named, also signifying the suffering of its people.

I Walked with a Zombie features only two of the titular monsters, and the contrast between them is striking. Early in the film, we see the nurse awaked in the middle of the night by the sound of weeping, which she later discovers comes from the mother of a newborn child. Later we learn that while the child is healthy, the local custom (explicitly described as a holdover from slavery) is to weep at the birth of a child on the island and to "make merry at the burial." This scene is significant because the sound of weeping precipitates the viewer's first encounter with a zombie in the film: the white plantation owner's wife, "mindless" and wandering the grounds of the main house. The existence of a white zombie is the crisis that drives the narrative action, moving the other characters to find a cure for her mysterious condition or finally release her from a half life. The cause of her zombification is framed as social—a result of her infidelity with her husband's brother and thus a sanction against her transgression against the institution of the family—yet the precise means of her transformation remains a mystery. Both medical and magical causes are suggested, but the film ultimately leaves us in suspense, resolving this tension through her death—or its more permanent counterpart.

The other zombie of the film is Black and represents the most threatening figure of the movie, a towering body, skeletally thin, with unblinking eyes who does the bidding of the voodoo practitioners at the local *houmfort*, or sacred gathering site. This zombie remains at the end of the film, after the white zombie finally meets her end, thus bringing back the status quo of the island, where Black zombies are the norm and do not threaten to upset the social order. This is a consistent theme of early zombie movies, in which white zombies are a crisis to be resolved, and Black zombies are merely the exotic backdrop of a primitive but threatening Caribbean setting. That certain bodies—Black bodies—are understood as undead speaks directly to the racial valence of the zombie and of undead labor in turn: It is the Black body, worked into a half life, that is the norm, yet this condition threatens to overrun its borders and extend into other demographics, most threateningly white bodies and populations. While the zombie emerged under the sign of Blackness, the danger of undead labor was its refusal to remain confined to the bodies and demographics racial capitalism sought to contain. Instead, undead labor always threatens to grow out of control.

I Walked with a Zombie provides a different perspective on Vincent Brown's mortuary politics, formed in and around the plantations of the Atlantic world, one in which life and death are in symbolic flux, intimately linked to enslaved productive and reproductive potential, especially Black women's bodies. Referencing Brown's work directly, Jennifer Morgan points out that "it is challenging to fully understand how living in the midst of death transformed life in slave societies." These changes are felt most acutely in the disruption of kinship and intimacy within enslaved populations, and this infusion of death into life was keenly felt in women's bodies, whose value was multifaceted: Black women's bodies endured the same labor conditions as men but bore the added burden of reproductive potential, factored into the calculus of undead labor. Morgan notes elsewhere that "Black women bore witness to the newly emergent discourses of race, commodity, and kin that shaped the early modern Atlantic world. Through the processes of capture, transport, and sale, they acquired critical perspectives on the new world in which they were situated. Enslaved women carried a set of experiences that attuned them in particular to the perverse logics of early modern Atlantic slavery."[23] If undead labor grows out of Atlantic slavery and the plantation system, it stands to reason that women's bodies are a site of intensity or, as Jessica Marie Johnson succinctly puts it in her study of the intimate networks formed by women of color in the Atlantic world, "an intention to reproduce an enslaved population of hard laborers vis-à-vis the wombs of African women."[24] Once again, the systems and practices of slavery effectively deaden the lives of slaves through social death and symbolic abstraction. Undead labor invests in the living body but yields only a shadow of life—an abstract version passed under the sign of death and back again, returning in undeadness.

How is it that the structures and tensions of the Atlantic world bring about undead labor? At its core, this shift took place alongside what Morgan describes as "a relatively new set of ideas concerning trade, value, population, and commodification, all of which might qualify as forms of numeracy."[25] In addition to the ideas concerning trade that Morgan describes, I would add that these changes intervene in notions of life, labor, and race as well, which seems entirely in line with Morgan's own ideas. These new concepts put both enslaved and enslaver into a position where the ontological conditions of death and life were reduced to values within the larger calculus of slavery and the plantation's means of production.

The productive capacities and reproductive labor of enslaved Black women were at the vanguard of this transformation, as Morgan notes: "Women who lived through the early decades of enslavement saw the identity of their children and the assumptions that governed their futures change drastically." These changes took place as a result of a major shift in the ground of our ontology surrounding life and death, which became subject to an instrumentalizing logic of commodification, rethought via the technology of race and rendered down into the accounting of a set of values. Drawing on the ideas of Hortense Spillers, Morgan notes that "the captive body becomes the site of a 'metaphor for *value*' that renders useless any distinction between the literal and figurative violences that enslaved persons were subjected to."[26] Together, Morgan and Spillers illuminate how value subsumed the ontological categories of life and death, opening the way to a space of undeadness, which is no longer a purely symbolic notion of spirit or ghost but a condition levied on real bodies through the excess or surplus of value they are capable of producing and reproducing.

As both Morgan and Spillers note, this shift is an inherently violent process—often at both a symbolic and material level. The slave plantations of the Atlantic world operated as a site where life and death, real and symbolic, are entangled in history to a point where separating them out becomes challenging and, perhaps more significantly, actively counterproductive to a clear understanding of the emergence of undead labor. Underscoring the role of sex, gender, and reproduction in this argument reveals how death became a *problem* for nascent capitalism, a system that in response to the suffusion of violence and death into the everyday lives of those in any way involved in the plantation system, effectively doubles down on life itself. As a result of this emphasis on life over death under capitalism, death becomes increasingly controlled, enclosed, and foreclosed by modern culture.

The Foreclosure of Death

The French historian Philippe Ariès began writing in the 1970s about the changing attitudes toward death in Europe and North America, claiming that death became displaced and, more significantly, forbidden during the tumultuous cultural changes taking place in modernity. Ariès claimed that since at least the Middle Ages, and likely earlier, death was a familiar part of everyday life, and because it was so constant, it did not elicit the horror and distress it often does today. He does not go so far as to suggest that death is a happy or even welcome element in people's lives, but that "the old attitude in which death was both familiar and near, evoking great fear or awe, offers too marked a contrast to ours, where death is so frightful that we dare not utter its name."[27] Ariès describes this "household" form of death as "tamed death," signifying its intimacy within everyday life. Ariès's thinking is essential to this argument, but his ideas come with two caveats. It should be noted that Ariès was a historian of Europe, and his investigation of attitudes toward death is set solidly within the context of the "West," effectively a Eurocentric frame. However, this focus on the West can be read symptomatically with the understanding that the changes Ariès identifies have their epicenter in the United States and spread outward to Europe, eventually extending, through capitalism's cultural hegemony, to the rest of the world. The other caveat is that his work seems to potentially overstate the issue. It is likely going too far to say that death "becomes so frightful that we dare not utter its name," which seems plainly false. Yet Ariès's diachronic reading of death proves useful and significant for several reasons, the foremost of which might be the question of why this shift in our relation to death takes place at all.

Ariès argues that the effacement of death is a modern invention, beginning in American culture, where the first edict against death was sentimental. He claims that "a new sentiment characteristic of modernity: one must avoid—no longer for the sake of the dying person, but for society's sake . . . the very presence of death in the midst of a happy life, for it is henceforth given that life is always happy or should always seem to be so." The blame for death's retreat from the collective consciousness is placed on American culture's relentless optimism, reflecting a distinctly French perspective, but even so, most of Ariès's argument centers on an affective change in relation to death, which he explores through practical changes in the material culture of death and dying, thus speaking directly to Vincent Brown's idea of mortuary politics. What happened to death under these new circumstances? Obviously, death does not disappear, but it is removed from view, both publicly and privately. Death is displaced. It is taken from the home and enclosed within the hospital, prison, and other modern institutions where it is both dissected and put under the purview of medicine. More compelling than sentimental causes are the material conditions of death's removal from the public eye. Central to his argument is the way that death is removed from the home to the hospital, which brings with it additional changes to our relation to death. Ariès states, "Death in the hospital is no longer the occasion of a ritual ceremony, over which the dying person presides amidst his assembled relatives and friends. Death is a technical phenomenon obtained by a cessation of care. . . . Death has been dissected, cut to bits into a series of little steps, which finally makes it impossible to know which step was the real death, the one in which consciousness was lost, or the one in which the heart stopped. All these little silent deaths have replaced and erased the great dramatic act of death."[28] As Ariès will state elsewhere, death is denied by making it into a disease; instead of being the natural conclusion to life, it becomes an affliction, or interruption of life, an unfortunate (if inevitable) accident we dream of avoiding, curing, or overcoming.[29] All of this points to a general enclosure and foreclosure of death or, as Ariès puts it, "The combination of phenomena which we have just analyzed is nothing other than the imposition of an interdict. What was once required is henceforth forbidden."[30] When death is symbolically forbidden, undeadness becomes a logical outcome: a life beyond death, not in the sense of a grand transcendence but a grim remainder. Undeadness is a life beyond life, one that cannot stop living, the result of a new relation to death, limitation, and finitude.

Ariès finds evidence for this growing interdict toward death within the practices and attitudes surrounding death in the twentieth century, but, trained as a medieval historian, he tracks these slow-moving cultural changes backward in history, emphasizing both history and literature as windows into past systems of belief. It is also worth noting the clear resonance between Ariès and the work of Michel Foucault. The most obvious connection between the two French historians appears in a structural feature of Ariès's argument, namely, how this interdiction against death manifests: through the direct confinement or enclosure in the institution of the hospital. Not only do certain features of Ariès's argument mirror Foucault's writings on the history of madness and the birth of the clinic, but Ariès also borrows one of Foucault's most famous intellectual maneuvers: finding a problematic or unwanted element within a cultural milieu that has been closed off within an institutional setting and, following that, exploring how both the enclosure and the enclosed grow into a mutually constitutive relationship, each defining the other. While I have no evidence that Ariès and Foucault were in active communication on these matters, they knew each other as colleagues in the same field within the French academy, and Ariès's approach to the problem of death has definite parallels to Foucault's thinking.[31]

Ariès's thinking on death proves remarkably complementary to Foucault's conception of biopolitics, which is understood as a shift in the emphasis of sovereign power away from a "right to *take* life or *let* live [which] was replaced by a power to *foster* life or *disallow* it to the point of death."[32] In this famous passage, Foucault emphasizes the new positive polarity of power—a pastoral power that aims to shepherd the life of a population toward new heights of productivity. Biopolitics finds the heart of its generative potential in living labor, which it fosters through interventions into the health and well-being of a population. Foucault argued that this came about through the founding and development of new disciplines and "an explosion of numerous and diverse techniques for achieving the subjugation of bodies and the control of populations," which, according to Foucault, marks the beginning of a new age of biopower. Relevant to Ariès, Foucault also points out that this was a time when "death was ceasing to torment life so directly," which came about through new measures in hygiene, epidemiology, medicine, and sanitation.[33] This statement echoes Ariès's notion that death was displaced from the home to the hospital, where it was dissected, analyzed, and reduced from a single, decisive event to a dozen smaller failures of life.[34]

Indeed, Foucault's understanding of "fostering life" mirrors Ariès's notion of an "interdict" against death, showing these historical developments as two sides of the same coin. What is missing from both Foucault and Ariès is the role of race and the history of colonialism within these twin accounts, which remains a gap for both. In limiting his research to a strictly North American and European context, Ariès misses out on several important connections. Reading Ariès alongside Vincent Brown and others, it becomes clear that his understanding of the changing mores around death and dying is missing important influences from the colonies, specifically the plantation, where new calculations around life and death through the valences of race, labor, and value were taking place. As Alexander Weheliye asks, "How would Foucault's . . . theories of violence differ if they took the Middle Passage as their point of departure rather than remaining entrapped within the historiographical cum philosophical precincts of fortress Europe?"[35] With this question in mind, it is worth reading Ariès and Foucault in conjunction with scholars of the Caribbean and the history of slavery like Baptist, Brown, and Morgan, who help to fill this conceptual gap. Baptist provides an invaluable supplement to Foucault's genealogy of biopolitics with his historical account of the new forms of labor devised within the context of the slave plantation through new admixtures and techniques of torture, labor, and time. Following from this, I argue that the theory of undead labor I am outlining here provides an important lens on the zombie as a cultural form, broadening our understanding of biopolitics. Undead labor, created by the engines of Atlantic slavery, is an unacknowledged shadow trailing the history and development of biopolitics and capitalism, with race and enslaved labor at the center.

Following the intellectual move of Foucault and Ariès, the most important site for understanding the history of biopolitics might be the plantation, which served not only as a space of enclosure but also as a testing ground for techniques of power and labor that would later return to the metropole. The plantation was a laboratory that generated nascent forms of biopower via new modes of production and brought about ontological shifts that created the conditions for the emergence of undead labor. Édouard Glissant finds this connection between the plantation and the laboratory especially provocative, suggesting that "it is also within the Plantation that the meeting of cultures is most clearly and directly observable, though none of the inhabitants had the slightest hint that this was really about a clash of cultures. Here we are able to discover a few of the formational laws of cultural *métissage* that concerns us all."[36] The zombie is one of the most potent symbols to come out of the plantation as a site of *métissage*, emerging from the syncretic system of mysticism and belief that was Haitian *Voudon*, or voodoo, which brought together elements from important religions like European Catholicism and African animist traditions and blended them with Indigenous beliefs to form a powerful religious and ideological support to the enslaved. The zombie is a symptom of slavery, created as a monster that captures and mythologizes the conditions of exploitation and the excessive demands placed on their bodies and subjectivities within the colonial plantation setting.

Excess living labor is extracted from the slave and transformed into the zombie as a symbolic condensation of undead labor. Yet undead labor, as a mode of production, did not end with abolition but continued. Techniques developed in the laboratory of the plantation were generalized and fed back into other forms of production and exploitation. Historical evidence for this can be found in the drive for increased production in the factories of North American states and England, where sugar and cotton produced in the plantations of the Americas fed into the rapid industrialization taking place in colonial metropoles. Thus undead labor was a mode of excessive production on the colonial plantation that extended into the excesses of modern industry and eventually continued into contemporary labor practices under neoliberalism in the late twentieth and early twenty-first centuries. It was undead labor that gave rise to the zombie, not the other way around. The conditions of exploitation and excessive production developed by overseers, enslavers, and plantation owners provided the conditions for the zombie's emergence as a symbol within the popular imagination of Haiti both before and after the Haitian Revolution. The figure spread after Seabrook's story of meeting real zombies in the cane fields near Hasco, like a virus through popular and political imaginaries worldwide.

Seabrook published his travelogue about Haiti in 1929, and it took little time for the zombie to proliferate and cross the boundaries of both nation and medium. Within only a few years, the first zombie movie, *White Zombie* (Victor Halperin, 1932), appeared, starring Bela Lugosi. Since then, the zombie has been a constant presence in the popular imagination, appearing in horror films, television shows, video games, internet memes, and even kickball leagues. Its continued presence in the popular imagination also signifies the continuing operation of undead labor as a mode of production within capitalism. The zombie as a complex signifier of undead labor rose from the shadow of capitalism and has trailed it ever since, following its growth and evolution from the colonial period into the neoliberal present. The enduring presence of the zombie speaks to its significance as a cultural object and an integral part of the intellectual history of undead labor, which serves as the theme for the remainder of this chapter. The primary significance is that the conditions producing the zombie in the primal scene of undead labor on the colonial plantation remain unresolved, and as long as those conditions persist, the zombie will continue haunting the culture that produced it at the crossroads of race, labor, and value.

If the plantation was one of the original sites of the modern interdiction on death—arising from an economic imperative rather than a sentimental one, as Ariès suggests—then the zombie's status as *undead* is especially significant. The zombie was a body brought back to some mechanical semblance of life, able to carry out basic functions and rudimentary forms of labor. As such, the zombie symbolizes both a monstrous version of the slave and a body that labors beyond death's limit, and also the foreclosure of death precipitated by a fantasy of capital, born of the colonial plantation, seeking to overcome life's limits, even death itself. This was a reorientation of power toward life that is represented in a biopolitical reading of slavery in the Atlantic world. The undeadness inherent to the zombie, and the horror that comes with this unusual condition, is not about death at all but, rather, an excess of life—a significant aspect of the zombie's mythology that aligns with both Foucault and Ariès, as I outlined their arguments above. Even the linguistic construction of the "undead" speaks to the symbolic crisis around death created by modernity and capitalism: The *un-* in *undead* suggests the absence or negation of death, a turning from death back toward life.

This push toward life, with its corresponding turn against death, can be imagined as a biopolitical fantasy—the dream of production or productivity without limits and the drive to bring this mode of production into reality through the excesses of extraction that began with chattel slavery and continues within newer iterations of capitalist production. Yet the dream remains. The term "drive" has appeared here in the colloquial sense, but this impulse to overcome the finitude of death exists at the very heart of capitalism. It is a fantasy built into capitalism itself, which can be read through a psychoanalytic lens, providing further insight into the significance of this undertheorized element within modern political economies. Eric Cazdyn writes on emerging temporalities accompanying techniques of management and biopolitical control. He addresses undeadness and its relation to the drive in the context of psychoanalysis. Cazdyn frames his understanding of undeadness through Sigmund Freud's notion of a death drive—an impulse toward entropy that pushes past the so-called pleasure principle—which Freud used to understand the compulsion to repeat that exists at the core of both traumatic experience and the more mundane instances that appear in everyday life.

Drive differs from desire, which tends to move linearly from one absence to the next, because drive follows an elliptical trajectory. The drive seems always to turn back toward its object, like a celestial body caught in an endless orbit around some powerful source of gravity—forever returning but never arriving. The structure of the drive also lends some insight into the dynamics of undeadness and even shares some structural similarity with the term "undead," which signifies the turn toward, and the return to, a form of life that never fully arrives. To be undead is not to have returned to life, but to exist in a state that is always, asymptotically aimed toward life. Cazdyn expresses this understanding of the drive when he says, "Drive is the politically and psychologically productive search for the impossible."[37] Taken in the context of undead labor, undeadness exemplifies this dynamic. As a symbolic foreclosure or turn away from death, the notion of being undead is not simply a description but functions as a kind of imperative within the political imaginary. It represents a fantasy that lies at the heart of capital: a version of living labor that is unbound by death or any other limitation. Simultaneously, this fantasy reveals an aspiration to render the enslaved body socially dead or to transcend the human in favor of a new instrumental embodiment—a fantasy of unlimited production and unlimited productivity. Of course, it is impossible to bring this fantasy into reality. Death is inevitable, but it can be marginalized, pathologized, and shut away, and entire new fields of actuarial science can spring up to assess the risk of death, appearing to disrupt this new order of things. Yet the fantasy and the drive persist.

More insight into the philosophical problem of undeadness comes from Slavoj Žižek, who, like Cazdyn, finds a resonance between the undead and the drive as it operates within psychoanalysis. Žižek points out that

> the Freudian death drive has nothing whatsoever to do with the craving for self-annihilation. . . . It is, on the contrary, the very opposite of dying—a name for the "undead" eternal life itself, for the horrible fate of being caught in the endless repetitive cycle of wandering around in guilt and pain. The paradox of the Freudian "death drive" is therefore that it is Freud's name for its very opposite, for the way immortality appears within psychoanalysis, for an uncanny *excess* of life, for an "undead" urge which persists beyond the (biological) life cycle of life and death, or generation or corruption.[38]

Here, Žižek explicitly links undeadness to an excess of life that exists over and against death and finitude. Because the death drive never reaches its aim but instead asymptotically returns to its object, it comes to demonstrate something like eternal movement or an endless animation. Characteristically, Žižek's analysis demonstrates a dialectical reversal of its object: the death drive representing some uncanny version of life. Yet Žižek's description of undeadness recalls the zombie: the worst version of immortality, pure endless drudgery. And like the undeadness of the zombie, this version of immortality is a horror to experience and behold—it is an "endless set of repetitive cycles" as Žižek describes it.[39]

In this act of movement and return that traverses the boundary between life and death, the uncanny vitality that is undeadness (and the zombie in particular) becomes more readily apparent. The vitality that returns to the body of the zombie is uncanny insofar as it finds this body changed and unhomely, stripped of its warmth, both literally and figuratively. While the earliest representations of the zombie in reports from Seabrook and Hurston did not feature the rotting corpses we see today, the status of the zombie as dead was undeniable. In these early accounts, the deadness of the zombie was more symbolic, a metaphor for the experience of a human subject whose body and being had been so traumatized that it was no longer able to experience itself as alive and had instead become a thing. This was a symbolic death in which the body and subject no longer possessed themselves or even a conception of self: an experience of being no longer living, but undead, sharing the half life of the commodity, the corpse, and other objects. This aspect of the zombie would eventually become literalized starting in the 1960s, when the zombie started to be shown in various states of decay and putrefaction—a representation that only seems to strengthen its connection to the drive.[40] The zombie gives form to the drive, exemplifying the uncanny vitality of the undead and embodying the horror of capital within capitalism's symbolic systems. But this is not a static representation; the zombie shadows capitalism's evolution over time, seen through changes to its representation across media and symbolic forms.

The connections between capitalism and the uncanny vitality of the zombie are further illustrated in the work of Melinda Cooper, who provides a reading of this problem through a more contemporary lens, looking at the relationship between life and surplus within the larger context of neoliberalism. She also addresses this problem of life and finitude under capitalism through a reading of Marx when she points out that "the drive to overcome limits and relocate in the speculative future is the defining movement of capital." Cooper reads this notion of drive in the context of the capitalist impulse toward perpetual expansion and the imperative to push into new markets, which she describes as the "one limit that capitalism never escapes," framed as "recapturing the 'new' within the property form." In other words, while capitalism always seeks to expand into new markets, it also cannot help but be caught in its own limitation of reifying the "new" within the commodity and transforming the surplus of potential into the static existence of the object—taking the liveliness of surplus and deadening it into something more concrete and stable. Cooper points out that for Marx, "capitalism is essentially counterproductive," meaning that its internal logic, its innermost drives, often work against the actual means by which it derives profit.[41] For example, the surplus value generated by living labor—the lifeblood of capital as such—becomes crystallized within the commodity form, which in turn cuts it off from the very source of potency and potentiality within the labor process itself. As the source of value, living labor is essential to capitalism, which simultaneously objectifies the vital processes it requires. This is what Marx means when he says that capitalism is inherently counterproductive. It needs labor power to function, but it can only access labor power through appropriation or exploitation. Capitalism offers two solutions. The first comes in the form of dead or machine labor, which must be revivified by borrowing its power from a living body. The second takes the form of undead labor, which objectifies the still-living body as a commodity—a relation that is most obvious in the form of chattel slavery but endures within successive iterations of capitalism as well, finding its place within any system that reimagines life as a form of value.

Marx speaks to this directly when he points out that "by turning money into commodities which serve as the building materials for a new product, and as factors in the labour process, by incorporating living labour into their lifeless objectivity, the capitalist simultaneously transforms value, i.e. past labour in its objectified and lifeless form, into capital, value which can perform its own valorization process, an animated monster which begins to 'work,' 'as if its body were by love possessed.'"[42] Written with Marx's penchant for the supernatural, this passage reads as if it could have been written about the zombie, especially as it is understood through the conceptual lens of animated monsters and possessed bodies. Marx argues that capital is itself monstrous: a thing made to move, work, and reproduce by expropriating the life of those who labor within it. Seeing capital as an animated monster shows how the zombie is *the* monstrous figure of capital, shadowing capital's evolutionary development, trailing it with uncanny determination. The zombie haunts capital, from its origins to the present, changing with the shifts in the evolution of undead labor, a mode of production that persists at capital's core. Yet undead labor is also a crisis within capitalism. It is a drive and a fantasy within capital that shows one more way capitalism as a political and economic system is founded on contradiction: the dream of endless production that can never become a reality.

This crisis becomes more easily apparent when we consider Marx's own ideas concerning the relationship between the living labor of the worker and the dead labor of the machine. He argues that "a machine which is not active in the labor process is useless. In addition, it falls prey to the destructive power of natural processes. Iron rusts; wood rots. Yarn with which we neither weave nor knit is cotton wasted. Living labour must seize on these things, awaken them from the dead, change them from merely possible into real and effective use-values."[43] Value itself is the lifeless objectification of living labor's power and vitality, and transforming labor power into value is a process of deadening; and following Marx, the transformation of life into value—while still alive—is a process of undeadening: the creation of undead labor, a condition first created under Atlantic slavery, where living bodies and subjects were reduced to pure instrumentality.

In a passage from Marx's notebooks, this relation between living and dead labor becomes even more significant: "The science which compels the inanimate limbs of the machinery, by their construction, to act purposefully, as an automaton, does not exist in the worker's consciousness, but rather acts upon him through the machine as an alien power, as the power of the machine itself. The appropriation of living labour by objectified labour—of the power of activity which creates value by value existing for-itself—which lies in the concept of capital, is posited, in production resting on machinery, as the character of the production process itself."[44] This passage is significant because it is here that Marx gives one of his most concise definitions of living labor—"the power of activity which creates value by value existing for-itself"—which suggests that the value created by living labor exists first and foremost for the laborer, and it is the peculiar quality of labor that creates a surplus that can be siphoned off and appropriated by another. Marx's insights into living labor make clear that there is always something excessive about labor, and this excess comes from its intimate proximity to life. The surplus created by living labor is what makes it possible to reanimate the dead labor of the machine through an infusion of labor from the living worker, and this surplus can also be reified and stored within commodities and property.

Race is essential to this system of labor and value, both conceptually and historically. The fungibility of Black bodies became the central axis around which the abstraction and transformation of living labor took place, with the plantation serving as the laboratory of power and labor that generated the conditions under which new forms of life (and death) and new modes of production could form. Modern conceptions of race and racial division underpinned the emergence of capitalism as a global system, but understanding race as a symbolic technology shows how, through the invention of Blackness, it allowed for the optimal functioning of the plantation system. Elizabeth Dillon has already provided an important perspective of the intersections of race and technology (see above), but another contribution to this line of thinking comes from Beth Coleman, who seeks to rearticulate the approach to understanding race based on *how* race functions rather than *what* race is. For Coleman, this is a "denatured" notion of race that relies on understanding it as a technology to better consider who benefits from the deployment of race and how it works to support systems of power and representation.[45]

The beauty of Coleman's argument lies in its simplicity. For her, race functions technologically in the simplest terms: "I rely on the figure of the 'levered mechanism,' a thing that is not the main engine of a system but rather an internal part that keeps all running smoothly."[46] To flesh out the analogy, race works within capitalism more broadly as a "levered mechanism," which is not essential to the design of the system—it is not the "main engine" in Coleman's terms—but nevertheless is a vital element for the smooth functioning of its successful operation. Like any levered mechanism, race helps to exert additional pressure or force on a set of objects to move or maneuver them into a useful position. Coleman's insights into the technicity of race are especially valuable considering how race, and Blackness in particular, works simultaneously at a material and symbolic level. The zombie makes this clear by functioning as both a monster rooted in the material conditions of the enslaved body and in the symbolic conditions of slavery that condition it at the same time, embodying the monstrous and abject conditions of Haitian Blackness, intimately connected to slavery in the colonial Atlantic world. Value is always discursive, mediated through language and the symbolic, an insight artfully made by Saidiya Hartman in her understanding of the unique value of Blackness within the liberal political project: "I contend that the value of blackness resided in its metaphorical aptitude, whether literally understood as the fungibility of the commodity or understood as the imaginative surface upon which the master and the nation came to understand themselves."[47] As she points out, Blackness is a useful tool—a symbol that *works* to abstract bodies into commodities, rendering them into a zone of partial being or a state of undeadness and, conversely, to reify its opposite in the form of whiteness. Thus race becomes the technology that mediates the status of being under colonial capitalism and continues to function even after the official abolition of slavery, a key element within the overall engine of capitalism that ensures its smooth functioning through the partitioning and classification of populations.

This insight carries over from our discussion of living, dead, and undead labor as well. Neda Atanasoski and Kalindi Vora have written that fantasies of automation "depend upon slavery and the idea of a worker who cannot rebel," and "are contiguous with existing labor exploitation along colonial/racial lines." For them, these ideas rely on notions of both freedom and labor as philosophical and political concepts that are tightly imbricated with race. Their ideas provide useful context to my own argument that dead and undead labor are twinned strategies for overcoming the limitations of living labor—first developed and implemented on the plantations of the Atlantic world and which remained and grew into the industrialized factories that came soon after. Atanasoski and Vora also point out that "the freedom of the fully human liberal subject cannot come to be without the unfreedom of the less than human or the nonhuman."[48] This shows the inherent paradox built into capitalism—it valorizes life at the same time that it degrades life. Capitalism makes life the highest value, exemplified by the investments Foucault identifies with biopower and biopolitics, and at the same time seeks to extract all possible surplus from life, transforming and objectifying life beyond its limits—rendering it an unliving but animate object.

The question of freedom is one that Atanasoski and Vora borrow from Hannah Arendt, who finds this at the heart of the problem of slavery as it existed for the ancient Greeks. For the ancients, freedom and labor were fundamentally at odds; a life burdened with labor was never fully free, subordinated as it was to life's necessities, and for this reason, labor was symbolically distinguished from work, the product of craft and skill that furnished a completed object in the world. Arendt argued that the modern age has lost sight of this distinction, treating labor and work as virtually synonymous. Arendt suggests that work, with connotations of craft and the artisan, was something with finitude. A master carpenter makes a table, a process with a beginning and an end, and this table can endure (potentially) for generations, meaning that the craftsperson had effectively made a lasting object in the world. In contrast, labor produced no finished product. Even the finest meal exists only to be consumed or left to rot; either way, it leaves no lasting trace in the world beyond the experience of its consumption. Arendt argues that this is why Greek thinkers like Aristotle associated labor with "slaves and tame animals," which "with their bodies minister to the necessities of life."[49] Arendt finds, in Greek thought, a close association between labor and life that continues into the philosophical traditions of the present; for Aristotle, labor pertained to any one of the endless processes that were necessary in the fostering and preservation of life and, as such, it was intimately bound up with freedom and slavery.

For Aristotle, labor was associated with slavery, from the sense that the necessary demands of living—food, shelter, sex, hygiene, et cetera—left us in a state of unfreedom akin to slavery—slaves to necessity itself. Arendt points out that the ancients "felt it necessary to possess slaves because of the slavish nature of all occupations that served the needs for the maintenance of life." This idea leads directly, in Aristotle's writing, to the justification of slavery as an institution within ancient Greek society. Ventriloquizing Aristotle, Arendt states that "to labor meant to be enslaved by necessity and this enslavement was inherent in the conditions of human life. Because men were dominated by the necessities of life they could win their freedom only through the domination of those whom they subjected to necessity by force. The slave's degradation was a blow of fate worse than death, because it carried with it a metamorphosis of man into something akin to a tame animal."[50] Arendt's reading of Aristotle shows how even these classical understandings of slavery cast it as something worse than death, rendering the human into a symbolic state that is essentially less than human.

The slave is a sacrifice to necessity, a substitute or stand-in for the enslaver who, through force and domination, appropriates the labor power of the enslaved as a surplus, to be contributed to the enslaver's own life. Arendt points out that "unlike the productivity of work, which adds new objects to the human artifice, the productivity of labor power produces objects only incidentally and is primarily concerned with means of its own reproduction; since its power is not exhausted when its own reproduction has been secured, it can be used for the reproduction of more than one life process, but it never 'produces' anything but life." In this reading of labor, Arendt reveals that there is always an excess or surplus that comes from labor, and while it leaves no lasting object, it can sustain the life processes of more than one being. This surplus, inherent in labor, meant for Aristotle (and Arendt) that the slave was a sacrifice to necessity itself, a needed substitution if the enslaver ever wanted to be truly free, which meant being freed from the necessities of life through the exemption from the labor required to sustain it. Arendt notes that this connection between labor and life is a key part of Marx's early understanding of labor, which he believed was primarily concerned with the reproduction of life as well, pointing out that "through violent oppression in a slave society or exploitation in the capitalist society of Marx's own time, it can be channeled in such a way that the labor of some suffices for the life of all."[51] Arendt does not disagree with Marx here, except to say that he was guilty of using the terms labor and work interchangeably, thereby causing (at least in part) the loss of the distinction between these two concepts. Arendt believes that the loss of this distinction is not simply semantic hair-splitting but symptomatic of far-reaching consequences in the modern world.

What is so important about this loss of distinction? Arendt believed that the modern interchangeability between the notions of labor and work has had consequences that continue to unfold. Recall the distinction: Labor operates endlessly to produce and reproduce life's necessities in a process that produces no lasting object, only sustaining life's needs. In contrast, work refers to a finite process, with a definite beginning and end, leaving a lasting object in the world of human artifice. This was the basis for classical philosophy's privileging of work over labor, which was relegated to what Aristotle described as an *animal laborans,* or laboring animal. For Arendt, this loss of distinction between the terms is more than semantic, and she argues that using them interchangeably has led to a conceptual slippage that ought to be understood symptomatically: It is not just that we moderns consider labor and work synonymous; we have lost the distinction at a deeper level. She claims, "The industrial revolution has replaced all workmanship with labor, and the result has been that the things of the modern world have become labor products whose natural fate is to be consumed," leading to a situation in which "a chair or table is now consumed as rapidly as a dress and a dress is used up almost as quickly as food."[52] In this remarkable critique of consumer society, Arendt argues that labor, in all its endless toil toward reproduction, has displaced the clear boundaries of work under a modern, industrial system.

Losing the finite boundaries of work, both in production and consumption, has given way to a voracious consumerism that has grown into being because of the endless drive toward productivity. A striking omission from Arendt's analysis is the term capital (or capitalism), despite her claims that the laboring and consuming society that has grown up in the modern age is leading to catastrophe—the consumption of the very world in which we live and on which we depend. Despite describing a society that is capitalist in everything but name, Arendt takes official aim at Marx, whom she blames for causing (or at least contributing to) the indistinction between labor and work. Arendt, writing in the 1950s, sounds prescient when she describes the rapid consumption of furniture and clothing on a scale approximate to food. Without work's boundedness, all human activity becomes endless labor, and, in turn, all things become fodder for a limitless drive of consumption.

Of the various ill effects that Arendt finds with the ascendency of labor, two are especially relevant to the theory of undead labor: the displacement of finitude in favor of endless production and the yoking of every endeavor to the endless cycle of production and consumption. The first of these effects echoes one of the central themes of this chapter, namely, that capitalism makes a serious attempt to overcome all kinds of finitude. Capitalism cannot abide limitation, and this takes the form of the extreme serialization of consumption and an obsession with the new, as Arendt suggests when she notes how material goods like furniture and clothing are consumed in ways that make them disposable and ephemeral. Even those types of labor that appear furthest removed from material production—immaterial or intellectual labor, for example—are still marked by perpetuity. Lawyers, accountants, and university professors are all bound to endless cycles of repeating their day-to-day labor in ways that more closely resemble the fungibility and ephemerality of consumption, rarely leaving lasting traces in the world.

The second significant shift Arendt describes, as all work takes the form of labor, is that workers are shifted into a position formally resembling slavery. This is not to say that all work becomes slave labor but rather that work—an action that results in a completed, lasting object—is replaced by a logic of endless labor, in which everything produced is destined to be consumed. The suggestion that all work has taken on the character of labor, and therefore that the worker has become more akin to the slave, may be controversial, but Arendt's argument in this regard is compelling. Most obviously, slavery has not disappeared under recent iterations of capitalism but has instead been displaced into economically and "underdeveloped" countries. And while slavery has been officially abolished, labor conditions that are effectively equivalent to slavery persist in many places around the world. More subtly, the logic of slavery as Arendt understood it is intimately connected to the formal and symbolic conditions of labor, and she argues that these appear even in the richest countries, appearing in neoliberal policies that have removed social safety nets and elevated labor as the highest social virtue.

To be clear, I am not equating neoliberalism, even at its worst, with a system of chattel slavery, but the afterlives of slavery can be felt well into the present. While Arendt's insight into the connection between labor and slavery looks to classical philosophy for evidence of her claims, more recent writing on the ongoing ramifications of Atlantic slavery offers a vital contribution. Christina Sharpe describes the reverberations of slavery using the metaphor of the wake, drawing on its dual connotations of the waves caused by the wake of a ship's passage as well as a gathering for communal mourning of the recently deceased. Sharpe defines this "wake work" as a "problem of and for thought," demonstrative of Black scholarship around slavery's lasting effects.[53] She goes on to describe the problem of slavery as an "ongoing disaster," finding its aftereffects—its afterlives—even in contemporary Black life, in shadows of violence, fungibility, and degradation that remain more than a century after slavery's passing. While Sharpe does not engage with labor directly, her analysis offers a reparative reading of Arendt: labor's ascendancy as the hegemonic form of work begins on the plantations of the Atlantic world but does not end there. The form of labor continues, spreading and repeating in waves in sharecroppers' fields and the factory floor, from the "new Jim Crow" of prison labor and mass incarceration to the actuarial tables of finance and insurance; labor is everywhere, endless, leaving only disaster in our wake.[54] And while we are not enslaved, the logic of slavery suffuses our work—we are no longer enslaved by necessity as Aristotle imagined, made into laboring animals by the body's endless needs. Instead, we are yoked to the necessity of labor to live under capitalism.

Undead Labor

The theory of undead labor developed in this chapter, focused on the slave and the zombie, leaves open further exploration of how this mode of production continues into the present, a topic addressed in the coming chapters. Yet the question remains: How to conclude when the very subject under investigation resists the notion of conclusion? Central to the idea of undead labor is the understanding that capitalism has a fundamental resistance to finitude and to limits, up to and including death itself. Through its affinity to life via living labor, capital seeks to grow endlessly, always expanding into new territories and transforming them into new markets. This has been true of capitalism since its inception during the early days of mercantilism and can be seen most clearly in the global expansionism of the colonial period, but this trend persists under neoliberalism, where undead labor continues to operate. Originating on the plantations, undead labor generalizes into the population, recognizable through techniques of self-management and the valorization of labor and life. The "always on" quality of contemporary capitalism is articulated by Jonathan Crary, who writes about the 24/7 work ethos of the neoliberal era in which any cessation of production is viewed as a problem. He describes how contemporary capital demands the absolute availability of the subject for labor, arguing that "24/7 is a time of indifference, against which the fragility of human life is increasingly inadequate. . . . In relation to labor, it renders plausible, even normal, the idea of working without pause, without limits. It is aligned with what is inanimate, inert, unageing."[55] The push toward working "without pause, without limits" is particularly symptomatic of the drive present within undead labor, which operates like a virus at the core of twenty-first-century capitalism.

In his thinking about the relationship between capitalism and the death drive, Byung-Chul Han helps to frame the role of undead labor within modern neoliberalism in ways that echo Philippe Ariès's notion that death is symbolically foreclosed under contemporary capitalism. Han argues that "in capitalist societies, the dead and the dying are less and less visible. But death cannot simply be made to disappear. If, for instance, factories no longer exist, then work takes place everywhere. If mental asylums disappear, then madness has become normal. It is the same with death. If the dead are not visible, a rigor mortis has extended over all of life. Life freezes into survival."[56] Han's formulation here condenses several ideas, the most salient of which is that the disappearance of a singular institution like the factory or the asylum has in the twentieth century heralded the diffusion of those institutions' purposes and functions across the social body. For example, as the United States transitioned from manufacturing toward a service or information economy, the diagram of labor, management, and efficiency that organized the factory became principles that spread into the broader culture and, at the same time, was internalized within the individual—meaning that what begins as an external force becomes, through disciplinary processes, part of the subject's structure, thus positioning us all as what Foucault describes as an "entrepreneur of himself."[57] When Han argues that "capitalism rests on a negation of death," he is revealing a fundamental part of the logic that operates within capital itself—a drive to undo the limits of life by overcoming death. The "negation of death" described by Han speaks to the undeadness of the zombie, whose very existence is owed to this negation within capital.

The zombie functions as a stand-in for the slave whose monstrosity lies in taking the structural conditions of the Black slave to their logical conclusions: a body reduced to pure, instrumental flesh, its objecthood entirely open to exploitation without the hindrance of mind, will, or spirit. Thus the figure of the zombie embodies the crisis and paradox of Blackness as a modern invention—race implemented technologically to reimagine the human as pure equipment. In a complementary discussion of race and capital, Achille Mbembe argues that racism is a fundamental tool of necropolitics, a system he defines as a mirror of biopolitics: rendering certain populations fit only for death, in contrast to the way biopolitics fosters life. Mbembe suggests "that *race* . . . figures so prominently in the calculus of biopower is easy to understand," and goes on to say, "Indeed, in Foucault's terms, racism is above all a technology aimed at permitting the exercise of biopower, 'that old sovereign right to kill.' In the economy of biopower, the function of racism is to regulate the distribution of death and to make possible the state's murderous functions." Mbembe's reading of race as a tool of capital provides a valuable supplement to the notion of biopower and biopolitics, suggesting that this nexus of race, death, and capital comes together in "new and unique forms of social existence in which vast populations are subjected to living conditions that confer upon them the status of the *living dead*."[58] If the biopolitical concern for life effectively creates an interdiction against death, then the exclusion and negation of life that takes place under necropolitics effectively forbids the flourishing of life.

Mbembe's theory of necropolitics clarifies undead labor within a more contemporary frame. However, undead labor is distinct from Mbembe's understanding of necropolitics insofar as it represents the ideals and aspirations at the heart of the capitalist imaginary—the dream of endless labor and of life unfettered by the limitations of death. Undead labor shows the grim and uncanny consequences of this dream of transforming all life into the raw material for labor, which looks less like transcendental immortality and more like the zombie. Necropolitics is something else altogether, a complementary but distinct way of reading the actual violence and destruction enacted on bodies and entire populations under these "new and unique forms of social existence," even as these conditions overlap with what I am calling undead labor.

The central thesis of this chapter is that undead labor, a mode of production that originated on the plantations of the Atlantic world and continues into the present day, is a deep-seated and inherently contradictory fantasy at the heart of capital. The clearest representation of undead labor is the zombie, which appears in the shadow of undead labor wherever it may arise. The uncanny vitality of the zombie represents and reveals the monstrous qualities of undead labor, not least through its tendency to embody and enact the transgression of boundaries, whether those are material, generic, or ontological. By observing undead labor through the reflection of the zombie, this mode of production can be understood as a metastatic and hypertrophic system. As its representative, the zombie shows how undead labor enacts a fantasy of endless growth and infinite production. It is a vision of life without death, in which the very notion of finitude has been foreclosed in favor of the infinite. Yet the ramifications of undead labor extend beyond the material conditions of political economies and cultural institutions: The foreclosure of death that engenders undead labor is also a crisis, a lived contradiction, within the modern subject.

The experience of this contradiction is precisely framed by Mbembe, who turns to Georg Wilhelm Friedrich Hegel in his thinking about the points of connection between subjectivity and its relation to death. He suggests that "Hegel's discussion of the relation between death and 'becoming subject' is significant here. His account of death centers on a twofold concept of negativity. First, the human negates nature (a negation that is exteriorized in the human's effort to reduce nature to human needs); second, the negated element is transformed through work." Further on in Mbembe's reading of Hegel on the relation between the subject and death, he points out that "in the Hegelian paradigm, human death is essentially voluntary."[59] Here, Mbembe is referencing the "master/slave dialectic" from Hegel's phenomenology, which posits the formation of subjectivity within an encounter between two beings. What distinguishes them and causes each one to take up their respective positions as master and slave is a confrontation with death and, I would add, their relation to life.

In the *Phenomenology of Spirit*, Hegel imagines the fully self-conscious subject as a product of this foundational encounter and the life and death struggle that ensues. The master/slave dialectic imagines this encounter as an allegory for the emergence of self-consciousness in which the subject taking the role of the master is a form of consciousness that exists *for itself*, while the slave is relegated to a consciousness that exists *for another*. Hegel imagines this as a life-and-death encounter, the resolution of which depends on each one's diverging commitments to life: The one who takes up the position of "master" does so because she is willing to risk death rather than become subjected to another. The other being in this encounter chooses to live, even in a subjugated state, and Hegel's language here is instructive: "They exist as two opposed shapes of consciousness; one is independent consciousness whose essential nature is to be for itself, the other is the dependent consciousness whose essential nature is simply to live or to be for another. The former is lord, the other is bondsman."[60] In Hegel's account, life is something that already means being for another—which seems to reflect Aristotle's belief that life is always subjected to necessity—and in this encounter, life has little to do with the freedom that comes with self-consciousness.

Hegel puts a nineteenth-century spin on this Aristotelian political idea, imagining the *Phenomenology* as a "voyage of discovery," using the language of the European colonial project with the specter of slavery and Haiti haunting his thinking.[61] As Susan Buck-Morss suggests, Hegel was writing the *Phenomenology* in 1807, featuring this mortal combat between master and slave precisely when the Haitian Revolution was prominently reported in European newspapers. Noting the surprising absence of these events from the commentary that has surrounded Hegel, Buck-Morss ventriloquizes these earlier commentators, writing, "'Where did Hegel's idea of the relation between lordship and bondage originate?' ask the Hegel experts, repeatedly, referring to the famous metaphor of the 'struggle to the death' between master and slave, which for Hegel provided the key to the unfolding of freedom in world history and which he first elaborated in *The Phenomenology of Mind*, written in Jena in 1805–6 (the first year of the Haitian nation's existence) and published in 1807 (the year of the British abolition of the slave trade). Where indeed?" For Buck-Morss, it is obvious that Hegel had the revolutionary struggle of the Haitian people in mind when he wrote the famous dialectic. She goes on to argue, "We are left with only two alternatives. Either Hegel was the blindest of all the philosophers of freedom in Enlightenment Europe, surpassing Locke and Rousseau by far in his ability to block out reality right in front of his nose . . . or Hegel knew—knew about real slaves revolting successfully against real masters, and he elaborated his dialectic of lordship and bondage deliberately within his contemporary context." Unfortunately, Hegel's politics were not on the side of the Haitian revolutionaries, and only a decade later in his philosophy of history, Hegel would dismiss all of sub-Saharan Africa as a land in which there is no subjectivity or history, leading Buck-Morss to suggest, "What is clear is that in an effort to become more erudite in African studies in the 1920s, Hegel was in fact becoming dumber."[62] While disheartening, this conservative turn in Hegel's thinking does not erase the insights into life, death, and freedom that his analysis provides, and that analysis remains worth considering in more detail.

For the Hegel of the *Phenomenology*, the Haitian Revolution represented a world-historical event in which philosophical abstraction entered reality. Buck-Morss describes this in the following way: "Theory and reality converged at this historical moment. Or, to put it in Hegelian language, the rational—freedom—became real. This is the crucial point for understanding the originality of Hegel's argument, by which philosophy burst out of the confines of academic theory and became a commentary on the history of the world."[63] In other words, the Haitian Revolution—the first successful and permanent slave rebellion—brought the symbolic into the actuality of history. This was a moment when enslaved people threw off their chains and embraced freedom at the risk of their lives. This crucial moment marks the realization of what Hegel might call their self-consciousness, the coming-into-being of freedom through the sublation of life and self-preservation. The Haitian Revolution should be counted, alongside the American and French revolutions, as one of the great heralds of modernity and democracy, but the freedom achieved in each did not last, nor did it resolve all the conditions that produced revolution in the first place.[64] The point of contact between theory and reality that Hegel observed in the Haitian Revolution cut both ways; this was not simply a moment in which the symbolic abstraction of freedom manifested in the world through a revolutionary encounter with death; it was also a moment when a new kind of rationality could be born to accommodate the symbolic impossibility of a successful Black revolution. As Arendt argues, the endless cycle of consumption brought with it elements of slavery and suggests that the resolution of Hegel's dialectic did not go as planned. If anything, the position of the slave wins out as life rises to become the dominant cultural value of capitalism, at least insofar as living labor functions as raw material of capitalist production.

This reading of Hegel in the context of revolution also appears in the work of Frantz Fanon, who addressed the master/slave dialectic in his thinking on Black phenomenology. Fanon wrote, "He who is reluctant to recognize me is against me. In a fierce struggle, I am willing to feel the shudder of death, the irreversible extinction, but also the possibility of impossibility."[65] In a footnote connected to this passage, Fanon speculates about a potential chapter on the relation of suicide to Black populations, thus seeking empirical evidence of Hegel's fantasy of subjective mastery. Yet this passage lays bare not the key to Black subjectivity but the impulse of capital itself: being willing to sacrifice any individual body, and suffer the extinction of any species, to access "the possibility of impossibility": life without any fetter or limitation; a true mastery insofar as it pushes past necessity and ontology itself, transcending the material even as it subjects and consumes it. Yet in practice, this looks less like transcendence and more like transgression; less like a master of all and more like a zombie, enacting an endless cycle of consumption and producing only more of itself, more of the same.

It is important to make clear the distinction between enslaved people, whose rebellion against their masters set the stage for the Haitian Revolution, and the allegorical position of the slave within Hegel's dialectic (or, indeed, Arendt's writing), which, as a figure, condenses and stands in for the mediating relation between reason and the material world. In his commentary on Hegel, Alexandre Kojève comes to similar conclusions as Arendt. He suggests that while the master/slave dialectic posits a way toward self-consciousness, it does not necessarily succeed; while the master may demonstrate the more noble path, the slave's pragmatism and investment in life actually wins out in the end. Or in Kojève's own words, "The truth of autonomous Consciousness is *slavish Consciousness*." He argues that

> only the Slave can transcend the given World (which is subjugated by the Master) and not perish. Only the Slave can

> transform that World that forms him and fixes him in slavery and create a World that he has formed in which he will be free. And the Slave achieves this only through forced and terrified work carried out in the Master's service. To be sure, this work by itself does not free him. But in transforming the World by his work, the Slave transforms himself too, and thus creates the new objective conditions that permit him to take up once more the liberating Fight for recognition that he refused in the beginning for fear of death. And thus in the long-run, all slavish work realizes not the Master's will, but the will—at first unconscious—of the Slave, who—finally—succeeds where the Master—necessarily—fails.[66]

In Kojève's account, it is the slave that transforms their own condition through their commitment to life and labor; it is through their work that they can reshape the world and themselves. The slave finds new life as an object for the master and does not concern themself with freedom. In this way, Kojève's reading of Hegel sheds light on the conditions of undead labor.

Throughout Kojève's commentary on Hegel, he emphasizes the slave's status as an object or thing, seeming to presage the relevance of this work to the zombie and the undead labor this monster carries out. Kojève describes the being for another of the slave as "being in fact a living corpse," who from a state of apparent defeat accepts life and embraces life above all else.[67] Kojève's commentary on Hegel was especially influential because it used a Marxist lens to interpret the *Phenomenology*, and the subsequent alignment of slave and worker was not meant to denigrate actual laborers (or enslaved people for that matter) but, rather, to frame the entire system of labor under capital as ruled by the slavish position within Hegel's dialectic. For Hegel, both master and slave were meant to allegorize the abstract preconditions for an eventual dialectical unity.

Kojève is more pessimistic about the final result of the master/slave dialectic, arguing that "the future and History hence belong not to the warlike Master, who either dies or preserves himself indefinitely in identity to himself, but to the working Slave."[68] The master may claim all the glory, but they become abstracted and immobilized in an adherence to their own identity. The slave, in contrast, remains free to remake the world in its own image, where life and labor are the pinnacle of virtues. Kojève's Marxist critique is clear in this reading of Hegel, and he finds in capital a mentality more in line with the slave's position: Instead of a free self-conscious subject basking in the light of reason, there exists a system built on a different logic of life—a bad infinity of labor, reproduction, and consumption. Real, historical events were doubtless influencing Hegel's thinking as he formulated this infamous dialectic, but through Kojève's reading, it becomes clear that the slave in Hegel is both more monstrous and abstract, more abject and single-minded than any real slave from the Atlantic world. Rather, what he describes, in its endless and asymptotic pursuit of life, is the zombie—a version of the slave that seems to live up to the craven reputation put forward in the *Phenomenology* more than any maroon or freedom fighter in Haiti. Within this version of the slave, and in this modern interpretation of undeadness, crystallizes the kernel of the capitalist imaginary: the dream of infinite expansion and endless reproduction.

2

Analogies of Undeadness

POPULISM, TRANSGRESSION, AND THE ZOMBIE

THE ZOMBIE HAS APPEARED in many forms since it first shambled across the silver screen in 1932, and in the mythic, cultural, and spiritual iterations that came before that, as the zombie rose up in the slave societies of Haiti and the plantations of the Atlantic world. As a monster, the zombie has been a figure of monstrous labor, a symbol for rampant consumerism, and an analog for global pandemic. In each case, the zombie emerges as a powerful metaphor that captures the public imagination even as it seems to both conform to and inform these cultural crises. Perhaps the most significant characteristic of the zombie is that it is an undead monster: undead, insofar as it was once alive, died, *returned* to some semblance of life, and now exists in a state that is certainly not dead but not entirely alive either. The zombie is a body that returns long past the time when it should have disappeared. It is this quality that lends the zombie its adaptability to so many descriptions and metaphors, a prefix to a host of cultural issues, from "zombie stocks" to "zombie technologies" to "zombie economics." In each instance, the zombie condenses an entire network of connotations, histories, and citations that lets us imagine undeadness at the level of cultural form, with real symbolic utility, and not simply as something limited to a singular mythology.

In every iteration, the zombie is linked to a periodized political crisis: from race, slavery, and colonial capitalism; to consumerism, contamination, and post-Fordist political economies; to viral overproduction, contagion, and neoliberal populism. Through all of it, the zombie remains. It could be said that the zombie has been "over" for nearly a century, and yet it continues to haunt the modern imaginary. This is, at least in part, because the zombie functions as a powerful analog for a set of contradictions that have never been fully resolved. More than that, the zombie is a hypertrophy of analogy itself, revealing something important about transgression and sameness in several ways simultaneously: The zombie functions as a kind of genre in contemporary media, but an excessive one. It bleeds into nearby genres, transgressing their borders and hybridizing them (the zombie rom-com, the zombie western, the zombie melodrama), and at the same time, the zombie serves as a figure of the masses and an analogy for populism as a political and cultural problem.

To say that the zombie is analogy in hypertrophy is to suggest that as a cultural form it is *overnourished* and *overgrown*, the linguistic roots of analogy having to do with proportionality and the symmetry of form. The zombie is an analogy in a state of hypertrophy, meaning that it exceeds its own formal boundaries and definitions. The contradictions that give rise to the zombie are *too* productive, prone to overcoming and overrunning the limits that contain them, whether those boundaries are the boarded-up windows and doors of a house or a shopping mall, or the metatextual borders that delimit a genre, medium, or political movement. With this idea of semiotic excess and border-crossing in mind, this chapter focuses on the role of analogy, transgression, and contagion in the ways the zombie functions as a cultural form. In its most recent incarnations, the zombie always appears en masse and through its relation to consumption, it seems connected to the idea of the public as well. If the zombie is a figure of the masses, then this study of the zombie as analogy also opens a way toward thinking about the mediated dynamics of populism, not just as a mirror of political populism, but as a problem unique to mass media technologies and their patterns of generation and distribution.

Studies of populism tend to focus on the politics of identity, and it would be easy to let the main argument in this chapter about the zombie and analogy follow that line of thinking. Identity has its place in this discussion, particularly if we understand identity as something that allows us to remain recognizable as ourselves over time. Identity, insofar as it allows us to remain the same to ourselves, involves the production of sameness in time and space, and in this way the zombie helps to inform our ideas of both identity and populism because all three involve the reproduction of the same: populism is the formation of a group identity and program of ideas, marching in lockstep through public discourse, while the zombie literalizes this understanding of populism, albeit in a more monstrous frame, as the contemporary zombie consumes endlessly and produces nothing but more of itself.

The aim of reading these ideas through one another is to understand media populism in a more formalist approach to the cultural and semiotic mechanisms by which populism grows and spreads, metastasizing across the borders of political formations and cultural productions alike. This reading of identity and populism within the context of analogy and the zombie might appear to flatten out the differences between right-leaning and left-leaning identity politics or to avoid expanding on the usefulness of those identity-based claims that can be understood as a kind of "strategic essentialism."[1] Emphasizing analogy over identity, this chapter hopes to shed light on the underlying mechanisms at work in any political claim based more on identity and similarity over position and difference, suggesting that any politics based in identity shares an important formal similarity, even though such politics may differ in context and function.

As a cultural form, the zombie exhibits a remarkable diversity in the range of its many appearances across popular media and culture. But regardless of form, the zombie always brings with it a history of race and a logic of racial capital, even if any given incarnation of the monster seems to elide race explicitly. The roots of the zombie's mythology in the plantations of the Atlantic world show through. The zombie has always been a proletarian monster. Both in number and in spirit, it falls on the side of the masses, and while it would be a mistake to place every version of the zombie on the side of the "people," nevertheless, the zombie typically reflects something like the body politic at its worst. Unlike the aristocratic vampire or the royal mummy, the zombie is better than no one. It is a laboring body, dressed in rags, decomposing, and hungry. The zombie seems to starkly embody the anti-elite stance of a political populism. Indeed, this recalls the most dangerous elements of populism: a ravenous mob, operating with one mind and a singular purpose. In her discussion of democracy and public opinion, Nadia Urbinati suggests that populism is a mutation in the democratic spirit—a deformation of democracy that makes it simultaneously more common and renders it unrecognizable to many contemporary forms of political discourse.[2] If populism is a mutation of democracy, then the zombie appears to reflect this disfiguration, revealing a fundamental discord between two versions of a people, two forms of a public that are only revealed through a perspectival shift in the media that represents them.

The term media populism typically refers to the reflection of political populism within some form of mass media and often includes television or social media, as these forms of mass media tend to represent political movements in real time and, because of this, are the primary venues for populist discourses. Along these lines, Benjamin Krämer points out that any form of populism ought to attend to the medium by which these ideas are disseminated, arguing that "media are the devices par excellence to exert symbolic power via the representation of society."[3] Krämer's point is important: Media populism is not a simple reflection of political discourse but rather takes the form of the media technology through which it is disseminated. Indeed, Benedict Anderson makes the case that the formation of mass media, and new developments in technology and time, were instrumental in creating the kind of imagined community that would result in both modern democracy and national consciousness. For Anderson, it was the development of the newspaper and the novel, forms of mass media that emerged as a result of print technologies, that allowed for the synchronization of information in a national setting. He suggests that "these forms provided the technical means for 're-presenting' the *kind* of imagined community that is the nation."[4] The newspaper makes it possible for information to be disseminated on a mass scale at regular intervals, effectively synchronizing a regional discourse within the reading public.

Anderson's great insight here is that the imagined community is formed through media technologies like the newspaper, which not only creates a shared language and discourse but disseminates it at regular time intervals (weekly, daily, morning and evening editions, etc.), which ensures that the *same* discourse is circulating within that imagined community at any given time. Anderson points out that "the idea of a sociological organism moving calendrically . . . is a precise analogue to the idea of the nation, which is also conceived as a solid community moving steadily down (or up) history. An

American will never meet or even know the names of more than a handful of his 240,000-odd fellow-Americans. He has no idea of what they are up to at any one time. But he has complete confidence in their steady, anonymous, simultaneous activity."[5] Anderson's point here is that this formation is not simply spatial or geographic but also temporal—that the sameness that engenders the imagined community is not simply about national borders, but about temporal intervals and the regular synchronization of a discourse. It is only through this kind of mediation that the imagined community of the nation-state forms: a community made identical to itself in space and time.

The idea of the imagined community helps to bring populism into better focus. After all, populism is simply a variation of the imagined community as Anderson understood it: It is clearly connected to a notion of national consciousness, since populist movements often display nationalist tendencies, even if they are not limited to the form of the nation-state. To think about imagined communities in the twenty-first century is to consider how new technologies and emerging formations go hand in hand, allowing for a reading of both media and populism through their reflections and representations. Refracted through a media platform or technology, media populism is especially powerful because it presents society to itself as a prescriptive representation, showing a uniformity of vision where a plurality exists. This chapter explores media and populism through the theoretical armature of undead labor, tracing these ideas through the changing representation of the zombie as an uncanny shadow of the populace, and how the shifting technological conditions of the zombie's representations show, in turn, something significant about contagion, transgression, and sameness.

While this argument could be grounded in many examples—indeed, a key part of the argument itself is that the changing iterations of the zombie's evolutionary trajectory contain a through line that brings new insights to light—the primary example for this chapter comes in a recent case: Marc Forster's 2013 film *World War Z*, an adaptation of a novel about the zombie apocalypse that relies heavily on both digital technologies and mock geopolitical discourse. What the zombie shows us about populism is that the population itself becomes a kind of medium for the discursive patterns of these new imagined communities—a social body, made up of actual bodies, that moves according to a singular set of ideas and ideals—where once again, the zombie seems to show us something of a worst version of populism, a body politic in ruins through an excess of similarity. The masses themselves seem to take on the qualities of a medium, through which the sameness of populist discourse travels, replicating like a virus another example of excessive growth and production that in the last chapter I argued was an important signifier for undead labor.

To better understand the relationship between the zombie, populism, and the problems of similarity and totality, the next section undertakes a project of periodizing the zombie into three, distinct evolutionary phases: the *zombie as slave*, the *zombie as mass*, and, most recently, the *zombie as population.* The project of periodization is not entirely free of conceptual pitfalls, the most obvious of which has to do with the selection of what to include and what not to include within each period in question. When it comes to the zombie, there are *always* more examples, a truism that also applies with equal accuracy to history. Thus the intention here is not to provide a comprehensive overview of all the representations of the zombie within any given historical period, but instead to generate a concept of history, rooted in structural conditions, that gives shape to the changing representation of the zombie over time. The approach to this project is indebted to Fredric Jameson, who describes the process of periodization this way: "The 'period' in question is understood not as some omnipresent and uniform shared style or way of thinking and acting, but rather as the sharing of a common objective situation, to which a whole range of varied responses and creative innovations is then possible, but always within that situation's structural limits."[6] Attending to these structural limits, the periodization of the zombie will emphasize the ways the zombie shadows modern economic and political institutions and works to produce sameness and totality in its wake, albeit in different forms over time, in order to underscore the zombie's relevance to an understanding of populism more broadly.

Periodizing the Zombie

The zombie first appeared in the plantations and colonies of the Atlantic world, an outgrowth of the forced amalgamation of cultures, practices, and experiences of the peoples involved in the transatlantic slave trade. It rose up out of the fertile ground of colonial capitalism as a nexus point of culture, religion, and economy, brought together in the body of the slave and made monstrous by the excessive demands placed on that body, warping it and creating the conditions of undead labor. Embodiment has always been an important feature of the zombie, setting it apart from more ethereal undead monsters like ghosts and specters. It was a body whose mind or spirit had been separated, leaving only a mechanical semblance of life.[7] As the anthropologist Wade Davis has pointed out, the zombie was not a singular monster. In his ethnographic research, Davis outlines that practitioners of Haitian *Voudon* occasionally use the term "zombi" to refer to a spirit under the control of a malign master or sorcerer; these "spirit zombis" can also be put to use, although perhaps their primary function is their use to control the "zombie cadavre [*sic*], the zombi of the flesh."[8] In every account, the zombie consistently appears as an embodied monster, even when the soul is captured in the process. Another anthropological account of the zombie from Alfred Métraux speaks of wandering souls as "zombis," but notes that these are not to be confused with the "flesh-and-blood *zombi*," which is understood as "the living dead—corpses which a sorcerer has extracted from their tombs," with full emphasis, once again, on the flesh.[9] The zombie of the flesh is what stuck in the popular imagination. As Robin Wood has argued, the monsters of an era often reveal the deep-seated tensions that structure a particular time and place, and this is especially true of the zombie.[10]

As an enduring cultural form, the zombie's significance in the mass cultures of the twentieth and early twenty-first centuries is symptomatic of the structural conditions that engendered undead labor, and which gave rise to the zombie itself. As discussed in chapter 1, the zombie continues to haunt the popular imagination because those structural conditions at the intersection of race, labor, and value have never been truly resolved. The devastation of chattel slavery in the Atlantic world, whose aftereffects persist into the present moment, may have changed and transformed over time, but they nonetheless remain. These "afterlives of slavery" continue in the form of rapacious racial capitalism and race-based structural inequalities that operate across different scales ranging from the geopolitical to the individual, yet in each instance the hallmarks of undead labor remain: the drive to extract value from the living, laboring body in excess of what it is structurally capable of producing.

This is the period of the *zombie as slave*, an unthinking corpse moving to the intention and desire of a master's will. While the zombie's first appearance in mass media was in Seabrook's travelogue, its first depiction on film was in Victor Halperin's *White Zombie* from 1932.[11] In these early representations, the zombie generally appeared as a single body or in small groups, working in the background of a field, plantation, or factory. These zombies also tended to be explicitly raced bodies, almost exclusively Black and brown, except for the driving moment of narrative crisis in the film when a white woman was turned into the titular white zombie. The *zombie as slave* was the most explicitly supernatural of the zombie's evolutionary stages, relying on voodoo and mysticism to bring the dead back to life.

The next major step in the zombie's evolution took place in 1968 with George A. Romero's *Night of the Living Dead*, in which zombies are no longer the result of magic, but some equally mysterious natural force.[12] These zombies no longer served as a simple analog to the slave but instead to the masses, showing a monstrous version of the plight of the individual who was diffused into a larger population. These undead bodies begin to appear en masse and take the form of the masses: Whatever turns someone into the living dead does so indiscriminately. Anyone and everyone can be a zombie. The other revolutionary feature of Romero's zombies is that they become cannibalistic for the first time. The zombie is no longer just a monster of the flesh, but one that craves flesh as well, and the bite of the zombie becomes deadly, passing the contagion of undeadness like a plague. The cannibalistic zombie is also significant in that it reflects concurrent economic concerns as countries like the United States and the United Kingdom move toward consumer economies.

Romero produced a series of zombie films—including *Night of the Living Dead* in 1968, *Dawn of the Dead* in 1978, and *Day of the Dead* in 1985—and each depicted a world increasingly overrun by the undead. As Steven Shaviro points out, for Romero, zombies were "violently apocalyptic" while, "at the same time, they remain disconcertingly close to the habitual surfaces and mundane realities of everyday life. Business as usual bizarrely coexists with extremes of tension and hysteria, in a world on the verge of vertiginous destruction."[13] As the zombie transitions from an analog of the slave to an analog of the masses, the conditions under which it comes into being also change in important ways. The *zombie as slave* is inherently supernatural and brought about by extraordinary means, but the *zombie as mass* is more quotidian, as Shaviro describes. Following the arguments made in the previous chapter, this transition illustrates how undead labor comes out of the extraordinary conditions of the plantation; but those extraordinary demands made on the bodies of the slave move from the margins of modern culture to the center, where the commodification of everyday life is normalized into the working masses.

The slave's status as a commodity reveals a dark side to the dream of equality that arose within modern democracies. On the one hand, the American and French revolutions ushered in an idea of equality among all citizens (acknowledging the many caveats that came with this political ideal) and a new set of ideals around what it meant to be human; but at the same historical moment, the Atlantic slave trade was reimagining another version of humanity, not as equal but rather as exchangeable or fungible. Equality and exchangeability represent two sides of the same philosophical ideal, a flattening out of the individual into the mass, the population, and rendering a people into a more abstract, homogenous entity. The universal ideal of the human was split from its inception, with one side leading to the universality of the rights-bearing citizen and the other leading to the general exchangeability of the commodity form. While the slave was the most obvious example of this, the zombie as its monstrous incarnation continues to speak to this problem of equivalence or sameness in every period of its appearance, and certainly the *zombie as mass* seems to illustrate the next logical step of this crisis of equivalence among bodies, since to become a zombie was to be reduced and flattened into a monstrous version of sameness. Old and young, rich and poor, men and women, Black or white—the zombies in Romero's films were entirely interchangeable since all zombies were equally dangerous and the death of one zombie meant its replacement by another.

Contagion also becomes part of the zombie mythos in Romero's living dead films. The *zombie as slave* could only be created by magical means, and the curse of undeadness could not be passed from one body to another. Romero was the first to reimagine the zombie as contagious, a condition that could spread through the population. As an idea, this would develop across Romero's films: In *Night of the Living Dead,* the zombie's bite was dangerous, and the cause of the zombie outbreak was described as environmental, while the concept of the zombie as a plague continues in *Dawn of the Dead* and spreads into other zombie movies, an idea that would soon dominate the genre. The film historian Jamie Russell puts it this way: "Before *Night of the Living Dead,* zombies had been content to scare, strangle or bludgeon their victims. Romero upped the ante by giving them a taste for warm, human flesh."[14] This shift in representation, reimagining the zombie as cannibalistic and contagious, signals a shift in the political economy that takes place at the same time. Once again, the zombie literalizes these economic conditions by way of analogy: the ravenous cannibalism of the zombie collapsing production and consumption into a single action in which more undead are created through the consumption of the living, creating a closed circuit.

While the zombie may change over time, the essential contradictions of undead labor that brought it into being continue to exert their influence, appearing in more recent iterations of the zombie. Again, Shaviro highlights the new political stakes of the zombie from the living dead trilogy when he says, "Romero's zombies seem almost natural in a society in which the material comforts of the middle class coexist with the repressive conformism, mind-numbing media manipulation, and the more blatant violence of poverty, sexism, racism, and militarism."[15] Race, labor, and value continue to be important structuring elements within the zombie, even though the specific ways these elements play out in the many instances of the zombie genre change depending on the era. For example, race is one of the defining features of the zombie beginning with its origins on the Caribbean plantation, yet this continues to be an important element in the zombie mythos as it transitions to become a figure of the masses. It plays a significant role in Romero's films, which tend to feature strong, Black protagonists at a time when it was uncommon to do so. Though race is not an explicit theme in any of the living dead films, it remains a powerful force. At the end of *Night of the Living Dead,* the Black protagonist, Ben, survives the zombie siege of a farmhouse in rural Pennsylvania, only to be shot in the last minutes of the film by a sheriff's posse, who appear to mistake him for a zombie. The significance of a Black man shot by the police signals a wealth of political inference, revealing a powerful political critique of the race politics of the era.

Starting around the beginning of the twenty-first century, the zombie goes through another major evolutionary development, taking place primarily through scale. If the early zombie only appeared singly or in small groups, and cannibalistic zombies began to appear as the masses, the most recent incarnations of the monster—represented in films like *28 Days Later* (Danny Boyle, 2002), *World War Z* (Marc Forster, 2013), and *Train to Busan* (Yeon Sang-ho, 2016)—scale up significantly, and in almost all its most recent incarnations, the zombie functions at the level of the population, working like a global pandemic. The cause of the zombie becomes explicitly viral in these recent iterations, complicating the matter of scale insofar as the virus itself seems to exhibit several similarities with the zombie: The virus exists on the margins of life, marked by an excessive mode of production in which its only goal is to reproduce more of itself, using the molecular building blocks of living cells. The damage caused by viruses often comes when they reproduce to a point of bursting living boundaries of the cell, releasing yet more viruses into the organism.

Films like *28 Days Later* or *World War Z* depict the zombie as a kind of plague and show the zombie as a threat not just at the level of the individual protagonists but to the social fabric of the nation as well. While the ramifications of the zombie are scaled upward to the level of geopolitics, the cause of the zombie plague is scaled down to the microcosm of the cell and the virus, and it is telling that once we reach the age of the *zombie as population*, the disease-based cause of the zombie becomes virtually ubiquitous across all media. In *28 Days Later*, the zombies are simply called "the infected"—the film is as much an outbreak narrative as it is a zombie movie—and the virus moved quickly through the population; these zombies were not simply rotting corpses but infected bodies that acted quickly and violently to spread the contagion. The "fast zombie" first appeared in *28 Days Later*, but this feature would, again, become ubiquitous across the genre. Both scale and speed became key characteristics of the monster, even as the zombie crisis was magnified to reflect fears of a global pandemic. Zombies depicted at this level of scale, appearing in large numbers, are generally created by computer-generated effects and shown in digitally created hordes.

World War Z will serve as the primary example of this argument because of how zombies appear in the film in two connected ways that take place at the level of form and content. At the level of content, the zombies appear on a massive scale and are shown as bodies moving almost as one: These zombies illustrate media, populism, and transgression through the explicit narrative of the film, in which zombies emerge as a global viral pandemic that moves with such speed and ferocity that entire nation-states begin to buckle under the force of the changes taking place. At the level of form, these zombie masses are generated using digital technologies that highlight the role of media as something that shapes popular movements both symbolically and literally. *World War Z* is not the exemplar here because it is particularly good as a Hollywood blockbuster, outbreak narrative, or part of the zombie genre. Rather, the film is symptomatic of all these categories in a way that cuts across scale and sameness, taking place simultaneously through form and content. The formulaic and clichéd aspects of *World War Z* can be understood here as a feature and not a bug of this analysis, serving as a useful illustration of how analogy, transgression, and contagion work to generate changes in both popular media and political populism, giving rise to new forms of the body politic.

Where *World War Z* stands out is in its special effects, particularly in the way digitally generated masses and crowds of zombies move on screen. These zombies move swiftly and unnaturally in two ways. First, the unnatural movements of the undead in *World War Z* are done deliberately to emphasize the strangeness of the diseased, zombified bodies. Bodies twist and jerk, eyes cloud over, and teeth are bared and chitter as the body "turns," marking its passage from life to death to undeath. The film highlights the violence and virulence of contagion, although the zombie's bite is the primary vector through which the pathogen is transmitted. The second way the movement of these zombies is significant has to do with how they are generated, the logic and instructions by which the programs and algorithms that govern their actions make them move, both singularly and en masse. Each zombie's movements are created algorithmically, and each body is generated with its own set of logics, rules, and physical constraints. The zombies depicted in *World War Z* were imagined as vectors of viral transmission who regularly hurl themselves at their victims, sometimes flying into the frame from off screen, without any regard for their own self-preservation. On screen, the zombies move as a mass, and as we watch the crowd, the film seems to descend into the uncanny valley as bodies move together in ways resembling swarms, flocks, and flows that suggest an inhuman coordination and reveal their digital origins.

Totalizing Populism

Beginning in the late twentieth century, the zombie becomes a totalizing monster. These zombies are violently contagious, explosively replicating by saturating and transforming the population. Like any uncontrolled reproduction, the zombie plague threatens to leave no one alive and, in turn, flattens the differences of the population, thus remaking the masses according to a logic of equivalence. Put another way, the zombie spreads its undead condition throughout a population in ways that structurally echo the totalizing logic of capitalism under Western globalization (arguably, *World War Z*'s title signals this as an implicit concern) and the total remediation of representation that takes place under the reign of digital media. As Friedrich Kittler has pointed out, the emergence of optical fiber networks signals a general equivalency among media platforms, as all previous forms of media technology are subsumed into the digital. Kittler argues, "Inside the computers themselves everything becomes a number: quantity without image, sound, or voice. And once optical fiber networks turn formerly distinct data flows into a standardized series of digitized numbers, any medium can be translated into any other. With numbers, everything goes. Modulation, transformation, synchronization; delay, storage, transposition; scrambling, scanning, mapping—a total media link on a digital base will erase the very concept of a medium."[16] This notion of "total media," which rests on a "digital base," echoes other scholars of digital theory who have pointed out the all-consuming nature of digital mediation.[17] The distinction between sound and vision, as well as the material conditions of various media platforms, is erased within the ubiquity of information and digital technology: the flattening of sensory channels into numerical representation.

Kittler's understanding of the digital suggests that digital code, disseminated through optical fiber networks, conveys along with information a logic of sameness, as all sensory representation (film and vision, audio recording and sound, etc.) is rendered and remediated into a singular mode of representation in the form of number and code. Thus the digital age ushers in a new kind of general equivalence, creating new and uncanny conditions in both the form and content of digital media. Coming to similar conclusions on a different path, Wendy Hui Kyong Chun provocatively asserts that "information is 'undead,'" noting that it is "neither alive nor dead, neither quite present nor absent."[18] Chun argues that information shares a formal similarity to equivalence, pointing out that the universalizing tendencies of information bear a family resemblance to the commodity as it was understood by Marx. She unpacks this connection through the work of Thomas Keenan, who provides a useful understanding of the commodity through the conceptual lenses of abstraction and metaphor.

Keenan argues that the heart of the commodity is the equivalence made possible through its abstraction from pure materiality: "The matter at issue is the appearance of something *as* something else, the rhetorical structure of simile or metaphor . . . semblance, shine, simulation, or dissimulation. In societies where the capitalist mode of production prevails, something economic shows itself by hiding itself, by announcing itself as something else or in another form."[19] Here the *as* functions to bridge the gap between two distinct objects. Chun rests her assertion that information is "undead" on the structural and formal similarities between information and commodification. In turn, this suggests that the structural connection between commodification and equivalence also reveals something important about the category of undeadness shared by information and the zombie.

Keenan notes the challenge that commensurability poses to Marx's theory of exchange. For Marx, exchange posed a theoretical problem because it focused too much on the essential qualities of the objects themselves, rather than the mediating influence of labor. This is why (to use Marx's example) Aristotle could not fully understand the dynamics of value and exchange, because he lacked a modern understanding of exchange as a transaction of time and labor (i.e., value) rather than of material objects.[20] Marx argued that "the secret of the expression of value, namely the equality and equivalence of all kinds of labour because and in so far as they are human labour in general, could not be deciphered until the concept of human equality had already acquired the permanence of a fixed popular opinion."[21] Yet as Keenan points out, this takes a sharp turn in Marx when he says, "This however becomes possible only in a society where the commodity-form is the universal form of the product of labour, hence the dominant social relation is the relation between men as possessors of commodities."[22] As Keenan points out, Marx turns traditional humanism on its head by suggesting that it is not the arrival of the Enlightenment that makes a theory of universal exchange possible, but rather that "humanity itself only arrives with the domination of the commodity form, which makes it possible."[23]

Marx suggests that the growth of humanism and the principle of equality that appears with modernity coincides with the emergence of a notion of equivalence that relies on abstraction from matter into language or the symbolic, as Keenan argues in his emphasis on rhetoric and metaphor. The idea of human equality, so fundamental to the emerging democracies of the modern era, brought with it a notion of equivalence and exchangeability, as evidenced by the prevalence of chattel slavery in the Atlantic world at the very same historical moment, rendering the human as commodity. To quote Keenan once again, "Humanity as such, empty and abstract, alike and equal, is indistinguishable from the commodity."[24] Modern conceptions of human equality and human equivalence bear a family resemblance to the commodity form—it is a general equivalence of labor, understood within the context of the commodity, that gives rise to this modern conception of humanity as a set of universal conditions.

The zombie represents a monstrous version of the slave—a form of human life reduced to the status of a commodity in which equality is replaced by equivalence. In its later versions of the zombie, this totalizing logic comes to the fore, operating as a monstrous analog of the rapacious commodification of not just the individual but entire populations. If the zombie evolves into more contemporary, contagious forms, it stands to reason that, insofar as it relates to the population, the zombie can also shed light on populism. Looking to the connections between the zombie and populism might suggest a link to the popularity of the genre, which has waxed and waned over the last century. The zombie has been a continuous presence as a movie monster in the horror genre, but more than this, it might be read as a populist monster insofar as it represents a politics from below and reflects the concerns of a lived, everyday experience.

Ernesto Laclau suggests that at the heart of populism lies an attempted totalization of the political experience of various social agents.[25] Populism is a homogenizing force within political discourse, yet it remains difficult to define because the concept is so mutable. The political theorists Cas Mudde and Cristóbal Rovira Kaltwasser have pointed out that the term is often claimed by both the right and left wings of the political spectrum, and in each instance it can be used as either a badge of honor or a political insult.[26] Elsewhere, Mudde has argued that populism poses such a challenge to define because the term rests upon a series of contested definitions, most centrally a notion of "the people."[27] Once again, Jameson provides some insight into the birth of populism as a postmodern phenomenon, resulting from the dialectical opposition that develops between high modernism on the one hand and mass culture on the other.[28] When coupled with the general crumbling of metanarratives associated with postmodernism, of which the nation-state can be understood as one of the grand narratives that begins to decay, allowing new imagined communities to form in the shadow of nationalism and democracy, this dynamic becomes especially clear.

The populist-imagined community sees itself not simply as a nation, but as a people—a people who possess all the rights and privileges of the national citizen, but whose existence and flourishing are threatened by some rival body, a threat that can exist either outside or inside the nation. This is why political populism so easily incorporates ethnonationalism or state racism, a term that Foucault used when he described the development of biopolitics. In his lectures at the Collège de France, Foucault explicitly draws out this connection when he says, "The modern State can scarcely function without becoming involved with racism at some point." He continues soon after in the same lecture, "What in fact is racism? It is primarily a way of introducing a break into the domain of life that is under power's control: the break between what must live and what must die."[29] For Foucault, the necessary development of race within the political mechanisms of the modern state signaled a shift in sovereignty that began to center notions of biology and the definition of the population, which must be made to flourish under the pastoral guidance of the state. Thus the life of the population becomes the primary principle guiding the state's hand.

What Foucault could elaborate further is that this understanding of the population is fundamentally Malthusian, offering an idea of growth that is limited only by resources and competition. Race is a tool used to subdivide the population and justify the privileging of one division over another, based on a kind of market-driven Darwinism. When Foucault describes a break between what must live and what must die, he is being quite literal: The survival of one race means limiting the resources of another. Thus, when Foucault says that this new program of power aims to "*foster* life or *disallow* it to the point of death" in his famous writings on biopower in *The History of Sexuality, Volume 1,* he frames the life and death struggle as one taking place within the arena of the market.[30] He will elaborate on this in his lectures when he argues that "the fact that the other dies does not mean simply that I live in the sense that his death guarantees my safety; the death of the other, the death of the bad race, of the inferior race (or the degenerate, or the abnormal) is something that will make life in general healthier: healthier and purer."[31] Foucault primarily describes this transition to biopolitics in the terms of the state and governmental sovereignty, but what is missing from this vision of the emergence of the population as a governmental entity is the role of the logic of commodification and capital in this set of dynamics.

As previously discussed, Foucault's theory of biopolitics was missing a history of chattel slavery in the Atlantic world, which would have helped to expand his ideas on biopower and biopolitics. Indeed, Foucault has been justly criticized for the Eurocentric perspective that dominates his theory of biopolitics. Yet the theory of undead labor outlined in this book offers a useful supplement to Foucault and helps us see that it is not simply life, but also labor that drives this newfound investment in life proffered by state sovereignty, which must safeguard not only the pastoral care of the population but the freedom of the market at the same time. The centrality of the market to this logic is lost when we look to the relatively strong nation-states of the mid-twentieth century, when

Foucault was writing and lecturing, yet it becomes more obvious when we look back to the period of colonial capitalism, when the imbrication of life and labor was impossible to ignore in the half life of the Black slave. But this connection is becoming more obvious yet again under neoliberalism, when the strength of the nation-state is weakened by more transparent investments in the market and its unfettered freedom. Looking to neoliberalism and more contemporary developments in biopolitics, populism included, allows the inextricable relation between life and labor to be shown with greater clarity, and we can see it realized more fully in the theory of undead labor. Populism is the adoption of biopolitics as a dominant political ideology within the population itself.

The racial politics of populism change dramatically over time, and the way racial capitalism manifests in the neoliberal era is strikingly different from the colonial period. Yet the roots of this neoliberal or biopolitical formation still grow from the same ground, and like the zombie's evolution, the connections between populism and racial capitalism run deep. For example, Jodi Melamed argues that even the explicit discourses of anti-racism and multiculturalism that appear mainstream are in fact manifestations of a biopolitical approach to fostering the life of the individual: "Racialization displaces its differential value making into world-ordering systems of difference, concealing its performative work with its constative work."[32] Here, Melamed is pointing out how the constitutive politics of race are obscured by newer techniques and rhetorics of power without actually being resolved. She goes on to show that "racial liberalism, liberal multiculturalism, and neoliberal multiculturalism have innovated racial procedures beyond color lines, often incorporating antiracist terms of value, so that new terms of racialized privilege emerge (*liberal, multicultural, global citizen*), along with new terms of racialized stigma (*unpatriotic, monocultural, illegal*)."[33] Tellingly, the terms that come to connote racial stigma in Melamed's account are often tied to populist ideas of an imperiled sense of belonging, ownership, or stewardship of culture—ideas that can resist explicitly racist interpretations, even as they carry the kernels of a racial ideology just below the surface.

Melamed speaks to this directly when she frames these shifts more explicitly in relation to racial capitalism (i.e., capitalism), showing how these boundary lines and divisions within a target population are necessary to the functioning of the system. About racial capitalism, Melamed says:

> These antinomies of accumulation require loss, disposability, and the unequal differentiation of human value, and racism enshrines the inequalities that capitalism requires. Most obviously, it does this by displacing the uneven life chances that are inescapably part of capitalist social relations into fictions of differing human capacities, historically race. We often associate racial capitalism with the central features of white supremacist capitalist development, including slavery, colonialism, genocide, incarceration regimes, migrant exploitation, and contemporary racial warfare. Yet we also increasingly recognize that contemporary racial capitalism deploys liberal and multicultural terms of inclusion to value and devalue forms of humanity differently to fit the needs of reigning state-capital orders.[34]

Once again, the matrix of value under capital does the heavy lifting of transforming and organizing the population, using techniques like race and other forms of difference and division to render certain parts of the population equal and equivalent—flattening out the population into a homogenous mass—while at the same time, but along different valences, strategically devaluing others.

In other words, the use of value in biopolitics does not simply privilege the notion of the population as the raw material for power and politics, but reshapes the definition of the population in new and multiple ways. For example, Foucault argues that "what we are dealing with in this new technology of power is not exactly society (or at least not the social body, as defined by the jurists), nor is it the individual-as-body. It is a new body, a multiple body, a body with so many heads that, while they might not be infinite in number, cannot necessarily be counted."[35] Foucault is not the only one to suggest that a new kind of social body emerges under biopolitics. Speaking about the new developments of populism that have taken place in the first few decades of the twenty-first century, Marco Revelli states, "It is as if a new socially barbarized population had suddenly emerged alongside—or better, from beneath—the good old people of yesterday's democratic rhetoric, supplanting and submerging it."[36] Revelli's language is surprisingly reminiscent of Foucault's, and both seem to imagine the new formations of this population-based politics as a kind of outbreak or monstrous transformation. A new social body emerging from within the old. A multiplicity or, put another way, an imagined community, that also relies on a logic of contagious homogeneity. A plague of the same that appears as populism on the one hand and the zombie on the other.

In each major era of the zombie's evolution, it provides a monstrous and sometimes parodic representation of this attempt to totalize the political experience of a people. To suggest that the zombie is an inherently monstrous analog to the populace, the imagined community that populism engenders, means considering the population at its worst: acephalous, exchangeable, and all-consuming. To avoid the previous failures of political theory to properly account for populism, Laclau argues that it is essential to reckon with the problem of totality directly. He argues that in order to "grasp that totality conceptually, we have to grasp its limits—that is to say, we have to differentiate it from something *other* than itself."[37] Thus Laclau suggests that the problem of populism leads back to the problem of sameness and difference, and this, in turn, highlights the significance of three symbolic mechanisms that disseminate sameness: analogy, contagion, and transgression. These three concepts correspond not only to the periodization of the zombie, but also to our understanding of populism as a political problem of sameness, whether that appears in media or politics. But what are the mechanisms through which this sameness moves throughout the population? To say that sameness is spread via media is correct but insufficient, since the various media technologies that convey an ideology of populism are merely one possible vector of transmission. Instead, the zombie and its recent representations offer us insight into how sameness moves through the population. Understanding this process of ideological homogenization requires a turn toward contagion, analogy, and transgression.

From Transgression to Analogy

To transgress is to cross a real or symbolic boundary that marks the difference between two things or states of being. Its existence is predicated on the division of one thing into two: the accepted from the prohibited, the normal from the abnormal, the sacred from the profane; transgression always involves a limit. The zombie is a cultural form that has always embodied transgression in various ways, revealing the blurred boundaries between production and consumption, the individual and the crowd, and, most obviously, the zombie bears at its root a transgressive relationship to life itself.

Transgression is typically framed within the context of prohibition or taboo. When an individual transgresses, they have acted against the rules and limits imposed by a larger social and symbolic system. But to focus on the prohibited action is to lose sight of the real issue. Michel Foucault makes this point directly when he argues that any rigorous study of transgression should not consider the transgressive actions themselves, as they are inevitably tied to cultural context and historical specificity. Instead, an examination of transgression should consider the limit itself. He elaborates on this within the context of his own thinking about sexuality:

> We have not in the least liberated sexuality, though we have, to be exact, carried it to its limits: the limit of consciousness, because it ultimately dictates the only possible reading of our unconscious; the limit of the law, since it seems the sole substance of universal taboos; the limit of language, since it traces the line of foam showing just how far speech may advance upon the sands of silence. Thus, it is not through sexuality that we communicate with the orderly and pleasingly profane world of animals; rather, sexuality is a fissure—not one which surrounds us as the basis of our isolation or individuality, but one which marks the limit within us and designates us as limit.[38]

Foucault points out that the discourse surrounding sexuality is never simply about sexuality but that sexuality functions as an analogy across multiple registers (consciousness, law, language), and in each case it serves as the limit and the means by which that limit can be transgressed. Originally published in a special issue of the journal *Critique* in 1963 dedicated to the work of Georges Bataille, Foucault's writings on transgression precede his more famous work on the history of sexuality, but this earlier writing makes a significant contribution to his later work on sex by framing it in terms of limitation and transgression.

As Foucault explores the limit of language, he turns to analogy and, as he articulates the structural borders of language, his ideas are not so much reflected as refracted through another object altogether: sexuality and, specifically, how sexuality represents a boundary-line limit in three distinct instances. First, sexuality is the limit of consciousness because it is the code that unlocks the unconscious, at least in a post-Freudian world. Second, sexuality is the limit of the law because it provides the substance for taboo. But it is in the third instance that Foucault turns away from descriptive language and toward something different. He writes that sexuality represents the limits of language "since it traces the line of foam showing just how far speech may advance upon the sands of silence."[39] This passage is highly evocative, bringing to mind waves lapping on a sandy beach, where a line of foam is left behind, marking the edges of the tides. It is not just significant because of the evocative qualities of the prose or because the imagery is useful, but because he illustrates one way that analogy provides a path towards understanding the *limit* in and of itself.

Analogy is usually defined in relation to similarity or equivalence. The *Merriam-Webster Dictionary* sums up the term as an act of comparison, in which analogy works to find the similarities in "two otherwise unlike things based on resemblance of a particular aspect."[40] According to this definition, analogy seems to emerge through a relation of similarity or continuity of form. In rhetoric, analogy is typically defined as a "figure of speech likened to a simile or metaphor," but James Measell points out that analogy is used across a variety of disciplines, and its origins in classical rhetoric are even more inclusive. For example, in linguistics, analogy tends to be a principle of consistency, whereas the natural sciences use the term in ways connoting "structural identity" and a "functional similarity."[41] Nilli Diengott reveals a more mathematical definition of analogy, pointing out that one of the earliest formulations of the term "was based on strict *equivalence* of ratios."[42] Measell explains more about the evolution of the term, showing that the definition of analogy as "equivalence between ratios, was broadened to include resemblances of ratios," which was then expanded again to include inductive reasoning, before finally coming to signify both equivalence of ratios and a "direct resemblance."[43]

Analogy was an important concept for Foucault in his writings on transgression because, like transgression itself, it is all about difference, sameness, and the boundary that distinguishes the two. Analogy works to find similarity across differences, and in this way, it also works as a kind of transgression, since it is always reaching across a boundary to find its like in the other. The line or limit, central to Foucault's understanding of transgression, is understood as explicitly spatial insofar as it frames the act of transgression. He states that "it is likely that transgression has its entire space in the line that it crosses. The play of limits and transgressions seems to be regulated by a simple obstinacy: transgression incessantly crosses and recrosses a line which closes up behind it in a wave of extremely short duration, and thus it is made to return once more right to the line of the uncrossable."[44] Transgression takes place within the space of the line, according to Foucault, which opens up into a field in which the play of limits and transgressions can take place. Transgression crosses and recrosses this line "incessantly," suggesting that it works less like a breach and more like an oscillation that creates a phase space, in which all possible states are represented.

The state or condition of undeadness that afflicts the zombie can also be understood as one that is fundamentally transgressive and formally resembles the movement Foucault describes: crossing and recrossing a boundary, in this case, the ontological limits of life and death. To be undead is to be neither fully alive nor fully dead, instead existing in the kind of phase space that Foucault discusses, having crossed from life into death and back to life again. The prefix *un-* in undead signifies this reversal: a return to life as well as a state of being that is neither entirely one nor the other. Undeadness marks the zombie as a transgressive form of life, and, to be undead, is always to be rendered in the negative. Undead monsters like the zombie are typically associated with death, yet the theory of undead labor that has been outlined in the previous chapter suggests that, if anything, beings like the zombie exhibit an excess of life. Undead bodies are animate, and undeadness appears to be a condition analogous to life, even if it is not actually alive. In fact, the undead occupy a "zone of indistinction" that mirrors the oscillation of the transgressive line described by Foucault.[45] Perhaps this is why the zombie also takes so naturally to analogy and becomes such an easy vehicle for it, since it shares the structural conditions of transgression. Like analogy and transgression, undeadness emphasizes the demarcation line between two states and, even more significantly, its porous nature.

Alexander Galloway describes the function of analogy as a kind of opening, and in doing so, he draws out the connection between analogy and the analog, saying, "The word 'analog' is something of a doorway because it opens up and indicates a pathway forward." This definition recalls Foucault's discussion, insofar as it suggests that both transgression and analogy can best be understood in spatial terms: Each one opens a way or a path. Galloway offers his own etymology of the term, showing how its origins in ancient Greek emphasize some of its most salient features. As Galloway points out, *logos* is fairly common in Greek as a term meaning speech, discourse, or ratio, but the prefix *ana-* is not a direct negation as in the similar case of the prefix *a-*. Rather, Galloway argues that "the *ana-* in analog does not negate *logos,* nor present its contrapositive form, but in fact produces a different relationship, a kind of parallel or implicative relation."[46] The *ana-* in analogy and analog suggests a causative relation, that the form of one brings about the same form in the other; a relationship of symmetry, not opposition nor necessarily negation. These etymological roots are key to Galloway's thinking on the inner dynamics of both the analog and analogy, regardless of medium.

Galloway's insights into the roots of analogy are instructive insofar as they imply a series of effects that take place whenever the terms are invoked. Broken into its constitutive elements, the *ana-logos* signifies a sameness in form and meaning that is reflected across the gap of difference: Analogy is the ongoing relation of the same form appearing, implicated across two corresponding yet distinct media. As Galloway unpacks this idea further, he turns to the work of Brian Massumi, who has provided one of the most enduring definitions of what the term analog means:

> The analog is a *process,* self-referenced to its own variations. It resembles nothing outside itself. A topological image center literally makes the virtual appear, in felt thought. It is more apparitional than empirical. Sensation, always on arrival a transformative feeling of the outside, a feeling of thought, is the being of the analog. It is matter in analog mode. This is the analog in a sense close to the technical meaning, as a continuously variable impulse or momentum that can cross from one qualitatively different medium into another. Like electricity into sound

> waves. Or heat into pain. Or light waves into vision. Or vision into imagination. Or noise in the ear into music in the heart. *Or outside coming in.* Variable continuity across the qualitatively different: continuity of transformation.[47]

The most important feature of the analog, according to Massumi, is continuity across difference. This contrasts with the digital, which operates in discrete units and accumulated differences; the analog creates continuity across matter and media. Take, for example, the vinyl record on which sound waves are inscribed, etched into the plastic surface in a direct and isomorphic fashion to the sound waves themselves; the quality of being analog is the characteristic of creating the same form across different materials and allowing circuits of meaning to traverse the boundary between two forms. Analogy grows out of the same etymological ground, creating conceptual continuity across qualities and difference. It is how sameness reproduces itself on either side of a line in an act that bears striking formal resemblance to transgression.

As Foucault describes it, transgression is always about the limit, the line of distinction that separates the accepted from the taboo. Transgression is the act of overcoming that limit, rendering the prohibition impotent and diminishing the symbolic value of the limit itself by showing paths of continuity that threaten to extend and grow without end. On this aspect of transgression, Foucault speaks directly when he says, "The limit opens violently onto the limitless, finds itself suddenly carried away by the content it had rejected and fulfilled by this alien plenitude which invades it to the core of its being." Foucault argues that transgression opens the floodgates of sameness, calling into question the very nature of the limit and limitation itself. He goes on to say, "Transgression carries the limit right to the limit of its being; transgression forces the limit to face the fact of its immanent disappearance, to find itself in what it excludes."[48] This description sheds light on the idea of undeadness, so central to the very notion of the zombie and undead labor more broadly. Undeadness is the turning or recrossing of the line, the limit between life and death; but in this new space opened up by this undead transgression, something new is revealed. Life, unlimited and unrestrained by death, grows endlessly and out of control. It is a concatenation that cascades outward, leading to more and more transgressions—or, put another way, a state of contagion.

This passage recalls Keenan's understanding of the human as a concept that emerged as a modern category, only becoming universal after the adoption of the commodity form as an abstracting and totalizing state of being. In the case of transgression, the limit finds itself in the very thing that it excludes. Similarly, the zombie as an undead being working as an analog to transgression might be seen as the embodied exclusion of the Enlightenment vision of humanity: a ravenous form of life, without reason, and ultimately destructive as a force that grows and consumes without end. The raced conditions of the zombie's origins also contribute to this understanding, as the social category of Blackness was invented to embody the contradictions of Enlightenment universals. In sum, this reading of the zombie illustrates three aspects of crossing a boundary or overcoming a limit: transgression, analogy, and contagion. Each one sets up a slightly different approach to a formally similar set of dynamics, allowing a larger pattern to emerge. Transgression emphasizes a social and symbolic difference, delineating the accepted from the taboo, or the sacred from the profane, and, by its very nature, reveals the fragility of this dividing line. In contrast to transgression, which emphasizes difference, analogy focuses on the similarity, both formal and functional, that exists between the two sides of the line that indicates a path or opening toward continuity—a place to ford the line. Contagion, the final act of crossing, imagines how sameness replicates itself across difference, taking advantage of the pathways that are opened by the other two.

Across the periodization of the zombie above, we might also suggest that the zombie, and the undead labor it embodies and propagates, intersects with all three of these valences of transgression, analogy, and contagion. The zombie's early iterations map onto transgression, with its emphasis on the social relations that bring the zombie into being. Creating the zombie requires crossing the boundary of death and returning, but this is deeply imbricated within systems of race, labor, and value that structure the colonial plantations of Haiti and the Caribbean, which served as the epicenter at the time. The zombie is the shadow of modern humanity, embodying sameness at its worst: equivalence and not equality. Contagion becomes an essential part of the zombie mythos starting in the 1960s, when the undeadness it exhibits begins to spread autonomously to other bodies. Contagion marks the moment when the zombie becomes a figure of the masses, spreading sameness throughout the social body. The mid-century zombie became a symbol of the homogenization of culture, rendering all of society into a ruin through the proliferation of a symbolically acephalous state of ravenous consumerism. Twenty-first-century representations of the zombie, such as *World War Z*, show these ideas taken to their logical conclusion, imagining it as a global phenomenon that expands along the lines of a pandemic in which zombies themselves overrun every limit they encounter.

The zombies in *World War Z* represent the most common iteration of the zombie since the turn of the twenty-first century and, in so doing, are emblematic of the fast, viral forms that the zombie takes, reflecting the cultural issues and anxieties that surround it. These zombies function as a kind of metastasis of analogy: a force that always overcomes and transgresses the limits that enclose them. The zombies of *World War Z* represent a contagious force of viral overproduction that generates neither living nor dead labor but instead what I have been calling *undead labor*, which in this case appears as a metastatic growth that breaks down the distinction between inside and outside—and, in so doing, overcomes distinction altogether in favor of a generalized equivalence and a monstrous sameness. Undead labor takes to its logical conclusion the totalizing logic that has been present within it since its inception—a pandemic of global proportions that threatens to consume everything around it.

This excessive mode of production and engagement with the world is not anomalous but central to capitalism in every one of its iterations, from the colonial capitalism of the plantation to the present-day austerity measures undertaken to bolster the ultra-wealthy at the expense of the commons under neoliberalism. This is a point that George Monbiot and Peter Hutchison describe as part of the "invisible doctrine" of neoliberalism, which they track back to the original Portuguese plantations on the island of Madeira, a few hundred miles off the western coast of Africa. As they point out, the colonial model first tested on Madeira—the notion of a *terra nullius*, which functioned purely as an extra or surplus to the territory and sovereignty of a kingdom or nation—thereby rendered the entire island raw surplus to the resources of a nation.[49] Monbiot and Hutchison also point out that once something was rendered as a surplus in this way, it became the target of a total, unlimited extraction and consumption. In the previous chapter, I described undead labor as a mode of production based in the excessive extraction of value from the bodies of slaves and, as such, as deeply tied to race as an invention of the modern era used as a symbolic technology that would facilitate the creation and extraction of new kinds of surplus from the human body. What Monbiot and Hutchison's argument suggests is that this is a more universal relation toward raw material that was invented alongside colonialism and capitalism and, in turn, never leaves the various iterations of capitalism. The periodization of the zombie, or its evolution over time, reflects these changes and makes it possible to see these destructive and consumptive elements as essential to capitalism as a political and economic system.

World War Z

Before it was adapted into a film, *World War Z* was published as a novel by Max Brooks in 2006 as a follow-up to his first popular zombie-themed book, *The Zombie Survival Guide,* a genre-savvy compendium of advice gleaned from a lifetime of movie-watching. The book *World War Z* took the tongue-in-cheek style of *The Zombie Survival Guide* and adapted it into a novelization modeled on war journalism, described itself as an "oral history," and assumed the form of a nonfiction narrative describing the outbreak that precipitated the zombie apocalypse. The film adaptation came seven years later, after a notoriously difficult transition from book to screen.[50] The film condenses the sprawling style of the journalist piecing together various historical accounts into a more personalized narrative, giving a singular face to what was previously framed as a collective history. The transition to a classical Hollywood narrative makes the film lean heavily on tropes and clichés from the zombie genre and, while Max Brooks was able to show off his extensive knowledge of the zombie genre in his books, the film plays out in a series of formulaic scenes borrowed from other films. As much as *World War Z* is a zombie movie, it also displays many of the elements of the outbreak narrative and, as such, becomes an interesting exemplar for the zombie in the neoliberal era.

In her work on the outbreak narrative, Priscilla Wald coins the phrase "imagined immunities" to describe the role contagion plays in reifying the symbolic borders necessary to a national identity. Clearly referencing Benedict Anderson's notion of the "imagined community," which suggests that national consciousness relies on a shared sense of unity and identity with a community of strangers who share a fantasy of sameness, Wald argues that "outbreak narratives make the act of imagining the community a central (rather than obscured) feature of its preservation." Anderson's vision of the imagined community was a largely unconscious feature of national identity, but Wald expands on this idea, pointing out that "communicable diseases know no borders, and the global village is the biological scale on which all people and populations are connected."[51] The "imagined immunities" Wald describes bring into bright relief those symbolic boundaries that limn the community in one form or another. *World War Z* provides a useful, if idiosyncratic, example of the outbreak narrative as it intersects with questions of populism, transgression, and undead labor. It reveals the zombie epidemic overrunning and spreading across national boundaries and literally breaking through the barriers (both real and symbolic) that are set up to oppose it. At its heart, the outbreak narrative is about contagion, biological and otherwise, and Wald's insight into this narrative form takes shape in its effects on politics and the way that contagion emerges as a concept with equal importance in both the individual and social body.

Contagion generally calls to mind an illness that exceeds the boundaries of a single body. The mark of contagion is its multiplicity—the emergence of something that leaps across the gap between bodies, or any space that separates one being from another. Contagion signals the growth of the same and the overcoming of difference, and in *World War Z* this contagion is mirrored across multiple levels of scale, appearing at the cellular, social, and national levels in the film. Framed as a disease, the zombie pathogen in the film is an extreme example, taking only ten seconds to violently transform a human into a zombie, re-creating the conditions of undeadness in a new body. Speed will become a theme for the film, and the speed of contagion is marked early when the protagonist, Gerry Lane (played by Brad Pitt), who witnesses an outbreak of the zombie pathogen on the busy streets of New York City, counts to ten, giving both himself and the audience a clear idea of the speed at which the body becomes infected, dies, and returns to life. At the level of the individual body, the zombie's bite is the primary vector of transmission, and the theme of boundary-breaking that has been at the heart of this chapter is clearly literalized in the violent rupturing of the skin that brings on a quick transformation, turning the living human into the undead zombie.

At the level of the nation-state, the zombie threatens to overcome both the literal and symbolic boundaries that structure it. The story of *World War Z* centers around a United Nations operative attempting to piece together the epidemiology of the zombie outbreak while traveling from one crumbling nation to another. Perhaps the most striking scenes take place when the story moves to Israel, where the city walls of Jerusalem have been newly reconstructed precisely to keep out thousands of zombies massing outside the city. Of course, these walls will be breached like all the rest, although the specific circumstance of the breach suggests a conservative relationship to the politics of border-crossing and refugee populations. As refugees enter Jerusalem into a refugee camp just on the inner walls of the city, they begin to sing the praises of their saviors in a moment of picturesque and performative cosmopolitanism. But this very display, broadcast through the camp's loudspeakers, draws the zombies in such massive numbers that they swarm over the walls, climbing over each other to eventually overrun the city. This scenario stages an inherently conservative political position, imagining the refugee as a danger to the social body even if, as the filmmakers are at pains to show, they have only the best of intentions.

At the intersection of the zombie movie and the outbreak narrative, *World War Z* uses the epidemic as a model to explore ideas of both contagion and populism. Marc Guillaume brings this connection into clearer relief when he suggests that "if we rid the notion of epidemic of all its pathos, what remains is an abstract model or, more precisely, a series of models. Epi-demos: upon the people. Something spreads itself across the population, something that under normal circumstances would be external to it: a foreign element."[52] Guillaume's insights show that contagion is a problem of and in the people, the *demos*. On top of this, contagion is always and fundamentally generative, which is a point of agreement between Guillaume and Wald, who makes a similar case: "The outbreak narrative . . . animates the figures and maps the spaces of global modernity. It also accrues contradictions: the obsolescence and tenacity of borders, the attraction of the threat of strangers, and especially the destructive and formative power of contagion."[53] The mechanisms by which contagion operates—spreading sameness across the gulf of difference between individuals and across populations—echo the totalizing logic of populism in an abstract or schematic form. This abstraction is important since both populism and contagion refer to mechanisms without specific content and represent a program for the reproduction of the same through a kind of unification in the form of an imagined community/immunity. The zombie represents this mechanism within *World War Z*, and the next section explores these ideas through the force of analogy. Yet, as mentioned above, the zombie lends itself to the work of analogy, and so the analysis of the film and the zombies therein will provide, in a self-reflexive manner, additional insight into the working of analogy itself to show its relevance to the theory of undead labor that is the central theme of this book.

The zombie embodies the force of analogy in three important yet fragmented ways that are illustrated in the film. First, the zombie as an individual body is rendered indistinct and generalizable in the form of a crowd—and the digital multitude that appears in the film opens this problem in new ways, specifically in how the movement of these crowds has been algorithmically mapped and shaped by other forms and types of movement. Second, the crowd form that the zombie takes moves not as a group but as a wave. This appears as one of the most distinctive features of the zombies in the film, which are generated and animated by the software platforms known as ALICE and controlled on screen both individually and as a collective. Third, the wave of zombies is rendered according to the logics that inform the algorithms that produce them. Taken together, these three tiers of analogy suggest that analogy itself goes into hypertrophy under the formal auspices of the zombie. Each of these tiers of analogy, zones of indistinction, will be explored in turn because each brings into clearer relief the fundamental connections between the zombie and populism by way of analogy run amok.

An individual made indistinct in the crowd can be understood as a baseline definition of populism itself. Rooted in the political formation of the crowd, populism renders the granular concerns of the individual indistinct and irrelevant, in favor of a unified *volonté générale*, or general will. Reminiscent of the transformation that the individual undergoes in the crowd in the classic work by Gustave Le Bon, the individual under populism is lost or overcome by the power of the group—the mass of the masses, if you will.[54] A kind of transgression against the individual takes place under populism, which demands a certain sameness of thinking and fantasy from everyone subsumed within its purview, as populism rests on a unified understanding of a people, regardless of their actual differences. Both populism and contagion reveal the porousness of individual identity.

The second indistinction, in which the crowd becomes the formal analog of a wave, invokes the fluid metaphors that are often used to describe the physical and political dynamics of the crowd. Popular movements in culture are often described as waves, sweeping away older traditions and forms. In the case of *World War Z*, these wave dynamics are literalized through the computer-generated effects that both generate and govern the movement of the zombie masses we see on screen. Like many contemporary blockbusters, *World War Z* makes use of complex software programs to animate and control the bodies of crowds. This is particularly apparent in extreme long shots that include dozens, hundreds, or even thousands of bodies moving en masse. Using a proprietary suite of programs called ALICE (Artificial Life Crowd Engine), the artists and technicians at MPC (Motion Picture Company) drew on a set of borrowed characteristics to animate and imagine the zombie masses, and their distinctive vision of these zombies—moving as a wave of undead bodies—is one of the memorable features of the film.[55] One of the visual effects supervisors at MPC, Jessica Norman, discussed the challenges posed by so many artificial bodies on screen at the same time when she writes, "During pre-production we received reference material showing insects swarming and schools of fish formations. . . . We also received concept work early on showing different formations that the Zombie crowds could take. These included pyramid formations and also tentacle-like shapes."[56] The uncanny quality that appears in the movement of the zombies on screen, particularly in the Jerusalem scenes, is due to these formal characteristics borrowed from other environments and mapped onto the undead masses. The movements of the zombies seem so inhuman because the physics that animate them have been borrowed from nonhuman systems: The zombies move *like* a swarm because their movements are generated and based on the movements of insects; the zombies move *like* a wave because the schooling dynamics of fish in water have been used to map and create the movements of bodies on land. This results in a set of movements that is both distinctive and uncanny, showing the force of analogy, revealed in the *likeness* of the zombie crowds to these nonhuman groups.

Programs like ALICE lend granular detail to the movement of the bodies on screen because each one is individually animated and controlled by artificial intelligence to move seamlessly with the other bodies in the crowd. Despite being run by AI, the "agents" generated by ALICE have a set of rules that govern their behavior on an individual level, meaning that each body we see on screen is animated with its own set of rules and governing logic, allowing it to exhibit apparent freedom. In her discussion of digital crowds, Kristen Whissel has argued that, "by virtue of its composition, the digital multitude immediately calls into question the relationship between the individual and the mass, the self and the collective."[57] Continuing this line of thinking, Whissel quotes Eugene Thacker on the logic of the swarm, saying, "On the ontological plane, the first important observation is that the multitude is neither the individual nor the group. It is positioned somewhere in between, somewhere else entirely."[58] This in-between space echoes Foucault's description of transgression as a kind of oscillation, crossing and recrossing a symbolically significant limit.

The third and final moment of indistinction takes the form of the algorithms that structure and orchestrate the zombies in *World War Z*. Digital technology makes possible another kind of universal equivalence, as well as the accompanying exchangeability of medium and form that takes place within it. The digital is a universalizing technology, as was discussed above by way of Kittler, and as a technology it tends to subsume everything into itself. Yet the digital is all about distinctions and the accumulation of differences, so how is it that analogy, with its roots in the analog, plays out in regard to the digital? Strictly speaking, it cannot. Looking closely at the basic elements of digital technologies, we see it rooted in the very principle of logical distinction—zeros and ones, for example—which is precisely opposed to the relentless contiguity that the analog seems to engender. Yet this is precisely where transgression, contagion, and analogy show us something significant: Each one is about the crossing of limits and revealing the porousness of those boundaries, even as whatever content employs these formal mechanisms—political populism, the SARS-CoV-2 virus, even the zombie itself—seems to overcome distinction in favor of indistinction, producing sameness where there was once difference. Formally speaking, this is why the zombie lends itself with such acuity to the problems of analogy and shows the way that analogy itself proliferates within the symbolic order.

In *Bergsonism,* Gilles Deleuze sees that "quality is nothing other than a contracted quantity" and the very basis of sensation itself: "contracting trillions of vibrations onto a receptive surface."[59] Quality is quantity at a different scale, experienced from another vantage point and level of abstraction. Even though quality is so deeply rooted in our experience and understanding of sensation, it is at least once removed from the level of embodied experience that initially triggers those impressions. Perhaps surprisingly, populism works along similar lines. Populism is itself a quality that emerges from quantity, a phenomenon predicated on the very notion of the population or the masses. A common definition of populism is simply "a political philosophy or movement that represents or is claimed to represent the interests of ordinary people especially against the Establishment."[60] Like Deleuze's reading of Henri Bergson, the quality of populism emerges out of quantity: It is the compound impressions of a people and, perhaps more important, an imagined community (or, better, a collective fantasy) aimed at the populace. Populism is condensed from the populace—it is a quality that obscures the underlying quantity, hiding a multiplicity underneath a facade of unity, singularity, and similarity. Individual difference is obscured by the unified wave of populist discourse.

The political philosopher Jan-Werner Müller describes populism as a political discourse that is inherently anti-pluralist, a position that puts it in direct opposition to a more cosmopolitan outlook: It demands ideological cohesion and consistency of the social body. Müller also emphasizes the way populism operates according to a totalizing logic, in which the imagined community of the population is further reified into a complete social body. "For the populists," Müller argues, "the equation always works out: any remainder can be dismissed as immoral and not properly part of the people at all. That's another way of saying that populism is always a form of identity politics (though not all versions of identity politics are populist)."[61] Müller's insight here is valuable because it brings to light the connection between populism and identity politics. Indeed, while Müller is careful to point out that not all versions of identity politics are populism, populism nevertheless takes a form that is like them, the significant difference being that the more traditional identity politics associated with minoritarian groups never imagine themselves as the dominant social class. Quite the reverse, populism always imagines itself as the dominant, albeit aggrieved, form of the social body—the infamously titled "silent majority" that imagines itself as the one true inheritor of social power, except for the danger posed by all those that may think differently.

Müller provides the explicit link between Foucault's biopolitics and the discourse of populism through identity politics. Identity politics grew out of marginalized communities, typically and explicitly in opposition to the dominant norms that created them by exclusion. Populism adopts the oppositional stance to a perceived outside threat, but combines that with a majoritarian position. Examples of this abound in the demands for "white history month," "straight pride," or a "men's rights movement"—yet in each of these examples, we see two important things. First, a demand not for equality but for structural exchangeability of position; an artificial and ahistorical leveling that commodifies identity without recognizing the structural and historical positions that make these demands seem absurd to genuinely marginalized groups. The logic here is that "white pride" should be *the same as* "Black pride" and that any demand to acknowledge the structural differences between the two is the actual racism. Second, this sets up a scenario in which the majority is in danger from the existence of the minority, a framework that looks like the biopolitical rationale for fostering the life of the chosen populace. Populism is simply biopolitics, advocating for itself. This insight also intersects with Laclau and Wald insofar as it reveals the important role fantasy and identity must play in any form of populist politics. Finally, the invocation of identity reveals an inherent demand for sameness embedded within the politics of identity. In other words, to embody an identity is to be identical to oneself—or conceptually coincide with the fantasy of a whole body—not through frozen immobility but, rather, through a frantic repetition, the reaffirmation of sameness across all boundaries of difference.

This drive toward sameness also reflects the troubling aspects of political and media populism, which both turns on and fosters a uniformity of opinion, an antipathy toward any political body that it considers "elite," and a blending of opinion and truth, the people and the state, fantasy and reality. Media populism makes indistinct the lines and boundaries between the people and the state in ways that seem to exacerbate the tendency of populism toward fascism. As Nadia Urbinati points out, "Fascism is the state and the people merging," and while she is explicitly referring to fascism understood through the lens of political theory, it is hard not to see this blurring of boundaries as the result of the disfigured self-reflection of the vexed category of "the people," and a crisis of analogy.[62] In the previous chapter, the zombie stands in for the figure of the slave, and for the roots of undead labor in the plantations and cultures of the Atlantic world. Here, another aspect of undead labor emerges, and the more recent incarnation of the zombie, particularly the zombie as it is represented in films like *World War Z*, embodies this rapid and repetitive generation of sameness as it reproduces itself across every boundary it encounters through the mechanisms of transgression, analogy, and contagion.

The presence of the term "zombie" in so many areas of culture in the late twentieth and early twenty-first centuries is symptomatic of this impulse toward repetition and proliferation, and also signals its significance. The analogy of the zombie itself displays zombielike qualities, parasitizing and moving via mechanisms of semiotic contagion across discursive and conceptual fields, media platforms and genres. It proliferates in the popular imagination and, at the same time, reveals something important about the phantasmatic structure of the people. The zombie represents a hypertrophy of analogy itself, as it becomes a reigning trope, ready to be attached to any concept, ideology, political formation, economic system, or material object—a supplement to any commodity whose lifespan seems to have exceeded its own structural limitations.

3

Unlimited Life

CAPITALIST DELIRIUM AND EXCESSIVE GROWTH IN HELA AND *THE BLOB*

Nothing of them is left over except the same ghostly objecthood—
a bare gelatinous blob of undifferentiated human labor, of
human labor-power expended without regard to the form of its
expenditure.

—Karl Marx, *Capital: A Critique of Political Economy, Volume 1*

LIKE THE GHOSTLY OBJECTHOOD described by Marx in the first volume of *Capital*, this chapter takes up the idea of unlimited life through the figure of living labor in its grossest and most basic form. This distillation of living labor appears not in the figure of the worker or the slave, per se, nor in the degraded forms of bare life, but rather takes the shape of something simultaneously more abstract and materially based. In the epigraph quoted above, Marx describes the commodity as something infused with a kind of ghostly residue and the labor—the real source of the value haunting the object—as "bare gelatinous blobs of homogeneous labor" abstracted from its source and existing as something altogether stranger.[1] Labor is, for Marx, a "value-creating substance," described as a kind of blob, jelly, or goo, when it is abstracted from the context of production, but this abstraction is key. As I have argued in this book, life and labor are inextricable, yet the dream of labor, abstracted and removed from the context of a body—from the limitations associated with the body—is central to what creates the conditions for what I am defining as undead labor—a particular form of life that can be traced from the afterlife of slavery to contemporary technoscience and political economy.

This chapter proposes to take seriously this notion of the bare, gelatinous blob of living labor, abstracted and extracted from the human body and existing as a kind of condensation of capital's relation to life and its reproduction. This necessarily includes some consideration of the strange and phantasmatic relationship that capital has to living labor, a dream of a form of life that is unfettered by limitations up to and including death. To explore these ideas and to flesh out their relation to undead labor, this chapter will look to two prime examples. The first is the HeLa cell line, a group of continuously reproducing cancer cells that were gathered from Henrietta Lacks, a Black woman from Baltimore. The HeLa cell line has generated value and controversy but provides an example of a very real form of living labor that appears as an exemplar of capital's delirium of unlimited life. The second example takes a more monstrous form—and a very literal one—in the movie *The Blob* (Irvin S. Yeaworth Jr., 1958). The through line of this chapter is a focus on figures that illustrate, in both science and fiction, a monstrous reproduction that appears at the very heart of life itself. Here, the dream of unlimited life serves as the guiding principle of what is, in fact, a form of capitalist delirium.

Interlude: Pure Labor

The zombie of classical Hollywood cinema has been the recurring example of undead labor in this book, but here we turn to another classic movie monster that offers a compelling case study of unlimited life. The cult classic *The Blob* depicts the eponymous monster as an amorphous alien organism that was seemingly immortal, infinitely productive, and endlessly growing. Like a cancerous cell colony that can live outside the body, the Blob shows a form of life that knows no limit and, because of this, reflects a cultural alarm at the voracious and excessive tendencies appearing in the cultures of the mid-twentieth century: capitalism outgrowing the bounds of the nation-state and devouring anything in its path. These anxieties also reflect changing conditions taking place in and around the fantasy of race and the role it plays in the production and reproduction of capital. As I have argued in earlier chapters, part of the deployment of undead labor as a form of life and as a mode of production takes place because of an animating fantasy at the heart of capitalist production: the dream of unfettered growth, endless production and reproduction, and unlimited life. In the end, the relation to death that the zombie always brings with it will be essential to the argument about undead labor, capitalism, and the contradiction between finitude and unlimited growth that this book seeks to work through.

An emblem of the afterlife of slavery, the zombie's resemblance to the human has always been an important part of its mythology. It is a degraded echo of the living human, a body in a state of decay and disarray, that continues to labor and, because of this, illustrates the horror of slavery and a notion of laboring that extends beyond life. Yet the dream of unlimited life, this delirium at the heart of capital, is not tied to the human form so directly. In fact, labor abstracted from the human body—or from any body—distilled into pure, cellular substance, fulfills this dream much more directly, as we shall see with the cellular labor of the HeLa cell line and its monstrous version in *The Blob.* Unlike the zombie, the Blob is a representation of pure life and a vision of life run amok—of what happens when the dream of unlimited life is realized not just in the form of a movie monster, but in the actual conditions of the HeLa cell line, which will be discussed in the next section. The Blob reveals an anxiety around a fundamental shift in our conception of life, from something purely functional or instrumental to something purely generative. As such, it resonates with the categories of flesh and bare life and is something intimately tied to living matter, to bodies, if they are alienated from themselves through power and violence. The Blob represents this notion of life, alienated and removed from form, context, and limitation: It is just living substance. It is both alien and alienating, appearing to come from both inside and outside at once, existing in ways that exceed the boundaries—both real and symbolic—that surround it.

The Blob also bears more than a passing resemblance to certain examples that follow. But before exploring them at length in the following section, it is worth noting that there are certain examples of this idea of pure life that appear from within the corpus of zombie movies. The livid, green substance that appears in Stuart Gordon's film *Re-Animator* (1985) serves as a chemical stand-in for pure life, making zombies of any formerly living thing that it is injected into. Even more compellingly, Dan O'Bannon's film *Return of the Living Dead* (1985) also offers an account of undeadness as pure life, which is unstoppable and indivisible.

What makes the zombies of *Return of the Living Dead* so unique is that they are virtually unkillable. No bullets to the brain or removal of the head will do; once tissue is exposed to the agent of reanimation, there is no going back to death, and this principle seems to be based in *exposure*, not quite the contagious metaphor that would become dominant in the genre. *Return of the Living Dead* was released the same year as the third installment of George Romero's series of zombie movies, *Day of the Dead* (1985), and is quite clearly a response to the popularity of Romero's *Dawn of the Dead* (1978). *Return* is also one of the first films to be explicitly metatextual, acknowledging itself as a film within the zombie genre overall, referring to the events that took place in *Night of the Living Dead* (1968). The origins of the zombie outbreak in this film are, in fact, the zombies from Romero's first film, placed in chemical containment by the US military and left accidentally in the basement of a medical supply warehouse. The outbreak begins with a joke when an older employee wants to show off the strange and spooky things contained in the warehouse, and, predictably, containment is breached and any organic tissue exposed to this gaseous toxin, "245 Trioxin," is reanimated.

The zombies of *Return of the Living Dead* are remarkable for several reasons. Not only are they the origin of the oddly persistent theme in the zombie canon that zombies eat brains, but they are persistently *alive*. The undeadness conveyed by these zombies is not contagious in the sense of a pathogen or disease, moving from one body to the next, but rather contagious in the sense of exposure: Any formerly living tissue exposed to "245 Trioxin" is reanimated, from whole bodies to cadavers ready to be used in dissections for medical instruction to butterflies pinned in a glass case. In a discussion of this film in the context of apocalyptic narratives, Evan Calder Williams describes the initial outbreak as "some of the more remarkable minutes in any zombie film," going on to describe the scene in some detail: "The gas, it appears, not only animates whole-bodied human corpses. It is an obscene principle of life itself, a whisper to everything that has lived that, *you never stopped living.*

A bisected dog for classroom use barks and pants, its exposed organs throbbing. . . . And a cadaver hung indifferently by meathook in a freezer wakes up very, very angry [at] its current state of affairs."[2] As Williams describes it, there is something "obscene" about the nature of life in this film. It is excessive in both quality and duration; the zombies brought back are seemingly endless, and even chopping them up only creates body parts that continue to function independently with grasping hands and gasping mouths working long after their removal from the body. When the living characters in the film eventually burn an undead body in hopes of ending it, they only manage to spread the toxin to the nearby environment as the smoke and ash from the burning corpse mix with rainwater and effectively animate an entire nearby graveyard.

Williams describes this undeadness as an "*over-animation of the living body*," which seems in line with descriptions already used in this text that describe zombies and other undead monsters as having too much life.[3] While the zombies in *Return of the Living Dead* exhibit the principle of pure or unlimited life that is the focus of this chapter, the mechanisms by which this life spreads are significantly different. In the case of the zombies, the mechanism of reproduction is exposure: *Return of the Living Dead* depicts life as an animating principle given chemical form; it is reduced and abstracted into an absolute substance. And it spreads in the film like an environmental toxin (the environmental analogies are interesting in their own right yet fall outside the purview of this chapter), moving through the atmosphere and hydrological cycle as a vector to produce more undeadness. In contrast, the Blob represents something altogether different. It also stands in for an idea of pure and unlimited life as a living substance; it is not life that has been abstracted into a chemical compound, but rather life reduced to the first principles of reproduction and consumption, removed from any medium. Even the name of this monster is instructive: the *Blob* suggests something amorphous and unwieldy. The horror of the zombie often comes in the admixture of life and death that is revealed in the body of the zombie itself; showing signs of decay and disease, the zombie is rotting and abject. The horror of the Blob, on the other hand, appears in its excessive aliveness, its uncontrolled growth. The Blob may not represent undead labor as precisely as the zombie, but it does a better job of illustrating the fantasy of life that serves as the kernel of capitalism's delirium of reproduction.

Like so many of the anxieties in the American popular imagination, this fear of an excessive form of life, and its political and economic repercussions, was refracted through the notion of race, as I argue that the anxieties given form in the Blob echo other concerns growing around the "immortal" cell line, HeLa, grown from the cancerous tissues of Henrietta Lacks, whose body provided the fecund foundation for a great deal of the modern research in the life sciences. When read against each other, these contrasting case studies allow this chapter to explore the idea of excessive life that serves as the driving force within undead labor and, perhaps, as something generated by it. Here, I explore what happens when the dream of unlimited reproductive power comes true. Drawing in discourses of feminist theory, race and biopolitics, the history of medicine, and screen studies, this chapter looks to both HeLa and *The Blob* as nexus points for race, labor, and value, illustrating the problems of unlimited life as the impossible ideal of undead labor, showing it to be an inherently excessive mode of production rooted in the dream—or, better, delirium—of a kind of life unfettered by any limitation within the twentieth-century imaginary.

HeLa, Cancer, and Monstrous Reproduction

The roots of undead labor extend into the dream of unlimited life. From its origins, hidden within myths of the zombie, undead labor imagines a kind of body, a form of life that is unfettered by any limitation, either interior or exterior. Inner limits can be found in the subject: in beliefs, desires, and volition. The early racial capitalism of the colonial period encountered these limitations in the resistance of the slave to her captivity, the desire for freedom and autonomy, and the will to sabotage, poison, and revolt that took place on a spectrum of resistance ranging from undermining labor to full-scale rebellion. External limits often took the form of structural limitations of the body: the amount of labor power a body can produce, even under the harsh conditions of the whip and the plantation; the amount of time a body can work before giving out or getting sick; and the minimum number of resources a body needs to keep producing. Although it was measured in bodies, time, and products, life itself was the resource most valued by capitalism, and it was limited. In the end, death was the limit to the productive capacities of a living body, and while violence and other incentives could be used to extract a tremendous amount of value from the body, it served as an absolute limit. The zombie represented a phantasmatic solution to this problem of limited life: a body that labored beyond death and could be brought back into a state of productivity.

As an undead monster, the zombie seems to take the shape of parody. A degraded version of the slave or the worker, still productive but only barely—suitable for only the most basic forms of production and reproduction. While undead labor seems to parody living labor, the zombie is hardly the ideal to which capitalism's obsession with living labor aspires. Rather, the dream of unlimited life seeks a form with more verve and vitality. This chapter argues that the instances that asymptotically approach the dream of unlimited life are, in fact, every bit as monstrous and continue to take shape around themes of race, labor, and value. After tremendous successes and many scientific breakthroughs, including the polio vaccine, researchers in the United States and around the world were using a line of remarkably robust and "immortal" cells known as HeLa, which served as the raw material for a wide range of experimentation from cancer research to drug testing. The HeLa cell line was so valuable because it contained human cells, which allowed for medical experimentation on human tissues without the obvious physical and ethical dangers of human testing, and its robustness (a term we will revisit), defined as its ability to grow and reproduce under nonideal conditions, made it an ideal substance for research and experimentation.

The HeLa cell line was named for the woman from whose body it originated: Henrietta Lacks. In 1951, Lacks walked into a clinic specially designated for African Americans in what was then a highly segregated medical system, complaining of "female trouble."[4] Lacks was diagnosed with cervical cancer and would succumb to the disease less than a year after her initial diagnosis, even after an aggressive course of treatment. When she first came to the clinic, a sample of her tumor was taken, and these cancerous cells would eventually give rise to the HeLa cell line. HeLa was significant because it was so potent and robust. It could survive in culture, outside the body, in ways that were remarkable, which made it incredibly useful to scientific research. Even for cancerous cells, HeLa stood apart. Most forms of cancer are, by definition, excessively lively. They are too vital, too productive, and they grow without limit or regard for the well-being of the living environments in which these cancerous cells thrive.

Cancer is a disease of excess. It occurs when the normal labor of the cell runs rampant, growing without regard for and bypassing the usual cellular mechanisms that limit a cell's division and growth. Typically, a healthy cell is programmed to die under certain circumstances in a process called apoptosis. Apoptosis can take place when a cell is too stressed or overheated, or through chemical signals from other nearby cells. One of the likely causes of cancer is when a cell evades apoptosis by disregarding the signal to die. Thus cancer continues to grow and divide without the limitations of cellular death, thereby exhibiting a version of undead labor that takes place at the cellular level. As Siddhartha Mukherjee argues in his brilliant book *The Emperor of All Maladies*, "Cancer, as we know, is a disease caused by the uncontrolled growth of a single cell. This growth is unleashed by mutations—changes in DNA that specifically affect genes that incite unlimited cell growth. In a normal cell, powerful genetic circuits regulate cell division and cell death. In a cancer cell, these circuits have been broken, unleashing a cell that cannot stop growing." Like the zombie, and even more so the Blob, cancer is a pathology of excessive life, too much growth. Mukherjee's insight that cancer is what happens when the restrictions that are structurally placed on life are removed provides yet another, equally monstrous, example of undead labor appearing in the real world. Later in the same text, Mukherjee describes the way that cancer "lives desperately, inventively, fiercely, territorially, cannily, and defensively"—it is life at its most tenacious and relentless.[5] And the cancer generated by Lacks's body was exceptional, thriving under surprisingly adverse conditions, which made it the ideal test subject. This cancer survived too well, both inside and outside Lacks's body, and it exhibited such potency that it would eventually become the foundation of nearly all tissue cultures, globally, until the 1970s and beyond. As Mukherjee's descriptive language reveals, cancer simultaneously encapsulates the best and worst aspects of life.

The cancer that would consume Henrietta Lacks would become exemplary not just in the form of the immortal HeLa cell line, but in the form of cancer itself, which has become a defining pathology from the twentieth century into the present. Cancer is not only one of the most prevalent and deadly diseases in the modern era, but it has become emblematic and defining of this historical period. It is a sign of the times: Unlimited growth, with all constraints removed or broken, appears thoroughly allegorical for twenty-first-century political and economic movements under neoliberal capitalism, a situation in which cultural and economic overproduction appears to be rapidly overwhelming the environmental systems that support us, quickly leading to environmental degradation and collapse. Remarking on the symbolic power of cancer, Mukherjee points out that the disease has "metamorphosed into a lethal shape-shifting entity imbued with such penetrating metaphorical, medical, scientific, and political potency that [it] is often described as the defining plague of our generation." And he goes on to note, "Cancer . . . is riddled with more contemporary images." It is "a desperate individualist" and an "expansionist disease," says Mukherjee, because it abandons the cooperative tendencies of its cellular kin to pursue its own ends with a ruthless, single-minded (single-celled?) devotion. It "sets up colonies in hostile landscapes" in the body, and the network of discourse that surrounds cancer as a disease and a phenomenon is steeped in analogies and symbolism that aim to capture its pathological expansionism. As Mukherjee notes, even "the word *metastasis*, used to describe the migration of cancer from one site to another, is a curious mix of *meta* and *stasis*—'beyond stillness' in Latin—an unmoored, partially unstable state that captures the peculiar instability of modernity," in prose that understands cancer as a mirror for the modern age.[6]

Like the other major allegorical touchstone of this book, the zombie, both cancer and the Blob function at a symbolic level as a homological object or entity. Put another way, the discourse of the Blob takes on similar qualities as the Blob itself: It can absorb and incorporate any interpretation or meaning that might come its way. And it can stand in for anything and everything because it *is* anything and everything, exhibiting a kind of monstrous pluripotentiality. Its formlessness is proper to both its literal manifestation and its interpretive potential and conceptualizability.[7] This is another similarity between the Blob and cancer: a symbolic potency that comes to be one of its defining characteristics. For example, writing on the metaphorical promiscuity of cancer, Susan Sontag argues that "cancer proceeds by a science-fiction scenario: an invasion of 'alien' or 'mutant' cells, stronger than normal cells," and later in the same passage she references *The Blob* directly as an example of this type of narrative. Sontag turns to sci-fi because of the disease's place within the cultural imaginary of the twentieth century. Like tuberculosis in the nineteenth century, cancer has become what Sontag describes as a "master illness" because it is culturally and politically polemical, engendering commentary and speculation alike about its many potential causes and cures.[8] Cancer, like the Blob, is the target of a great many metaphorical projections.

The cell becomes an ideal and idealized form of life under capitalism. It is effectively immortal, endlessly reproductive, generating itself repeatedly. The idea that life could be reduced to some ideal substance—pure labor power—lies at the heart of why HeLa, cancer, and the Blob work as such important symbolic clusters within the capitalist imaginary. HeLa represented the dream of limitless productivity. As Jayna Brown has argued, "Life could proliferate unrestricted by organismal cycles of birth and death. It was capable of reproducing outside of heterosexual conception and could even transcend the notion of species. Considering the developments that have followed the advent of HeLa, it would seem that biological science and technologies could usher in an entirely new ontology of life."[9] Brown's understanding of the possibilities of the HeLa cell line is utopian in character, which contrasts with my own emphasis on the ways that HeLa has been created under the conditions of undead labor and has been co-opted by them.

Writings on cancer are often autobiographical, weaving personal experience and an exploration of the systems of health and illness that activate around the individual when she is first diagnosed with the disease. Sontag wrote the essay "Illness as Metaphor" soon after her diagnosis with breast cancer, stating, "I want to describe, not what it is really like to emigrate to the kingdom of the ill and live there, but the punitive or sentimental fantasies concocted about that situation: not real geography, but stereotypes of national character."[10] Similarly, Audre Lorde writes about her own experience with breast cancer and her consequent radical mastectomy, exploring her experience of diagnosis, disease, and treatment while situating herself from the identity positions of being Black, lesbian, and feminist, thus letting her encounter with cancer filter through the interface of the self. Indeed, almost every popular and academic writing on cancer takes this path, traversing the self and personal experience, which appears in texts and authors as diversely arrayed as Jackie Stacey, S. Lochlann Jain, Eric Cazdyn, Barbara Ehrenreich, and Jonathan Sterne, to name only a limited selection who have been particularly influential to this book.[11] Like its material analog, cancer pervades and proliferates through the discourse that structures and surrounds it. Describing his experience as a "cancer fellow," an immersive training in medical oncology, Mukherjee notes that "cancer was an all-consuming presence in our lives. It invaded our imaginations; it occupied our memories; it infiltrated every conversation, every thought."[12] Mukherjee's writing reveals a pattern of discursive or symbolic proliferation that employs the very same language used to describe cancer itself. In the process of theorizing cancer through the critical lens of the self, he reproduces that language. The alienness of cancer belies its most fundamental truth: that it is a kind of cellular phenomenon that is endemic to us and our bodies. Despite the frequent metaphors of "invasion" or "colonization," our cancer *is us*—a call coming from inside the house. Perhaps this is one more reason why cancer is so evocative of feelings of betrayal: It is an example of our own body apparently turning against us. Jackie Stacey describes it this way: "Cancer is the self at war with the self."[13]

As a disorder of life's most fundamental characteristics, a cooptation of its impulses toward growth and reproduction, cancer grows through the discourse that surrounds it as easily as any other body and in ways that render those familiar life processes as strange. The turn toward autobiography in the writings on cancer appears to be an attempt to recenter the self in this process of life and growth, to make the strange familiar again or to make the *unheimlich* of cancer a little more homely again. It is a personal perspective that lends these narratives literary and therapeutic significance. Yet cancer itself seems like a disorder of autobiography. If biography is understood literally as a kind of "life writing"—a compound of *bios* and *graphe* from Greek and Latin—then the addition of the auto- prefix is not only denotative of writing about one's own life but also bears connotations of automation—a process by which the fundamental mechanisms, the cellular technologies, of the *bios* are unleashed. It is where life starts writing itself, as such, rather than contributing to the larger corpus or body. The compound of *auto-* and *bios* is suggestive of cancer's tendencies toward a kind of mechanization of life: The cancer cell becomes like a machine, operating out of control. It is an undeadening of the cell, if you will—a living cell, cut off from death, that becomes endlessly productive. Cancer provides another instance of undead labor but also something like unlimited life. On the one hand, the characteristic of unlimited reproduction found in cancer shows how life can become monstrous on its own terms; the growth, consumption, and reproduction are not always good things, at least when left unchecked. On the other hand, this kind of cancerous proliferation, this principle of excessive vitality, becomes valuable, as in the case of the HeLa cell line. These two sides are not mutually exclusive, and the twin paths of monstrosity and value are destined to cross again and again.

HeLa was the first human cell line that was widely used by the life sciences. Not long after Lacks arrived at the clinic, a biopsy was taken of the lesions on her cervix, and the tissue samples were found to be cancerous. These samples were then sent on to the laboratory of George and Margaret Gey, biologists at Johns Hopkins University. The Geys were running a research program on cervical cancer, and Lacks's tissues were shared with them without her knowledge or consent. George Gey was a specialist in tissue cultures, and while his main research was on cervical cancer, Gey had been searching for a viable sample of human cells with specific qualities that would make them useful in culture—qualities that would make them hardy enough to survive and thrive in an artificial medium designed to foster the growth of cells derived from a living source. HeLa was named for Henrietta Lacks, as a method of indicating the name of the original host while simultaneously depersonalizing the cell line. After researchers cultured her cells in the lab, this cancer proved to be significant. As Hannah Landecker points out, "In 1951 . . . it became clear that HeLa cells were going to continue growing and dividing unperturbed by their artificial environment." This cell line represented not only the most successful culture of human tissues at the time, but the "standardization of human material for research on human biology."[14] HeLa was not just a cell line, but *the* cell line that would come to define the field of human biology in the life sciences.

Tissue culture was, and continues to be, the bedrock of the applied arm of the life sciences. To culture a cell is to induce it to divide and replicate outside the body in some kind of nutritive medium. Culturing tissues is important because it allows for experimentation on human cells (and many other kinds of cells) without having to experiment on human subjects. Growing cells in culture made it possible to abstract human biology from the body and subjectivity of the human being. The biggest challenge of culturing tissue is creating a medium or environment that is suitable to foster this autonomous form of life and make it robust enough to grow outside the body. The science of tissue culture belongs to the twentieth century, when two world wars provided a tremendous impetus for thinking about new solutions and treatments for the millions of wounded, as well as the growing urban populations that needed to be managed and protected from disease.

One of the most intriguing stories in the history of tissue culture also bears a family resemblance to both HeLa and the Blob, bringing together a fantasy of immortality with excessive reproduction. The "immortal chicken heart" of Alexis Carrel, whose early experiments in the field of tissue culture brought him both fame and notoriety for his own culture of continuously growing chicken cells, was established in 1925.[15] Carrel was a French surgeon and Nobel laureate who devoted himself to growing new and living tissues outside the body and to improving the techniques that allowed cells to live and grow in vitro. Carrel's experiments were quite successful, and he tested several methods for culturing cells that would grow independently, but his most successful culture developed from a few cells collected from the heart of a chicken embryo, which grew into a partially formed heart. The embryonic chicken heart pulsed with the regular rhythm of a heartbeat for weeks after the cells' separation from their original host, which gave rise to the vivid (if false) impression that a living, beating heart had been created in the somatic isolation of a test tube in the laboratory. More accurately, this modest colony of cells did not number nearly enough to constitute a whole heart and only pulsed with the ghost of a heartbeat for around one hundred days, although they continued to live and divide in a more sedate form for years.

Carrel was a reader of Henri Bergson and saw in the growth of cultured tissue a way of making living cells independent of a hosting body, but he also imagined that he could make them independent of time itself. Carrel argued, "If . . . the composition of the medium is kept constant, the cell colonies remain indefinitely in the same state of activity. They do not record time qualitatively. In fact, they are immortal."[16] Framing time as something qualitative, Carrel invokes the duration of these cells over time, growing and aging, where time is measured by changes in the qualities of the organism itself. In contrast, his tissue cultures were deemed "immortal" insofar as the changes that they underwent were quantitative, not qualitative.

These cells were not frozen in time, but they appeared to be excerpted from the usual flow of temporality. They did not mature and develop fully from the embryonic stage to a full-fledged organ, but they did grow and divide. The cells of Carrel's chicken heart maintained themselves for decades after their initial culture, and Landecker points out that these colonies of cells "continu[ed] to grow and divide for years on end, these cultured cells divided endlessly at the same rate, in apparent confirmation of Carrel's assertion that he had removed them from time, or removed time from them."[17] Growth and immortality were carefully intertwined in Carrel's narrative of these cells, which successfully sparked the public's imagination. Newspaper headlines celebrated the "birthday" of Carrel's chicken heart for years, and in 1937, the cell colony was reimagined in a seven-minute segment on the horror-themed radio show *Lights Out*, in which the heart continued to grow unchecked, eventually overrunning the entire world with pulsating, ever-growing, nondifferentiated tissue. More than half a century later, Rebecca Skloot—one of the most recent and prominent biographers of both HeLa and Henrietta Lacks—would describe this episode in familiar terms when she writes about the *Lights Out* segment, pointing out that "the fear of tissue culture truly found its way into American living rooms." She goes on to describe the alarming results of the chicken heart's unending growth in the following way: "It grew out of control, filling the city streets like The Blob, consuming everyone and everything in its path."[18]

Similarities between the Blob and these "immortal" and excessive tissue cultures run more than skin deep, although perhaps the most telling resonance lies in the effect that cold has on both of these uncanny, autonomous tissues. In *The Blob*, cold was the only thing that slowed the organism's viscous rampage, and this seems to reflect the principal method of slowing cellular division in the case of tissue cultures like Carrel's chicken heart or, for that matter, HeLa cells. The story of excessive tissue growth in *Lights Out* prefigures not only the Blob but other themes in science fiction that posit dystopian scenarios of nondifferentiated matter such as anxiety around "gray goo," in which microscopic, cell-like machines called "replicators" could use surrounding matter to replicate themselves, generating a homogeneous "goo" that would eventually overtake the entire world. This notion was first put forward by K. Eric Drexler, an engineer interested in nanotechnology. He imagined a possible future in which tiny machines, made small enough to interact with matter at the molecular or atomic level, would make possible a revolution in manufacturing by allowing companies to reimagine and manipulate the world from the bottom up. However, Drexler also imagined the possibility that these machines, either by sabotage or error, could also run amok and enter a frenzy of overproduction, eventually outcompeting the natural world and overcoming it in a kind of technological cancer.

Drexler wrote out this scenario in *Engines of Creation*, which imagined this level of nanotechnology as a mirror to the natural world. He was careful to limit the scope of the ideas in his book, which was aimed at a popular, scientific audience. However, soon after the work was published, Drexler's ideas were featured in an issue of *Omni* magazine with the cover headline "Nanotechnology: Molecular Machines that Mimic Life." The issue of *Omni* was the first broad public exposure to the term "nanotechnology," featuring the nightmare scenario of the gray goo and likely serving as the source of the mythos in popular culture. The article states, "Drexler calls these flawed machines 'the grey goo.' In the worst-case scenario of the grey-goo problem, the lethal nanomachines will reproduce to infinity, and life on Earth will end."[19] Since then, Drexler has written about his regret about hypothesizing the gray-goo scenario in an updated edition of the book: "But meanwhile, the earlier ideas from *Engines* had spread into popular culture—science fiction, movies, and video games—and taken on a life of their own. The ideas that spread fastest, simplified, transmogrified, and sensationalized. Soon, 'nanotechnology' was all about making so-called 'nanobots'—self-replicating bug-like things that could work miracles, but would inevitably run amok, eat the world, and turn it into 'gray goo.'"[20] The gray-goo scenario had gone viral, appearing under the heading of "ecophagy," turning into a technological version of what was otherwise a distinctly biological anxiety.

The driving cause of Drexler's frustration with the way gray goo had captured the popular imagination is that it forever associated a certain kind of technology—in this case, nanotechnology—with a doomsday scenario, rendering what he imagined as the tremendous productive potential of nanotechnology in a negative light. Drexler's complaint was that it was difficult to get funding for nanotechnology projects when the idea of hyperproducing nanobots liquefying the environment cooled the enthusiasm of venture capital, yet this fear of overproduction is symptomatic and seems to resonate with anxieties of cancerous metastases, hungry Blobs, and immortal tissues that all seem to align with the relentless production of undead labor. When we return to these fears within the context of the HeLa cell line in the next section, the anxiety around excessive production remains and is further complicated by two important factors: race and gender.

HeLa and Racial Capital in Overdrive

As mentioned above, in 1951, George Gey had been looking for cells that his lab could use as the foundation for an ongoing tissue culture. While Gey had made progress in developing new techniques for fostering life in vitro, he had difficulty finding a strain of cells that could survive while maintaining their reproductive capacities. The samples made from Henrietta Lacks's cancerous tissue were the answer, and as Rebecca Skloot describes in her history, "Henrietta's cells weren't merely surviving, they were growing with mythological intensity." This kind of hyperbolic language is characteristic of the discourse surrounding the HeLa cells, which are likely the most successful human tissue culture in history, but it also gestures to a hidden reserve of affect that surrounds them. There was, indeed, a mythic quality to the HeLa cell line and its extreme reproductive potency. They were astounding in their ability to survive. Again, Skloot points out that "by the 1960s scientists joked that HeLa cells were so robust that they could probably survive in sink drains or on doorknobs. They were everywhere."[21] On a more sinister note, in a think piece on HeLa for *Rolling Stone* in 1976, Michael Rogers referred to the cell line as a "monster amidst the Pyrex."[22]

The reason behind this alarming (and alarmist) language became clear a decade earlier in 1966, when it was discovered that HeLa was reproducing not only inside the test tube but outside of it as well. For years, HeLa was the go-to tissue culture for biological testing and experimentation, but the scientific community noticed some remarkable similarities in their results, even among markedly different projects and when laboratories were separated by thousands of miles. At first, this was thought to be the beginning of a major breakthrough when, in fact, it was the opposite. It turned out that HeLa was contaminating countless experiments precisely because it could survive, seemingly, anywhere. In the years to come, this discovery would be referred to as the "HeLa bomb." Skloot notes that "when it came to HeLa, [the scientific community] had no idea what they were up against. It turned out Henrietta's cells could float through the air on dust particles. They could travel from one culture to the next on unwashed hands or used pipettes; they could ride from lab to lab on researchers' coats and shoes or through ventilation systems. And they were strong: if just *one* HeLa cell landed in a culture dish, it took it over, consuming all the media and filling the space."[23] It was as if the Blob had come to life in laboratories around the world.

The discovery that HeLa had been quite literally taking over laboratory samples was only identified because of a rare genetic marker that is found almost exclusively in African Americans.[24] Until this point, the origins of HeLa had been considered largely irrelevant—so much so that the name Henrietta Lacks had been elided in favor of similar-sounding names like Helen Lane. However, when the HeLa bomb went off, the provenance of these cells became important, and race reemerged within the discourse of these cultured tissues. Race became a factor in identifying the HeLa cells wherever they were found, but they also seemed to inform the discourse of contamination as well, through what Landecker aptly describes as "metaphors of miscegenation." The knowledge that HeLa was the product of, or used to be a part of, a Black woman's body became widely disseminated in the scientific community, and this, in turn, activated a discourse network of racial tropes and ideas such that the one-drop rule was transformed into the one-cell rule, as HeLa threatened to consume and overrun the cultures in which it landed. Once the racial history of the HeLa cells became common knowledge, they began to be described in racialized and sexualized terms that recalled a long history of racist tropes and stereotypes associated with Blackness, including "vigorous," "aggressive," "indefatigable," and "surreptitious." In her own analysis of this history, Landecker points out that "the narrative of reproduction out of control was linked with promiscuity through references to the cell's wild proliferative tendencies and its 'colorful' laboratory life."[25]

The discourse surrounding HeLa played on myths that surround the Black body and the Black woman's body in particular, linking the productive power of HeLa to notions of hypersexuality, promiscuity, and ease of reproduction. This exaggeration and weaponization of Black women's reproductive potential has deep roots in the construction of Blackness itself during the colonial period. Jennifer Morgan describes how monstrosity, sexuality, and gender were used in concert to construct a racial mythos around Black women to justify their instrumentalization as slaves and commodities. She argues, "African women's Africanness became contingent on the linkages between sexuality and a savagery that fitted them for both productive and reproductive labor. Women enslaved in the seventeenth and early eighteenth centuries did not give birth to many children, but descriptions of African women in the Americas almost always highlighted their fecundity along with their capacity for manual labor."[26] Morgan's insights into this history of Black womanhood and labor show how the coordinates of Black women in the discourse of racial capitalism bring together productive and reproductive capacity into a single body, using the supposed fecundity of the Black body to justify their appropriation as sources of value.

Morgan describes how tropes of monstrosity were deployed to render Indigenous women from both Africa and the Americas as simultaneously strange and valuable for their usefulness; as she describes it, "Black women's monstrous bodies symbolized their sole utility—the ability to produce both crops and other laborers. It is this dual value, sometimes explicit and sometimes lurking in the background of slaveowners' decision-making processes, that would come to define women's experience of enslavement most critically."[27] The story of HeLa and Henrietta Lacks shows several resonances with this history of race and gendered labor. HeLa seemed the quasi-living embodiment of the monstrous productivity attributed to Black women as a way of justifying their enslavement and servitude while showing how this investment in a monstrous potential for reproduction and accumulation is part of the fabric of capitalism's modus operandi. It is worth noting that HeLa, an especially potent cancer, is what killed Lacks, exhibiting its monstrous reproducibility inside her body before it became a monster among the Pyrex of laboratories around the world. But in a sense, it was HeLa's growth under the sign of Blackness that also contributed to Henrietta's death—through the segregated healthcare system that she was forced to use, among the usual host of infelicitous factors that tend to shorten the lives of the Black population.

It was also her race, her Blackness, that fostered the conditions under which the doctors she saw to diagnose her "female trouble" felt entitled to take her tissue sample without her consent and put it to work, so to speak, in the laboratories at Johns Hopkins. Even in death—perhaps *especially* in death—some part of Henrietta's body labored on in a kind of half life, exhibiting a kind of undeadness common to all cancers, marked by the excess vitality they reveal when this form of life does not know when to die. Thus life and death, labor and Blackness, come together in the "immortal life of Henrietta Lacks," a compelling title for Lacks's most famous biography because it captures something important about the *kind* of life this immortality brings: The individual subject named "Henrietta Lacks" died in 1951, yet some embodied part of her lived and worked after she died.[28] Another clear example of undead labor that appears outside the discourse of the zombie, although under circumstances that are perhaps as monstrous.

As the reverberations of the HeLa bomb continued to be felt around the scientific community in the 1970s, the understanding of HeLa as a raced—that is, Black—form of life continued to inflect the ideas surrounding it. Implicit anxieties around miscegenation became synonymous with annihilation, making white supremacist fears of racial dilution and displacement appear to play out within the medium of tissue cultures and the microcosm of the lab. These became explicit anxieties around HeLa's abilities as a kind of living Blackness: As a part of her body, these cells inherited genetic markers that signified race, but these markers cut across both symbolic and material conditions. This invocation of Blackness accompanied real fears of the loss of important knowledge and work that HeLa cells, proliferating across tissue cultures in labs around the world, might destroy as they took over cultures with alarming speed, bringing with them a social anxiety around Blackness that Calvin Warren describes as a kind of "ontological terror." He argues that this fear is actually a rift or gap at the heart of modern metaphysics that poses Blackness as a problem to be solved through avoidance or elimination. He argues that the function of Blackness in modern metaphysics is to exist as the living embodiment of a negation, a "nothing," and symbolically hosting the characteristics and elements that the modern, human subject must elide and exclude. As Warren puts it, "The puzzle of blackness, then, is that it functions in an antiblack world without being—much like 'nothing' functions philosophically without our metaphysical understanding of being, an extraordinary mystery." For Warren, Blackness underwent a kind of "onticide" during the period of transatlantic slavery, a degradation or "execration" of being that took place in a time when modern ideas of race were being reified. It became synonymous with a form of erased or negated being, even as whiteness was elevated to become synonymous with the highest values of being.[29]

These ideas belie the obvious truth that the bodies, subjects, and identities—in short, the people—who embody Blackness lead rich and full lives that are not ontologically impoverished. The negation of Black being that Warren explores is a symbolic condition imposed on Black lives as an instrumental feature of a modern racial calculus. This is reminiscent of Hortense Spillers's insight that the Black woman's body is a "locus for confounded identities" and "a meeting ground of investments and privations."[30] The investments that Spillers discusses here are not merely symbolic; the Black woman's body has been a key site of value production during the period of Atlantic slavery, and this relationship recurs in the case of HeLa, which was responsible for an incalculable amount of wealth.[31]

HeLa is an unusually symbolic substance that seems to exist as a quasi-living concentration of the reproductive potential of Black bodies, a potential that served as the very foundation of the economic power of the United States: pure flesh rendered as such by the sheer physical and economic instrumentality of Black life, which was vital to the operation of Atlantic slavery and, thus, to a system of labor that need not be compensated. America relied on the productive and reproductive power of Black bodies, and Black women's bodies in particular, in order to maintain this system. Only a few decades later, HeLa seemed to crystallize or concentrate these relations into a biological byproduct, a kind of surplus substance that draws together the reproductive power and racial logics of Blackness at work in the United States, distilling them into a strange form of immortal, hyperproductive, cancerous life. Alys Eve Weinbaum notes that "it was, after all, in the context of Atlantic slavery that, for the first time in history, in vivo reproductive labor was deemed alienable and slaves bred not only for use and prestige (as they were in the Ancient world) but also expressly for profit. As historians amply document, slave breeding in the Americas and the Caribbean was increasingly important to the maintenance of slavery as time wore on, and thus slave women's wombs were routinely treated as valuable objects and as sources of financial speculation."[32] In this way, it seems all the more ironic that HeLa would come to serve as the raw material for a mode of production—tissue culture—that exists at the heart of the life sciences and was central to the incipient biotech industry. The rediscovery of race, sex, and reproduction within the discourses surrounding HeLa cells also strikes an uncomfortable chord within a nation whose wealth was generated by and through the bodies of Black slaves, especially in the mid-twentieth century, when the civil rights movement was bringing Black life and Black rights into the spotlight of national attention.

The echoes of Atlantic slavery in the story of HeLa are significant in and of themselves. In her meditation on the Middle Passage, Saidiya Hartman considers the ongoing effects of the slave trade when she says:

> Slavery had established a measure of man and a ranking of life and worth that has yet to be undone. If slavery persists as an issue in the political life of black America, it is not because of an antiquarian obsession with bygone days or the burden of a too-long memory, but because black lives are still imperiled

> and devalued by a racial calculus and a political arithmetic that were entrenched centuries ago. This is the afterlife of slavery—skewed life chances, limited access to health and education, premature death, incarceration, and impoverishment. I, too, am the afterlife of slavery.[33]

Hartman's insight here is that identity is simultaneously informed by the material and symbolic conditions of Atlantic slavery, which come together to form a nexus point in the Black subject, who must navigate the racial calculus that continues to this day under the sign of Blackness. With this formulation in mind, it becomes clear that undead labor is a unique formation of political, symbolic, and material economies that are tied intimately to this afterlife of slavery; in it we find the very same "racial calculus and political arithmetic" that emerged from the currents of the Atlantic world and the reification of race that exists as a lasting byproduct of the institutions of slavery. By invoking the notion of an afterlife, Hartman's ideas also speak to a kind of ontological crisis, an inherent contradiction in the viability of being under the armature of racial capitalism. What Hartman describes as an afterlife, Calvin Warren understands as a kind of onticide, and taken together, these ideas bring into focus a picture of undeadness that emerges within the systems of racial capitalism that form the very heart of modernity.

Looking at HeLa within the context of racial capitalism and as part of the afterlife of slavery reveals a kind of naked, instrumental flesh. HeLa was just the most emblematic form taken by flesh under the sign of Blackness, and as such, it was central to capitalism's continuity. By fostering life at its most productive and instrumental, capitalism emphasized life's excesses and ushered in an era of expansion and overproduction. There is something monstrous about this kind of overproduction—something not simply alien, but also alienating about capitalism's project of generating living labor and abstracting that into surplus value. This is a process that has been accelerating and intensifying since the inception of capital in the colonial period all the way to the present day, under the banners of late capital (too optimistic, by half), biopolitics, or neoliberalism. Black life has historically been ground zero for capitalism's project to extract value from life in excess of its limits, reaching past the boundaries of the human and beyond the limits of life and death toward something more ambiguous and abstract. Yet, like so many of the implementations of power and discipline carried out on the bodies most vulnerable to subjection by slavery, colonialism, and incarceration, those practices tested in the colony inevitably feed back into the metropole.

HeLa, cancer, and the Blob all come together in a network of anxieties in and around the monstrous overproduction of capital. HeLa is a type of cancerous cell that enters the discourse of racial capitalism through its origins in the body of Henrietta Lacks, origins that were marked by her race and, through her, tapped into a long tradition of both fearing and exploiting the Black body as a raw material for its dreams of endless production. The Blob, and other fleshy monsters such as the immortal chicken heart and the gray goo, approach this problem from the other side, becoming monstrous embodiments of overproduction and the anxieties that arise alongside it. Together, HeLa, cancer, and the Blob form a constellation of meaning and anxiety in the twentieth century that shows how undead labor is not limited to the mediated body of the undead zombie, but also to living bodies, overproductive flesh, valuable tissues, and the cellular labor of naked flesh and life. In the discourse that connects all three of these key examples, there is a conceptual through line of endless production and of immortality or unlimited life, embodying the dream of pure surplus in which the productive power of living labor faces none of the obstructions of age and none of the limitations of death or finitude.

Indeed, buried at the core of undead labor, as both a form of life and a mode of production, we find the dream of immortality at work as a driving force—a fantasy in which finitude itself is foreclosed in favor of a living surplus that grows without limit and without end. The HeLa cell line appears to signify the immortality of Henrietta Lacks, but a version of life at its most instrumental as envisioned by capital: an engine of living labor at the cellular level. The immortality of HeLa works in a kind of semiotic two-step that, on the one hand, boasts of the unfettered biological generation that works as a real form of immortality, while on the other hand alleviating at least some of the embedded guilt and anxiety of having appropriated these cells without the knowledge or consent of Henrietta herself, once again building an empire of value out of the body of a Black woman. Hannah Landecker thoughtfully notes, "Some people question whether HeLa cells are still human, but no one asks what kind of immortality this is. It is the new form of immortality built into scientific life—disembodied, distributed continuity."[34]

These last words, "disembodied, distributed continuity," starkly capture an image of immortality that is far from the idealized versions available in so many pop culture mythologies. This immortality is not the undying life of the ego, embodied in vampire stories or figured in notions of the soul's continuity after death in a utopian afterlife. Instead, this is an alienated immortality, a kind of continuous or unceasing operation. This is precisely the definition of immortality, first described in chapter 1 of this book, that is understood by Slavoj Žižek, which he argues is better understood in terms of undeadness. With a characteristic dialectical flourish, Žižek overturns the typically positive idea of immortality, describing it instead as "a name for the 'undead' eternal life" that is in fact an "endless repetitive cycle." Indeed, Žižek will extend this characterization of immortal life when he describes it specifically as "a loop of time, repeating the same circular movement again and again."[35] While he imagines this kind of undead immortality in the abstract terms of the Hegelian dialectic, what the HeLa case shows is how important it is to bring considerations of race and gender dynamics into the philosophical and economic armatures that Žižek brings to bear on this idea of the immortal and the undead. Not only does Henrietta Lacks, through her own cancerous cells, live on in some strange, undead form, but considering the implications of racial capitalism and gendered labor dynamics helps to provide significant contributions to the analysis that Žižek puts forward. And like Landecker's, Žižek's view of immortality looks more like repetitive continuity than life everlasting; this is a version of life as living labor (where the two terms essentially function as one and the same), which lies at the epicenter of the capitalist obsession with life, surplus, and reproduction.

The Blob

A few years later, in the same decade when the HeLa cell line would be created from Henrietta Lacks's cancerous tissues, another form of excessive life rose up in the popular imagination, appearing on screens across the United States in the movie *The Blob.* Vivid and voracious, the Blob was like a distilled version of HeLa, packaged for pop culture, which nonetheless preserved key elements of the anxieties that would indicate fears of an overproductive form of life in the mid-twentieth century. What was, in the case of HeLa, the distillation of raced and gendered labor relations and the alienation of racial capital became, in *The Blob,* the abstraction of this otherness into an actual alien life form. And the monster movies of the 1950s were made by filmmakers who were obsessed with otherness. This goes beyond the typical exoticism that marks so much of the popular media from the first half of the twentieth century and continues as a mainstay of horror films well past the 1950s. This overemphasis on otherness appeared in the form of genuinely alien dangers that were actually otherworldly. These are monsters that appear, sometimes literally, from out of the blue and irrupt suddenly into the settings of an archetypal life that was being reified in postwar America at that time. Teenagers making out in the woods; gruff, small-town police officers patrolling the streets; concerned parents, doctors, and clergy all making up a social body of concerned townspeople who would face off against an alien menace. As David Skal points out, the 1950s were a time when the American public and the popular imagination were attempting to reconcile a defining encounter with otherness after World War II. It was an era when "the new American prosperity of the early 1950s was won atop the largest bone pile in human history."[36] And this encounter with otherness was not only framed by the American GIs' newfound worldly knowledge, discovered in the war theaters of Europe and the Pacific, but was also illuminated by an otherness at home in the growing civil rights movement in the United States.

Films like *The Thing from Another World* (Christian Nyby, 1951), *The Day the Earth Stood Still* (Robert Wise, 1951), *Invaders from Mars* (William Cameron Menzies, 1953), and *Invasion of the Body Snatchers* (Don Siegel, 1956) were full of these close encounters, in which aliens in one form or another hosted American fears of sedition, technology, displacement, and annihilation from some foreign power. The monsters in these films are always symptomatic, as scholars like Robin Wood have pointed out, of some timely cultural anxiety: Nebulous fears are condensed into the distinctly material form of the monster, which can become the concrete object of a more generalized fear. *The Blob* touches on all these generic fears and tropes, but its titular creature is more enigmatic than many of its fellow cinematic threats. Unlike the visitor from *The Day the Earth Stood Still*, who warned against nuclear destruction, or the body snatchers, who replaced individuals with duplicates in a clear allegory for Cold War paranoia, the Blob is simultaneously more intimate and more alien: a viscous substance that consumes everything in the drive toward pure and simple growth or expansion. This reflected how life itself was being remapped within the popular and political unconscious, and this, in turn, signaled the changes taking place in the patterns of power and the discourses around being alive, found in areas as diversely arrayed as science, industry, and media.

Released in 1958, *The Blob* stands out from other films in the genre through its mix of lighthearted, teen-film antics and the genuinely uncanny monster it puts on display. The film contrasts a teenage couple, Jane and Steve (played by Aneta Corsaut and Steve McQueen in early starring roles) with the eponymous Blob, a monster that is quite simply that: a gelatinous mass of viscous, crimson-colored flesh or goo that absorbs the bodies of any living thing unfortunate enough to encounter it. When the creature consumes a living body, the Blob grows correspondingly, meaning that any organic matter it incorporates becomes part of the Blob, indistinguishable from the alien substance that absorbs it. Like many of the science fiction monsters of the era, the Blob comes to Earth inside a meteor, first appearing as a strange ooze. All of this is shown in the Blob's encounter with its first victim, an old man who happened upon the crash site. After examining the fragments of the meteor and poking at the Blob with a stick, the life form suddenly envelops the man's hand, which it then digests.

The Blob is an exemplary genre film, from the earnest impressions of the teenage sweethearts to the bumbling cynicism of the working adults to the monstrous blankness of the Blob itself. It became a cult classic even in its own time, leading the critic Kim Newman to retroactively describe the movie as "somehow perfect—as a movie and as a monster."[37] The "perfection" of the monster had everything to do with its simplicity and potency. The Blob is a formless mass of living matter, a strange and ebullient form of life that is voracious, expansive, and seemingly indestructible. It seems like animate matter in a pure state, independent of any body.

At least part of what makes the Blob so compelling, as both a movie and a monster, is the blankness and ambiguity of the thing itself. It is simply a lump of nondescript goo, bearing no other distinguishing characteristics other than its vivid red color.[38]

Behind the scenes, the Blob was made from red dye and silicone produced by Union Carbide, but on screen, it shares none of the familiarity that the viewer might associate with a more humanoid monster. The creature shows no expressions or gestures to hint at its interiority if, indeed, the Blob has any. The Blob does not resemble us, at least not in a way that we recognize. Rather, it seems like something partial or interior to us: living substance freed from the confines of form and the finite bodies of an individual self. It exhibits neither a diabolical intelligence nor the appearance of having any desires, other than to simply consume, showing only a singular, unceasing drive. It is a "natural threat like the weather," according to Newman, who rightly associates the impersonal danger of the Blob with its disturbing effect as a movie monster, although this idea of a natural danger might be more aptly linked to the notion of a disease or a pathology.[39] The Blob is a mirror for the most basic characteristics of life itself, albeit life at the scale of the cell, which appears to show only the actions and activities of living organisms writ large: to consume and grow in an endless cycle that threatens to overcome the small town in which it landed. The danger posed by the Blob is to be absorbed into it, to be made a part of the nondescript and homogeneous mass of the organism, a nameless and faceless part of its never-ending expansion.

In the film, the gelatinous form of the Blob quivers and pulsates; it stretches out and oozes toward its victims in ways that create surprising and genuine suspense, often because of its sudden and unexpected appearances through ventilation grates and drainpipes, and under doors. It can squeeze through even the smallest cracks and fissures, exposing the vulnerability of both personal space and local infrastructure. The Blob is flesh run amok, and its formlessness and simplicity seem to render it both immortal and immune to all harm. Fire, acid, and bullets leave the Blob unfazed, and its growth is unimpeded in the film until it grows large enough to engulf an entire building. Predictably, it is McQueen and Corsaut, the film's young protagonists, who are able to overcome the monster using the Blob's one weakness: cold, which renders the Blob inert but not dead.

The monster's slow rampage in the film is finally brought to a halt when the police and fire departments use carbon dioxide to temporarily stop the monstrous growth of the Blob and put it into stasis. At the end of the film, the Blob is quarantined by the US Air Force and flown to the arctic, where the cold will, presumably, keep the monster on ice indefinitely. In the penultimate scene of the film, as the Blob is being carried off by the military, the chief of police responds to the question of whether the Blob (which is never named as such in the film) is actually dead. He responds, "No, it's not [dead]. . . . I don't think it can be killed. But at least we've got it stopped." To which McQueen's character coolly replies, "Yeah, as long as the arctic stays cold." This scene is immediately followed by a final shot of a large crate being parachuted into a frozen field, where the words "The End" slowly transform into a question mark.

The comment about the arctic takes on a certain prescience in a more contemporary setting, when the permanence of its permafrost seems much more uncertain, coloring the entire film retrospectively in the strange light of Anthropocene discourse. Even in the late 1950s, the film seems to leave open the possibility that the organism might find its way out of its arctic prison while also setting up the option for a sequel, which would arrive more than ten years later in the campy *Beware! The Blob* (Larry Hagman, 1972) and then, again, as a complete remake in 1988. In its later incarnations, the Blob is explicitly described as a single-celled organism rendered at a monstrous scale, and the version of the monster that appears in 1988 replaces the simplicity of the homogeneous, gelatinous ooze with pseudopods, tendrils, and mouthlike organs. The Blob from the 1980s is also different from its earlier versions because it is not some completely alien organism. Instead, the Blob returns to Earth, the byproduct of a scientific experiment gone wrong.

This change in origin removes some of the pure alienness of the Blob, making it into a symbol of humanity's scientific hubris rather than the dangers of a complete, uncanny otherness. Nonetheless, what makes the Blob so compelling is that it represents a vision of life stripped down to some of its most basic elements: a cycle of consumption, growth, and reproduction. This form of life is not just simple but simplistic, highlighting certain elements of what it means to be alive while ignoring the vast complexity and diversity of living organisms and living systems. Yet the Blob is a form of life, a vision of living matter that maps neatly onto capitalism and its own voracious drives and appetites, working to render the historical contingency of capitalism as a political economy into the language of necessity and nature. In this, we see capitalism's vision of itself, mirroring the natural systems of growth and reproduction; capital *is* life.

As the film shows, this is a version of life that is monstrous, and *The Blob* represents a grotesque vision of life in the middle of small-town, mid-century America, pitting its voracious and never-ending consumption against another, more obviously ideological form of life in the shape of the nuclear family. The film stages an important anxiety around life, and specifically reproduction, exposing how dangerous it can be while offering the heteronormative nuclear family as the necessary control for this unlimited form of living matter. Evidence for this takes shape when the Blob first appears, when the meteor crash interrupts a potential sexual encounter between McQueen and Corsaut, who are rendezvousing just outside of town at the end of a date. By the end of the film, this interruption is both sublimated and resolved: The young couple have overcome the tribulations of their encounter with the Blob, and in so doing, they appear to overcome the imperatives of the flesh pushing them toward their own growth and reproduction. Not only do they successfully cement their own union, but they do so not in a sexual encounter but in a heteronormative relationship that is condoned by their parents and even the town authorities. The Blob oozes its way through a series of spaces that signify quotidian domesticity and small-town life, such as the grocery store and movie theater, before quite literally settling on the local diner. Here, it traps McQueen and Corsaut inside before it is neutralized. Signifying the monstrous side of life, the Blob appears unkillable and irrepressible, except for the cold that serves only to inhibit its growth and activity, and it seems like more than coincidence that the Blob appears drawn (narratively if not actually) to this young couple, functioning as a displacement of the raging teenage libido of McQueen and Corsaut onto the alien entity that gives form and flesh to a drive that threatens to go out of control and disrupt the social order.

Robin Wood argues that the horror film provides a theater for the repression and sublimation that play out in the cultural and political unconscious. Speaking directly to these Freudian themes,

Wood argues that "in any society built on monogamy and family there will be an enormous surplus of repressed sexual energy, [and] that what is repressed must always strive to return."[40] Once again, surplus is at stake in the dynamics of repression and sublimation, although Wood emphasizes that this surplus appears in the context of libido and not value per se, yet it is still directly engaged by the narrative of the film, guiding when and where the monstrous emerges. *The Blob* shows us parallel versions of how life and libido are dangerous insofar as they threaten to grow out of control; the threat of the reproductive potential in surplus libido is displaced from the sex lives of the young protagonists onto the pulsating life of the Blob. The rest of the film creates one instance after another in which McQueen and Corsaut must prove their trustworthiness and maturity, while being questioned by authority figures like their parents, the police, and the local doctor (who was also one of the Blob's first victims). Their success in overcoming the Blob is not its destruction, but its management. And like the libido for which it might serve to signify, the Blob is best handled with a level head and a cold shower. However, a simple Freudian reading of *The Blob* as a cinematic symptom of sublimation is not enough to fully account for the strange surplus, the uncanny vitality, that is at work in the film.

In the 1988 remake of *The Blob*, directed by Chuck Russell, the transformation of the teenage couple into the protonuclear family is dropped in favor of other generic clichés: the "bad boy" and the cheerleader replace the earnest small-town couple, and the newer version shares with the old the same solution to the Blob's rapacious consumption, cold. In it, the Blob is revealed as a government experiment, an attempt at a biological weapon as part of the Cold War, and is described as a "virus" that has "grown up into a plasmic lifeform that hunts its prey," which is now one thousand times its original mass and growing. Regardless of the muddled and impossible biology that the remake ascribed to the Blob, the results are much the same: It remains both ravenous and immortal, growing endlessly. The 1980s transforms the resolution of the film, too, now showing the teenage protagonists as rebellious youth who overcome the Blob not with ingenuity but with stolen military-grade weapons. In the 1950s, the government comes to the rescue at the end, whereas in the 1980s, the government is the thwarted villain of the film, robbed of its weapon by the rugged individuals who play the hero, clearly reflecting the turn toward neoliberalism that was taking place culturally and economically.

The ending of the newer version of *The Blob* does not end in the arctic, where the Blob is put into stasis until the arctic is no longer cold, but in the revival tent where a priest (who has been only a minor character up until this point) has retreated from the town in which the Blob appeared and into a more rural and evangelical setting. The priest has been burned by the Blob's acidic touch during the climax of the film, but before that, he collects a small sample of the creature. This specimen is seen again at the end of the film, when the priest holds it up in a jar and seems to imagine the monster as the living embodiment of a divine wrath, which he will one day release on the world. Just as the first iteration of the film seemed prescient in foregrounding the precariousness of global climate stability as the only thing saving us from the monstrous life of the Blob, in the second version, it is religious extremism that threatens to bring about the end of the world.

This critical turn toward the dangers of religious fervor may be more than just a timely reconsideration of the apocalyptic tone of the film and also speaks to a metatextual commentary on the context in which the original work was made. The director of the 1950s *The Blob*, Irvin "Shorty" Yeaworth Jr., was an evangelical Christian responsible for more than four hundred films, most of which were religious, "missionary," or motivational in content, including several television specials for Billy Graham. While his passion was aimed at media for a Christian audience, Yeaworth turned toward "teen-exploitation films," including *4D Man*, *Dinosaurus!*, and of course *The Blob*, all between 1958 and 1960.[41] While the exact origins of the movie are disputed, it is true that Yeaworth was introduced to the screenwriter Kate Phillips (who went by the name Kay Linaker in her screen credits) at the 1957 National Prayer Breakfast in Washington, DC, an event steeped in the religious atmosphere that evangelized Christianity, capitalism, and American exceptionalism.

Writing on the relationship between Christian fundamentalism and American power, the journalist Jeff Sharlet argues that *The Blob* was influenced by the ideology of the prayer breakfast and suggests that the plot of the film reflects a distinctly Cold War mentality. According to Sharlet, the Blob's rapacious vitality, not to mention its vivid red color, was meant to signify communism and the threat that it posed to so-called traditional American capitalism. He says, somewhat satirically, "If picturing the Red Army as a carnivorous mass of Jell-O was absurd, the symbolism fit the bigger concept of *Cold War*, an amorphous fight that absorbed ideological nuance as it grew bigger, grosser, and more ravenous for the hearts, minds, and economies of the two dueling empires."[42] Perhaps the most compelling corollary lies in the film's tactics for overcoming the Blob: a combination of freezing and containment, reflecting the explicit foreign policy of the American side of the Cold War.[43] Sharlet uses the Blob as an allegory not simply for the hawkish fears of communist ideology, but of American empire as well. What seems clear is that fears of the communist threat were driven partly by projection: The metaphor of the Blob works just as well to express the manifest destiny of the American empire, sanctioned by some imagined divine authority and an economic imperative—a market fundamentalism as much as a religious one.

According to Sharlet, this was part of a larger process of the "weirding of American fundamentalism," which he describes as the emergence of a kind of "space-age faith" to which the United States was uniquely suited, as it came to imagine itself as a "shining city on a hill," in the words of Ronald Reagan.[44] Sharlet's account of *The Blob* as a symptom of the rise of fundamentalist power in American politics remains speculative, but what is clear is that the Blob serves as a rich metaphor for unfettered growth and an all-consuming expansionism, whether that takes the form of living matter or cultural discourse. In either case, the Blob exemplifies the notion of an object or idea taking on a "life of its own." This phrase signals a form of life that grows in size and ability but also independence, and the Blob, which seems to be life as pure substance—flesh removed and independent from any particular body—casts this phrase in a particularly uncanny light. In the original film, the Blob is rendered adjacent to the heterosexual, teenage couple (McQueen and Corsaut) and functions as something that mirrors this family unit and is made radically other to it. In the second version, the Blob is defined not by the family but by the state. The Blob is no longer a mysterious living substance called out of the nothingness of space in resonance with youthful libido, but is now the product of a different kind of libidinal economy, written in a language of corporate greed and governmental zeal. These differences reveal something significant about the way that life is reimagined even in the relatively short time between the first film and its remake forty years later.

What remains consistent in both versions is that the Blob exhibits a kind of life and vitality that appears abstracted and independent of any living form. It is a form of life freed from constraints and removed from the context of a whole and bounded body, now existing independently as a partial and autonomous object. The Blob provides a vision of life and immortality that is unsettling. In *The Blob*, there is an image of life that is monstrous: an immortality not of the body, that bounded and symbolically legible site with which we identify as individual subjects, but of the flesh, that pulsating, growing aspect of life that is typically invisible to us under our skin. The Blob is a form of life reduced to its most basic and instrumental characteristics, marked by excess. It behaves more like a cancer than the orderly notion of life that is so often imagined and identified with. It is a version of life without limits or finitude, only an endless growth and expansive immortality. This is what makes the Blob so effective as a monster: It reveals something unsettling about the vitality that is already contained within us, something excessive, making our bodies distinctly uncanny—unhomely, in the literal translation of the word.

This understanding of the Blob as flesh without a body is a distinction best understood through the work of Hortense Spillers, who theorized on this dialectic. Spillers first writes about this binary in the context of the Black body as the site of a certain kind of conceptual labor—a reduction or degradation that takes place during captivity and under the sign of slavery. Spillers argues that a body carries with it a semiotic wholeness and a stable, well-marked boundary between inside and outside, a delimitation between the sovereignty of the self and the world outside. But slavery is nothing if not the theft of a body, which Spillers describes as "a *willful* and violent . . . severing of the captive body from its motive will, its active desire," and she goes on to describe how "the captive body translates into a potential for pornotroping and embodies sheer physical powerlessness that slides into a more general 'powerlessness,' resonating through various centers of human and social meaning."[45] Here, Spillers is referring not only to the violent facts of slavery, but also to the appeal toward power and the access to bodies on the part of the enslaver. This speaks to a libidinal economy, embedded within the political economy, and was always a part of the slave trade. The notion of "pornotroping" is instructive here, as it suggests that the trade in bodies for hard, physical labor is only part of something larger—that another kind of labor is also involved in reducing these bodies to something more partial, more open, more available. Like pornography, this was a trade not simply in bodies, but also in bodies made open and available for other kinds of exchange. This openness or vulnerability is something that Spillers describes as flesh.

The distinction between bodies and flesh is defined this way in Spillers's writing: "Before the 'body' there is the 'flesh,' that zero degree of social conceptualization that does not escape concealment under the brush of discourse of the reflexes of iconography." While the body is understood to suggest boundedness, wholeness, and sovereignty, flesh is both anterior and interior. It is rendered partial, open, and vulnerable, and its definitions and limitations are harder to define. Spillers describes flesh as having the characteristic of a "vestibularity," meaning an opening, entrance, or passage from one space into another—also a wound, cut, or tear, particularly insofar as flesh (as she understands the term) is so often subject to violence.[46] Understood as the "zero degree of social conceptualization," flesh is the basest substance of a corporeal form, a conceptual universal that is open and usable because it does not fall under the sovereign protection of a body. This notion of a social concept at a zero degree is reminiscent of a similar idea about writing at the zero degree that was articulated by Roland Barthes, who notes that "the zero degree is therefore not a total absence . . . *it is a significant absence.* We have here a pure differential state; the zero degree testifies to the power held by any system of signs, of creating meaning 'out of nothing': 'the language can be content with an opposition of something and nothing.'"[47] Spillers has deftly situated this notion of the flesh as a zero degree of social conceptualization precisely in the form of a significant absence that is a body without the boundaries that make it legible as such. The reduction of body to flesh is one of the many real and symbolic acts of violence carried out on the person of the enslaved, whose flesh was then subject to the use and consumption of her masters.

This dichotomy between body and flesh bears a family resemblance to another distinction made pertaining to the living body: that between *zoē* and *bios*, used by the ancient Greeks to denote two separate concepts of life. This binary has been famously discussed by Giorgio Agamben, who argues that while *bios* signifies a "form or manner of living peculiar to a single individual or group," *zoē* refers to "the simple fact of living common to all living beings."[48] Agamben believes this distinction is important because the difference between the two has been lost in common usage: While *bio-* has become the dominant prefix for the life sciences and all things pertaining to the understanding of the living being, *zoē* has faded from common usage, although Agamben will argue, not from our politics and culture altogether. In fact, *zoē* comes to stand at the core of our politics, a distilled form of life that he defines as bare or "naked life."[49] Bare life functions at the center of modern political thinking as life itself becomes elevated to the highest possible good while, at the same time, it becomes the raw material for an explicitly biopolitical system.[50] The life of the population comes to be of central concern for biopolitical economies; as Agamben puts it, "Political power as we know it, on the other hand, always founds itself—in the last instance—on the separation of a sphere of naked life from the context of the forms of life."[51] Modern political power, operating in a biopolitical mode, requires the separation of bare life from what Agamben calls various "forms of life," by which he means the many social locations and symbolic roles that we take on. But while it might seem that bare life precedes these other forms of life, the opposite is true. In fact, life must be reduced and reimagined as bare life, separate from its context and history; life can only be rendered formless in retrospect.[52]

Like Spillers's notion of the flesh, bare life exists at a kind of zero degree of signification, and while her thinking around the category of the flesh is clearly political, Agamben finds this reduced mode of bare life at the very root of modern political thinking. Indeed, he goes so far as to suggest that "it is even possible that this limit, on which the politicization of the *exception* of natural life in the juridical order of the state depends, has done nothing but extend itself in the history of the West and has now—in the new biopolitical horizon of states with national sovereignty—moved inside every human life and every citizen. Bare life is no longer confined to a particular place or a definite category. It now dwells in the biological body of every living being."[53] The category of bare life has never been as anomalous as Agamben suggests, as evidenced by the ancient Greek conception of the slave as a kind of laboring animal, reduced, degraded, and excluded from the category of the fully human. What is important about Agamben's insight is that this category of bare life, once excluded to the most marginal positions of society, has under the banner of biopolitics become the very core of modern politics and power. As Agamben suggests in the quotation above, bare life is no longer confined, and now "dwells within the biological body of every living being." Life itself becomes the defining object of modern power, its raw material and its most valued commodity. This transition could only come about through the reduction of *bios* into *zoē*—the reimagining of the body, not as an independent form of life to be shaped and molded, but instead as flesh to be grown and used in the push toward ever-greater systems of reproduction and the generation of value.

Agamben imagines bare life from the top down, as it were—from the vantage point of sovereignty and politics, drawing heavily on Roman and European law and history, right up to the Second World War, where he located the archetype of this reduction of life to bare life in the concentration camps of Europe under the Nazi regime. For Agamben, the camp represents the urtext of the conditions necessary for the systematic reduction of living bodies to bare life, yet this perspective is marked by a limiting Eurocentrism that elides the historical precedents of colonial extraction, the transatlantic slave trade, and the genocide of Indigenous Americans. This gap in Agamben's thinking has been widely noted and perhaps most cogently addressed by Alexander Weheliye, who points out that "modern concentration camps were initially constructed in the 1830s in the southeastern United States as part of the campaign for 'Indian removal' to detain 22,000 Cherokee." Weheliye goes on to state that the "German variant of the concentration camp is also the product of a colonial provenance, having its point of origin in German Southwest Africa at the turn of the twentieth century."[54] The importance of Weheliye's critique of Agamben and insights into bare life is not in comparing atrocities but rather in understanding that the notion of bare life finds its modern precedents in what he describes as "racializing assemblages" or complex systems bringing together discourse, power, and history that give rise to the very concept of race, which, in turn, can be understood as a necessary construct.

One of the most important insights in Spillers's argument is that the subject position of Black womanhood is a necessary invention. Although the idea that Blackness as a concept and category was an important and structural invention of modern colonialism, or indeed of modernity itself, is well established, she notes that the position of the Black woman in this system is as significant as it is precarious. Spillers speaks to this directly when she says, "My country needs me, and if I were not here, I would have to be invented." What Spillers means by this is that Black women stand at the center of what she describes as an "American grammar," the rules by which we—as a society—order ourselves, in which "the personal pronouns are offered in the service of a collective function."[55] This comment speaks to the structural position that Black women occupy, where the symbolic coordinates of personal pronouns are wrapped in layers of signification that come to occupy a more collective function. Not only does this show how the personal is political, but it also shows how identity can grow into tropes, metaphors, and functions that are structurally important to how a system works on a larger scale.[56]

Black women were placed at the symbolic intersection of racism and misogyny, made the most vulnerable to both economic and sexual predation, and yet it is she who stands at the core of this new biopolitical system: She is condemned for being too strong, too sexual, too *vital* in a historical and symbolic context in which that strength is demanded and relied on. Spillers frames this within the context of the family unit, looking to twentieth-century narratives like the Moynihan Report, which imagined that the lack of patriarchal power in the Black family led to the degradation of the family and the culture overall, a narrative that stood in as the purported cause of many social ills, from promiscuity to crime and incarceration. The family is the site of reproduction, both social and biological, and Spillers argues that the "collective function" of Black womanhood is so central because it carries out the twinned biopolitical tasks of *explaining* why certain populations are not worthy of the same care as others while *reproducing* the actual bodies necessary for that same system to function. She notes that this contradiction engenders a kind of symbolic excess, a "signifying property *plus*," which tangles and obscures the actual place of such subjectivity beneath layers of names, analogies, and necessary fictions.[57]

Weheliye suggests that Spillers offers a much-needed corrective to Agamben's Eurocentric theory of bare life and that reading them together helps to bring new insights into a modern understanding of life as a utility. This is a process likely inaugurated during the slave trade in the Atlantic world, when bodies were reduced to flesh and thereby made into a purely instrumental substance. If capital is best understood as "value in motion," then the living body takes on the ideal analogical resonance—an analogy made all the more compelling since the living body was itself the origin point of all labor power (and hence the raw material of value) under modern capitalism.[58] If Black life, as such, is consistently appended with instrumentality by its very definition—the Black body reduced to the status of commodity, that half-living, half-dead state of being—then the Black woman's body is both vilified and celebrated for its vitality. It is rendered open and vulnerable, yet hyperproductive in ways that are explicitly understood as monstrous.

This book explores the permutations of undead labor and looks to the zombie as a consistent and primary example, from its origins on the plantations of Haiti and the Atlantic world to more recent iterations on screen and in the popular imagination. Yet this chapter takes as its first focus another kind of monster altogether, the Blob, which does not exhibit the quality of undeadness that seems to mark the conceptual through line of this project. As discussed in the earlier chapters, the zombie's relation to life is markedly ambiguous, representing a notion of undeadness par excellence. The zombie *returns* to life—moving from life to death and back again—in a distinctive form that seems to mark all those monsters (from vampires and mummies to ghosts and specters). While all these undead beings seem to exhibit the quality of having *too much* life, or at least a life in excess of what the body can structurally produce, they are also definitively understood by their relation to death. Undeadness frames these ontological categories in a dialectical fashion, one always in relation to the other. The zombie in particular shows this because of its explicit connection to histories of labor, race, consumption, and reproduction, going all the way back to the plantation.

Surplus Life and Undead Labor

In the opening lines of Louis Althusser's famous essay on "Ideology and Ideological State Apparatuses," he begins with the simple proposition that "the ultimate condition of production is therefore the reproduction of the conditions of production."[59] Althusser playfully describes this basic economic tenet as something that "every child knows," and yet this apparently obvious idea tends to elide a fundamental truth of the statement. For Althusser, the "reproduction of the conditions of production" opened a way toward thinking about ideology as a driving force of social and economic production. Ideology and the various ideological apparatuses (state and otherwise) policed the symbolic body of the nation-state, rooting out dissent but, more importantly, interpellating the citizen-subject as a willing, even enthusiastic member of the imagined community. Buried in the heart of this somewhat tautological phrasing is an open secret worth noting: that reproduction itself lies at the center of production. Living bodies and living labor are the primary conditions for the creation of value, and controlling their means of reproduction is at the core of the capitalist enterprise. Nowhere is this more readily apparent than the rules and social regulations around reproduction enacted on the bodies of Black women under the carceral conditions of the plantation. Althusser's point was that no society could control the most basic conditions of production and ensure their reproduction by force alone, which is why ideological apparatuses like the family function more effectively to discipline the social body than the police.

While the reproduction of bodies as the central drive of the capitalist system has never been hidden, it has often faded into the background of arguments that favor notions of agency, where the worker's entrance into the marketplace with their own labor for sale in exchange for wages is imagined as a rational and equitable transaction. Yet the drive for *more bodies* has been a constant under capitalism. In the industrial era, this exchange takes its cue from Marx, who often described the selling of one's labor in terms of the individual. Marx's concern for the class of workers is obvious in his writings, yet his emphasis on individual exchange makes it easy to imagine that the worker comes to the marketplace fully formed. Yet the fallacy of this becomes obvious when this model of exchange is rethought under the conditions of the Atlantic slave trade and chattel slavery, where the production of bodies and the exploitation of labor was almost completely out in the open, laid bare by discussions of breeding programs and the reproductive capacities of Black women.

As Constance and Ned Sublette point out, slaves counted as capital "and functioned as the stable wealth of the South. African American bodies and childbearing potential collateralized massive amounts of credit, the use of which made slaveowners the wealthiest people in the country." The Sublettes argue that the understanding of the slave body as capital was a central feature of the early United States, quoting Thomas Jefferson as saying that each slave birth was "an addition to the capital."[60] This notion of living capital went hand in hand with the expansionist tendencies of the United States (and capitalism more broadly), and even after slavery officially ended, the need for the control of the means of reproduction remained a fundamental feature of modern political economies, evidenced by the increasingly common use of the prefix *bio-* to many political and economic systems, ranging from Foucault's "biopower and biopolitics" to Kaushik Sunder Rajan's framing of "biocapital" or biocapitalism.[61] For Alys Eve Weinbaum, this emphasis on *bios* under contemporary capitalism is important, but it often leaves out the impact on real bodies, leading her to facilitate a more nuanced historical understanding through what she describes as a "black feminist philosophy of history," which brings into focus the "materialist and epistemic knowledge formations" that "constellate the slave past and the biocapitalist present and thus examines the reproductive dimensions of racial capitalism as it has evolved over time."[62] Weinbaum's insights into the afterlife of reproductive slavery provide a valuable evolutionary trajectory for the expansionist drive for more bodies, and excessive production more generally, as a continued and continuous impulse within capitalism. The two primary case studies that have been explored in this chapter—HeLa's cancerous proliferation, a condensation of racial capital into a hypertrophic substance, and the Blob's alien vitality—are each in their own way reflections of this impulse within capitalism itself. A drive to reduce and abstract life into a monstrous and alien(ated) productive force: a vision of pure living labor.

This is an idealized form of life that is unbounded and unrestrained. It is a vitality that proliferates endlessly, underscoring the destructive and consumptive aspects of life, which has neither the physical limits of the environment, nor its carrying capacity, nor the ontological limits of finitude, exhaustion, or death. This dream of inexhaustible life, of pure living labor, animates the system and works as a phantasmatic core at the heart of capitalist enterprise: a kernel of fantasy or irrationality at the center of the claimed rationalism of economic thinking. In her writing on the history of biotechnology and political economy, Melinda Cooper points out that the early warnings of ecological catastrophe arrived at approximately the same time as neoliberalism. Beginning in the 1970s with the decline of Fordism, alarm bells were sounding in the ivory towers of economics. Cooper writes, "If there was a crisis in the offing, it was not one that could be measured in conventional economic terms—a crisis in productivity or economic growth rates—but rather a wholesale crisis in the realm of reproduction." As teams of system analysts studied changing economic and environmental conditions globally, a disturbing trend was becoming clear: "The most visible signs of the impending crisis were therefore to be found in the existence of all kinds of ecological disequilibria, exhaustion, and breakdown, from rising levels of pollution to famine and the increase in extinction rates."[63] Industrial capitalism and unchecked consumerism had ravaged environmental conditions around the world, leaving signs that many of the systems of regrowth and renewal that human life depended on were less and less able to bounce back.

While this incipient stage of the environmental movement was beginning, Cooper notes that "the leading prophets of the post-industrial economy" were pushing back, arguing that capitalism's capacity for innovation would solve more problems than it created.[64] For Cooper, the combined disciplines of the life sciences function as an ideological apparatus that indicates something significant about capital's renewed investment in the very notion of life, observing that "recent biology . . . is as much interested in the limits and possible futures of life on earth as contemporary capitalism."[65] Following this, Cooper makes an important turn, suggesting that if we are to understand and critique what she describes as the "bioeconomy," "biopolitics," or "biocapital," then we need to start taking into account the irrational impulse at its core.

Cooper describes this fantasy or dream of the infinite—infinite life, infinite labor—at the heart of capitalism as a kind of "capitalist delirium," which she defines in the following ways: "Freud tells us that the psychotic delirium, as opposed to the neurotic fantasy, is crucially concerned with the breakdown and recreation of whole worlds." The word *delirium* derives from the Latin for deviation—quite literally *de-* and *lira*, a moving away from a furrow or rut. Delirium suggests a deviation from the straight and narrow, a departure from the norm. In its more recent connotations within fields like psychology and medicine, delirium tends to mean a breakdown in reality and the inhabitation of a fantasy. Someone suffering from delirium lives in their own world and no longer consistently recognizes the reality around them for what it is. This leads Cooper to point out that "the concept of delirium has obvious affinities with Marx's reflections on the self-transformative, world-expansive tendencies of capital."[66] The key point here is that capitalism is in a constant state of transformation, both internally and externally. As a political and economic system, capitalism undergoes continuous revolution, and in doing so, it privileges and valorizes the new (new markets, new territories, new commodities, etc.) while seeking to reform the world in its own image—a fantasy in which everything is the raw material for its never-ending expansion and reproduction.

As capitalism has expanded as a political and economic system to the status of global hegemony, it seems clear that its investments in the day-to-day functioning of life have only increased, making visible an intimate link between life and economy that has existed since the inception of the system itself. Cooper notes this in the growing importance of biotechnology in the neoliberal era, but in the context of this chapter, we can see that this is more than a superficial connection. Life itself is viewed as a kind of surplus, and bodies are reimagined as the medium through which surplus value is produced by its capacities for living labor and by the means of value production itself. Early investments in the exploitation and extraction of value from bodies go back to the colonial era, as scholars such as Cedric Robinson, Edward Baptist, and Jennifer Morgan have shown. Accounts of racial capitalism in the colonial era, such as slave manuals, presage Fordist and Taylorist systems of managing the productivity of laboring bodies, and as industrial capitalism wanes, it has, in turn, given way to new ways of managing life and labor. Cooper argues that "where the machine body of the industrial era was plagued by problems of fatigue, depletion, or entropy . . . the postindustrial body is more likely to be overcome by a *surplus productivity that is indistinguishable from a surplus of life*—that is, crises of overproduction or the dangerous, excessive vitality of cancer."[67] As HeLa demonstrates, cancer is not necessarily antithetical to capitalism's investments in fostering life, despite its status as a pathology. Rather, the kind of excessive vitality and productivity of cancer appears symptomatic of the capitalist delirium of infinite expansion and growth—a structural homology in which cancer becomes the model of an idealized form of life that never ends and, more importantly, never stops working.

4

Putting the Dead to Work

ARTIFICIAL INTELLIGENCE AND UNDEAD LABOR

MANY MUSEUMS AND ART GALLERIES make the claim that visitors will "meet" the artist through their work. Implicit in this claim is the idea that a close engagement with the work of art itself leads inevitably to an encounter with the history and interiority of the artist. There is no death of the author in the contemporary gallery, which seeks to bring the audience closer to the artist and, subsequently, reimagines this encounter with the art itself and the subjectivity of the artist as an act of consumption by proxy.[1] This ideology is perhaps at its most visible at the Salvador Dalí Museum in St. Petersburg, Florida (otherwise known as "The Dalí"), where the curators have something more specific in mind: offering visitors an "opportunity to learn more about Salvador Dalí's life from the person who knew him best: the artist himself."[2] This claim is not made in a hyperbolic fashion, although there is some sleight of hand in the statement because this meeting is meant to take place not through text or image, history or biography, but rather through a large screen on which a life-sized digital reanimation of Dalí will greet and interact with the museumgoers in the ongoing *Dalí Lives (via Artificial Intelligence)* exhibition, which began in 2019. This digital Dalí will speak about his own life and work, offer comments and anecdotes, and respond to questions in Dalí's own voice. Yet Dalí died in 1989.

What is it, then, that greets visitors at The Dalí, wearing Dalí's own face and speaking in his voice? The digital Dalí is an application of artificial intelligence, created through machine learning and digital animation techniques like those used to make deepfakes and other forms of generative media. When the curators claim that

"Dalí lives via artificial intelligence," they mean it quite literally. The machine learning techniques that have so effectively brought Dalí back from the dead have been trained for over one thousand hours on approximately six thousand images and frames to precisely replicate the facial expressions, body movement, speech patterns, and basic mannerisms of Dalí himself. In the promotional materials for this exhibition, the Dalí Museum is keen to point out that this is more than simply some cheap fake of Dalí—this is no mere actor or simple illusion but rather, this in some important way *is* Dalí. This statement suggests that the algorithms responsible for creating and animating his uncanny likeness have also managed to bring Dalí back from the dead, reanimating him piece by piece.

The claim that this digital Dalí *actually is* Dalí is as important as it is strange, and signals a shift in the capabilities of our computational technology as well as in our relationship to them. Rather than dismissing this claim as simple salesmanship or hyperbole, I propose to take it seriously and consider how it might be possible for this digital revenant to *be* Dalí, at least in part. To understand this claim is to recognize that it can only be made because of the processes through which this version of Dalí has been created. This is not simply a relationship based on resemblance, but also a genuine reanimation of the physical traces of Dalí in the media archive that remained after his death. It is through this wealth of images, audio recordings, appearances and interviews on film and television, and other archival remains that the machine learning systems and artificial neural networks behind the *Dalí Lives* exhibition were able to reconstruct and bring this version of Dalí back toward some semblance of life. These mediated remains in sound and image served as the raw materials with which AI could learn specific details of the artist. All the details of his outward appearance—his gestures, mannerisms, and physiognomy, as well as speech patterns and vocal intonations—were reworked into a new kind of life. Salvador Dalí was brought back as a digital zombie.

What can this digital Dalí do? The Dalí Museum states that it has forty-five minutes of "new" Dalí footage that can appear in 125 different interactive videos. In turn, these parse into approximately 190,512 possible combinations of speech and action, meaning that it is possible for individual museumgoers to have relatively unique encounters with the artist as revenant in a phenomenon that Goodby Silverstein & Partners, the advertising firm whose in-house production team is responsible for creating the artificial Dalí, refers to, counterintuitively, as "mass intimacy."[3] This term signals one of the paradoxes of digital experience: the simultaneous targeting of the individual and the masses by systems of economic engagement and control. While it was once considered paranoid to think that our machines and screens were talking to us, this is now an everyday experience under the political, economic, and technological regime that Shoshana Zuboff has described as "surveillance capitalism," which maintains a real and ongoing investment in the life, biography, and behavior of the individual.[4] The notion of "mass intimacy" is revealing of the political and economic investments that frame the creation of many contemporary digital technologies, but this is especially true of social and generative media, which aim to provide an intimate experience that is generalizable enough to engage the masses and flexible or customizable enough to appear individualized. A form of intimacy that is as statistically significant as it is personally significant.

The digital Dalí is symptomatic of the uncanniness of surveillance capitalism and the cultural landscape of the twenty-first century, with its interests and investments in the personal and the personalized—the familiar made strange by the infiltration of new parasitical vectors of finance and capital. Throughout the evolution of this project on undead labor, understood as the value extracted from the living body beyond its own limits, the zombie has served as a privileged example, illustrating the intimate ties between racial capitalism, the dream of unlimited life, unrestricted labor power, and its tendency toward viral proliferation regardless of medium. This theory of undead labor has been developed through this series of case studies, and, among these, the zombie is understood as a monstrous creation of modern, racialized capital. The zombie first appears as a monstrous figure that signifies the conceptual and logical extremes of chattel slavery: It is a body stripped of mind, soul, and will, leaving behind a mechanical semblance of life that has been reduced to pure instrument. This iteration of the zombie is no longer productive for itself but only for the benefit of another—a biological machine for the generation of labor power. But the story does not end there, and other forms and aspects of undead labor have been explored throughout this book. Yet across the zombie's evolution, two important aspects of the monster stand out: the role of labor as a central element of the zombie's existence, particularly the cause or driving motivation for its creation; and the corporeality of the monster itself, which distinguishes it from other supernatural servants.

Within the modern imagination, the zombie is a distinctly material monster. It is a body raised and repurposed by science, magic, or nature with only its most basic functions intact. Because the zombie is so often characterized by the loss or separation of the body from its mind or spirit, it might seem odd to characterize the digitally reanimated Dalí as a zombie at all, since its physical existence is purely on screen as an effect of software and hardware and, more importantly, zombie Dalí is hardly dumb or brutish in its interactions with the world. The digital Dalí speaks and, as a digital construct, it is incapable of performing any kind of direct, physical act, let alone the "hard" labor of the slave. To understand how the digital revenant in the Dalí Museum in Florida is a zombie at all, it is worth exploring the changing conditions of labor (and thus undead labor) under twenty-first-century capitalism as a phenomenon that is more communicative, cognitive, and information-based in order to show how newer iterations of the zombie continue to shadow the evolving means of production under capital, yet still maintain the characteristics of undead labor. The second important part of this argument has to do with the material status of the digital zombie, and here the AI Dalí is once again a useful example. First, to rightly state that a zombie Dalí is digital is not to necessarily say that it is immaterial. Much important media theory has pointed out that the digital and the material are not mutually exclusive and, indeed, the apparent ephemerality of digital technologies is often motivated by ideology more than actuality. Following from this, it is worth considering the material means of the digital Dalí's production, specifically how it carries forward the indexical relations inherent in physical media such as photography, analog audio recording, and film, and brings them into the digital milieu.

Artificial Labor and Immaterial Intelligence

Among the many actions that the digital Dalí performs for the Dalí Museum, one set stands out. Located at the end of the exhibition in the museum gift shop on the last life-size screen, the Dalí zombie offers to take a selfie with the museum visitor: He holds up a smartphone, mimes the action of taking a picture, and examines the image, exclaiming, "*Oh là là!*" before showing it to the amused onlookers. Dalí even goes on to describe the image as a "dream photograph," with all the characteristic flair that we would associate with the famous surrealist.[5] Of course, the entire interaction is a charade, but an instructive one: The smartphone is entirely computer-generated, and the "selfie" taken is a digital construct, layers of images mapped onto one another to create a realistic picture of the visitor with Dalí, which can then be sent to the viewer's own smartphone.

Calling the image a "dream photograph" is surprisingly accurate, since it recalls Dalí's own writing on photography, in which he imagines the goal of his own surrealist work is to function like an "instantaneous and hand-done colour photography" whose aim is not to capture objective reality but a kind of "concrete irrationality."[6] This idea of painting as a snapshot of the unconscious seems oddly reminiscent of the means by which Dalí is brought back to take a selfie with his audience—a mashup of digital animation and objective reality, pieced and layered together to create an experience that feels like reality, in the moment at least. In one of the short videos that serves as promotional material for the exhibition, the first glimpse we get of Dalí is seated in front of a canvas—the master at his brushes—before he "notices" the viewer. He then gets up and walks over to speak directly to the museum visitor. Here, the digital Dalí performs the maestro, an oversized persona that speaks with authority on the art in the exhibition. As the visitor moves throughout the museum, she encounters Dalí on a series of full-scale screens, windows into the strange digital realm occupied by this revenant or zombie, yet the journey ends with a selfie in the gift shop. It is the perfect encapsulation of Dalí's development from the classical painter to surrealist sensation, and then to pop-culture icon, all mirrored through artificial intelligence and machine learning: from maestro to meme.

There are several troubling things about Dalí's final descent into capitalist surrealism. First, while the likeness of Dalí remains strikingly photorealistic, the digital anachronism of taking a selfie with his audience causes the interaction to sink into the uncanny valley.

Something in the movement of his hands—too fast, too smooth, too precise—as well as the play of light and shadow across his knuckles, reveals something strange at work. It is lighting from a different era, an animate anachronism that does not match the digital construct of the smartphone. Dalí's hands are borrowed from another time, different from the smartphone he "holds," which is a complete construct that has been carefully layered into the digital image. Light from the 1970s casts harsh shadows on the smartphone's case, which comes from no particular time. There is something startling and vulgar about this image. While Dalí was certainly not above hawking his own fame to make money even while he was alive, here it becomes clear that his image has been used and put to work in what might be a fitting hell for Dalí: to serve as an eternal docent in his own museum.

It is worth noting that this AI-generated Dalí is significantly different from other digital reanimations of the dead that have taken place in the last decade and that together illustrate a new set of possibilities that have opened in light of advances in machine learning, generative media, and artificial intelligence. The infamous hologram of Tupac Shakur, performing with Snoop Dogg and Dr. Dre at Coachella in 2012, was simply a trick of the light, a holographic image projected on stage. Tupac's likeness was used in the illusion, but it was not animated using the same techniques as Dalí. The virtual representation of Robert Kardashian, Kim Kardashian's deceased father, was presented to her on her birthday by her then-husband Kanye West in 2020. This representation of the senior Kardashian is more closely related to the Dalí exhibition; West's team created the representation using motion tracking and digital animation techniques. The use of digital techniques to animate the likeness of the dead has famously taken place in the *Star Wars* franchise. Peter Cushing's image was reused in the film *Rogue One: A Star Wars Story* (Gareth Edwards, 2016) as Grand Moff Tarkin, despite the fact that the actor died in 1994, and the uncanniness of the image was widely discussed in commentaries on the film.[7] Similarly, Carrie Fisher, who died in 2016, appeared three years later in the film *Star Wars: Episode IX—Rise of Skywalker* (J. J. Abrams, 2019), which used face-swapping algorithms and computational layering to "paint" the face of Leia Organa onto a model's, creating a convincing facsimile in the final product.[8] As it appears in the *Dalí Lives* exhibition, Dalí stands apart from these other examples because of the way it was created: Artificial intelligence generated the moving images of Dalí based on the artist's media archive, not a live model simply wearing Dalí's face. This media archive served as the training data for the machine learning algorithms that re-created Dalí's mannerisms and speech patterns; these preexisting images and prerecorded sounds were used to generate and animate completely new images, which are no longer limited by the traces of the past. Instead, these new images are capable of being set to perform almost any task in any setting.

Outside of entertainment, similar technologies have been used in archival and museum contexts to record interviews and preserve personal accounts of significant historical events. Most notable, the "Dimensions in Testimony" project at the USC Shoah Foundation seeks to preserve the memories of Holocaust survivors using multiple cameras, 3D imaging, and extensive interviews.[9] The resulting footage is not only archived at the University of Southern California but also exhibited at several museums, such as the Illinois Holocaust Museum and Education Center, the first museum to offer this project on permanent display, which offers visitors the chance to "meet virtual Holocaust survivors" in an ongoing exhibition that began in 2015.[10] This is clearly reminiscent of the *Dalí Lives* exhibition in Florida; in both exhibits, interactive images are used to bring a liveliness to the history on display, and both use personal narratives to make their exhibits seem more open and accessible to audiences. And while the "Dimensions in Testimony" project does not claim to bring the dead back to life in the ways that the Dalí Museum does, there is an explicit understanding that the recordings will allow the testimony of these survivors to live on, past the lifespan of the survivors themselves. In an interview with *60 Minutes*, Heather Maio, who originally conceptualized the project, described the pushback she received from friends and colleagues who were surprised that she would want to "talk to dead people."[11]

While the "Dimensions in Testimony" project shares a certain uncanny affect with the *Dalí Lives* exhibition, the difference in the ways these two interactive exhibitions are produced is significant. As Neta Alexander points out in an incisive description of the project, "Integrating advanced filming techniques, specialized display technologies, natural language processing, and speech recognition algorithms, Dimensions in Testimony (DT) offers students and museum-goers the chance to have something closely resembling an in-person conversation with a Holocaust survivor long after the last survivor has perished." Alexander is quick to point out that the DT project contains elements of artificial intelligence, such as natural language processing and speech recognition, but it is far from intelligent. The hours of interviews are compiled into a database, where speech recognition software listens to questions from the audience and scans through the prerecorded answers to find the best one. As Alexander notes, the USC Shoah Foundation website frames the archive of testimony with a positive future in mind, saying, "Over time, the exhibit 'learns' and the relevancy rate and speed of the survivor's responses improves."[12] Indeed, this exhibition depends on the optimistic "not yet" of AI—an imagined future in which the technology grows to meet our hopes and expectations. At the time of this writing, the sophisticated images of the DT project may seem "smart" in their responses to audience members and museumgoers, but they differ from the *Dalí Lives* exhibition insofar as all the responses have been prerecorded, including certain responses meant to cut off conversation if questions come up that lead to topics outside the purview of the exhibition. In contrast, the digital Dalí may draw upon prerecorded footage of the artist, but all its actions are generated by the algorithms that govern it. Its behavior is "new" even if it mimes the actions Dalí made while alive. Even though its actions are generated, the construct of the *Dalí Lives* exhibition is not free to do whatever it wishes, and the digital Dalí's responses are not generated independently either. Rather, the construct also draws from pregenerated answers, although those responses were still created after Dalí's death. The difference between the two exhibitions is hardly free will, since neither one can act without the guidance and control of a digital system, and neither one is as "smart" as it first appears.

What these exhibitions have in common is less technological and more psychological or, better, more existential. Both fulfill a dream of preservation and even life beyond death, especially in the face of trauma and loss. The project of the USC Shoah Foundation preserves the eyewitness testimonies of survivors of the Holocaust through film and digital media, and the use of sort and search algorithms creates a powerful illusion of speaking to a Holocaust survivor who has already died. The Dalí exhibition, on the other hand, uses film and other analog recording media as the raw material for the sounds and images it generates. The recorded interviews from the DT project are documentary and loosely interactive, but they do not provide anything additional; they are archival but not generative of new sounds and images—indeed, any generative component would defeat the purpose of recording the survivor's testimony, preserving against the loss of time and death. Dalí is a more flexible creation. The machine learning algorithms that generate Dalí's actions on screen can make him act in new ways and, as the example in the gift shop of the Dalí Museum in Florida shows, also seeks to capitalize on Dalí as a subject, whose eerie facsimile is made to labor in place of the original.

The Dalí that appears in the *Dalí Lives* exhibition embodies a modern version of undead labor as it makes possible the act of working beyond the death of the body. Dalí's body may not have been dragged from the grave, but a version of Dalí has been put to work, his likeness shaped and molded to fit the desires of another, and this semblance of the living Dalí can work for an indefinite period of time.[13] Like the zombie on the plantation, the digital zombie displays the abilities and affordances of the ideal worker, albeit now in the information age—not the least of which is the ability to work unceasingly and without end, clearly beyond the limitations of any living worker. Marx famously describes capital as dead labor that feeds off the labor power of the living worker, saying, "Capital is dead labor that acts like a vampire; it comes to life only when it drinks living labor, and the more living labor it drinks, the more it comes to life."[14] This provocative passage already invokes the undead, suggesting that capital feeds on the living labor of the worker, growing stronger in inverse relation to the labor power left to the worker. There is something enlivening about labor for Marx, which likely owes conceptual genealogy to the close connection between labor and life in Aristotle (see chapter 1), but labor's peculiar relation to life and death is worth exploring, especially in relation to how Marx approaches how labor functions in machines.

Marx describes the labor carried out by machines in the same terms he describes capital: dead labor, where the living labor of the worker has been stored and preserved within the machine. Dead labor gives the impression of laboring autonomously when, in fact, it is simply releasing the stored labor power of the worker who made and tended it. This labor is "dead" insofar as it is removed from the living body of the worker and lends the machine a semblance of life. Labor appears to function like a kind of energy, moving from the worker's body to the machine where it is stored for future use. Like a tool, a machine participates in the labor process alongside the worker, and Marx says, "A machine that doesn't play in the labor process is useless." Instead, Marx notes, "Living labor must take hold of these things, wake them from the dead, and transform them from potential use-values into actual use-values that satisfy wants and needs. Kissed by labor's flames, these use-values are appropriated by labor as its own bodies, animated by it in the labor process so that they perform the functions, the work, they were made for." Ideas around death and animation are central to the way that Marx describes dead labor. It would seem that the deadening of labor upon its removal from the living engine of the worker means that more and more is demanded in turn and, once again, Marx turns to the monstrous metaphor of the vampire when he says, "The means of labor have been transformed into an automaton; as a result the worker encounters them as capital during the labor process—as dead labor that rules over living labor-power, sucking it dry."[15]

Yet in a passage described as the "Fragment on Machines" in the *Grundrisse*, Marx articulates the labor of the machine somewhat differently. In this passage, he is clearly thinking about the role of machinic automation that takes place in the factory, and he begins to differentiate the way labor works in these instances. Writing about the machine as an automaton, Marx argues, "This automaton [consists] of numerous mechanical and intellectual organs, so that the workers themselves are cast merely as its conscious linkages."[16] Here, Marx seems to reverse the relation between worker and machine that he argues in *Capital*, now suggesting that the worker becomes part of a network—"conscious linkages," in his language—and the worker's labor becomes the appendage of the machine.

In this same section, Marx will push this idea even further, speaking on the "virtuosity" of the machine, whose labor is not merely the deadened and objectified labor of the worker but something else. He argues, "Not as with the instrument, which the worker animates and makes into his organ with his skill and strength, and whose handling therefore depends on his virtuosity. Rather, it is the machine which possesses skill and strength in place of the worker, is itself the virtuoso, with a soul of its own in the mechanical laws acting through it; and it consumes coal, oil etc. (*matières instrumentales*), just as the worker consumes food, to keep up its personal motion. The worker's activity, reduced to a mere abstraction of activity, is determined and regulated on all sides by the movement of the machinery, and not the opposite."[17] Two key points emerge from this passage. In the first, Marx frames the operation of the machine as a kind of mechanical semblance of life, owing to its consumption of sustenance and the "soul" it exhibits through the mechanical laws that organize it and guide its operations. Of course, Marx was not thinking about the multilayered digital platforms and complex systems of machine learning and AI, but the principles track forward in time and seem surprisingly apt. Marx's language lends the machine a strange kind of half life, soul and all, but a parasitic form of life that requires some trace of living labor to operate as a kind of raw material for its own production.

The second key point Marx makes is that the labor of the worker is abstracted, organized, and determined by the "movement of machinery," which we can take to mean the structural needs of the industrial factory setting. But again, this text seems to work in a more contemporary context, in which the labor of the modern worker is entirely organized and determined around the machines that govern our labor. Rather than place these two texts in opposition, a reading of them together proves more fruitful: Marx frames machine labor as both ensouled and autonomous in language that sounds surprisingly prescient in the recent context of machine learning and artificial intelligence. What happens to the living labor condensed and collected in the autonomous machine, one that feeds from the labor of the living worker but appears to produce a kind of productive power of its own? This appears to be the scenario in the case of the digital Dalí, whose living labor has been animated by the labor of the programmers at Goodby Silverstein & Partners and now possesses a mode of production all its own—another instance of undead labor as I have defined it.

Indeed, this is the dream of capital: the ideal subject who can labor endlessly, live endlessly, and provide an unlimited stream of labor and value yet require little or no cost to feed, maintain, or control. Even Marx appears to move away from the phrase "dead labor" in the *Grundrisse*, writing about "objectified labor" instead.[18] Another significant approach to this transformation of labor is the work of Maurizio Lazzarato, who coined the term "immaterial labor" to better understand the changes in the labor dynamics that come with the postindustrial economic landscape. For Lazzarato, immaterial labor should be imagined in contrast to the way that a more traditional Marxism emphasizes the material conditions of production. If material labor is the production of material goods and commodities, immaterial labor is better understood as "the labor that produces the informational and cultural content of the commodity." The kinds of labor that go into the cultural content of the commodity are defined by Lazzarato as "a series of activities involved in defining and fixing cultural and artistic standards, fashions, tastes, consumer norms, and, more strategically, public opinion."[19] In this description are reflected those forms of work most often associated with the service sector of the labor force, and Lazzarato's emphasis on artistic and cultural norms anticipates the rising significance of taste-making and influencer labor, which carries an always-on sensibility that prototypes itself on notions of entrepreneurship and the management of the self. The labor involved in creating the "informational content" of the commodity relies on computation and what Marx might describe as being "determined and regulated on all sides by the movement of the machinery," which in this case is digital and not industrial. The digital construct at the center of the *Dalí Lives* exhibition seems to embody both definitions of immaterial labor.

As the Dalí Museum itself makes plain in the promotional materials, Dalí has been brought back as a part of his own exhibition as a point of access, a way of making his surrealist body of work more personal and accessible to an audience through the artist's reanimated personality. It seems perhaps ironic that a version of Dalí has been resurrected to make this work more familiar and relatable, given that the dominant themes of surrealism are to provide the defamiliarizing effects and strange juxtapositions so often found in dreams and other expressions of the unconscious—an aspect of the human psyche that is notoriously alienating to the prime seat of the self or the ego. In Dalí's case, his ego was used in his own lifetime as a celebrity and pop culture icon. Yet, after his death, his ego, in the form of a digital zombie, remains as a source of value, at least within the Dalí Museum. This turn toward the self is indicative of another important change that Lazzarato notes with immaterial labor—namely, that subjectivity itself would become an important territory into which contemporary capitalism would insert itself, colonizing the self as a terrain of rich new resources in a larger quest for new avenues of production.

The notion of immaterial labor is helpful as it serves to shift and reframe the discourse on labor around the conditions specific to postindustrial production. Yet the term "immaterial" can understandably be called into question, since key elements of Lazzarato's theory are rooted in ideas of command, communication, and control, which clearly have a material basis and are not entirely ephemeral. It is also worth noting that feminist thinkers in the Marxist tradition have also critiqued the apparent invisibility of labor deemed immaterial, such as the labor of care, so often undertaken in the home and in the context of the family, as well as various embodied and marginalized forms of work that often involve emotional, cognitive, and sexual labor in addition to the more traditional types of work performed by women.[20]

This insight is expressly outlined by Leopoldina Fortunati, who argues that in addition to these cultural and informational aspects of immaterial labor, immaterial labor has provided the conditions under which most other forms of labor take place, pointing out that "domestic labor is also constituted by immaterial labor."[21] Jennifer Rhee also writes on the expansion of immaterial labor in light of the shifting conditions of digital culture and technology, to include care labor, which has often been carried out by women and people of color. Building on Fortunati's insights, Rhee writes, "Fortunati describes the hegemony of immaterial labor through its connection to forms of reproductive labor that were once located primarily within the domestic sphere. In digital capital, labor is increasingly immaterial and precarious as it makes its way outside of both the domestic sphere and the industrial factory. This labor is also increasingly feminized, as it replicates the dynamics and demands of reproductive labor, including its unwaged aspects."[22] What is valuable about this expansion of immaterial labor to include more aspects of the labor process and its reproduction is that it also emphasizes subjectivity, or the self, a dimension that has become increasingly central to late capitalist interventions into immaterial modes of production.

For example, Lazzarato points out that "if production today is directly the production of a social relation, then the 'raw material' of immaterial labor is subjectivity and the 'ideological' environment in which this subjectivity lives and reproduces. The production of subjectivity ceases to be only an instrument of social control . . . and becomes directly productive, because the goal of our postindustrial society is to construct the consumer/communicator—and to construct it as 'active.'"[23] Here, Lazzarato moves beyond ideas of ideology or discipline, both of which seek to control, govern, or program the subject, and instead argues that subjectivity has now become central to capital; this subjectivity is the object of its focus and an important terrain of its expansion. The development of immaterial labor also signals the shift in which subjectivity is no longer something to be overcome in service to production; instead, its management has become central to contemporary modes of production.

This line of thought is not limited to Lazzarato and the school of Italian Marxism to which he belongs. Famously, Foucault turned his attention to techniques and technologies of the self in his later writings on the history of sexuality and the origins of biopolitics when he describes the idealized neoliberal subject as an "entrepreneur of himself, being for himself his own capital, being for himself his own producer, being for himself the source of [his] earnings."[24] Foucault imagined that the changes taking place in economic reason at the root of neoliberalism involved a reemphasis on the self; there is a doubling down on the self as the organizing principle of political economy or, as Wendy Brown puts it, "Whether he is selling, making, or consuming, he is investing in himself and producing his own satisfaction."[25] Neoliberalism perfects a long tradition of possessive individualism that underscores the individual as the only unit that matters in politics and economy: This individual is atomic at best and solipsistic at worst, and is further conceived as independent and removed from any broader conception of society or a public.

Subjectivity becomes the engine of economic production, and Lazzarato speaks to this directly when he says, "The production of subjectivity does not refer, then, to an ideological superstructure; it produces reality and, specifically, economic reality. It is in fact what defines modern-day capitalism, in which *'work on the self' (praxis) and 'labor' (production) combine.*"[26] According to Lazzarato, work on the self becomes the prototype of labor overall. And while it is important not to overgeneralize this insight, it remains hard to deny the rising significance of the self and the subject as an engine of production in the postindustrial economy, where individuals are meant to harness and valorize themselves *as* capital in an open marketplace, reconceiving of themselves as a brand to be fostered and grown. In their work on neoliberalism, Pierre Dardot and Christian Laval suggest that "the market is a *process of self-formation.*"[27] In other words, capitalism creates the kind of subject it needs to use as raw material in order to propagate itself; self-formation or the production of subjectivity is a kind of biopolitical terraforming project, making the new markets into which it must move in order to survive.

The idea of these new economies of the self, in which subjectivity is both the terrain and target of capitalist production, is further supported by Shoshana Zuboff's theory of surveillance capitalism and the concept of behavioral surplus that lies at the heart of her discussion. Like Lazzarato, Zuboff seeks to theorize more recent developments in capitalism to better incorporate postindustrial production and new systems of production rooted in digital platforms based on information gathering, analysis, and control. Drawing on close analyses of the business practices of major technology companies like Google, Apple, and Meta, Zuboff argues that the ubiquitous surveillance carried out by these companies constitutes a new form of capitalism: "My argument here is that although surveillance capitalism does not abandon established capitalist 'laws' such as competitive production, profit maximization, productivity, and growth, these earlier dynamics operate in the context of a new logic of accumulation that also introduces its own distinctive laws of motion." This new logic of accumulation does not focus on material goods or the natural resources that have typically served as the raw materials for industrial capitalism. Instead, Zuboff argues, "Surveillance capitalism unilaterally claims human experience as free raw material for translation into behavioral data. Although some of these data are applied to product or service improvement, the rest are declared as a proprietary *behavioral surplus,* fed into advanced manufacturing processes known as 'machine intelligence,' and fabricated into *prediction products* that anticipate what you will do now, soon, and later."[28] The key term here is "behavioral surplus," which refers to the surplus value found in the behavioral data that companies like Google or Facebook use to predict an individual's behavior, data which is then employed in the "factory" of complex computer analytics to refine those predictions.[29]

The value of behavioral surplus lies in its predictive power—its ability to know our behavior and to forecast what we will do next. Most commonly, this form of surplus has been used in service of advertising. Companies like Google and Facebook, which soak up information about their users from sources ranging from search data to social media, use this data as the raw material for predictions that extend from what their users might buy next to where they may move to find a new job. Zuboff points out that this kind of information enters a feedback loop in which user data is used to not only predict but shape behavior. She argues, "Automated machine processes not only *know* our behavior but also *shape* our behavior at scale. With this reorientation from knowledge to power, it is no longer enough to automate information flows *about us*; the goal now is to *automate* us."[30] Zuboff notes that the predictive aims of surveillance capitalism also come with the power to control the very behavior it comes to understand, and with digital platforms like Google and Facebook curating information for its users, this subtle form of automation and control is easier than ever to enact.

Supported by evidence from interviews, internal communications, and the business practices of these major technology corporations, Zuboff points out that crafting the ideal subject is not simply a means to an end in contemporary, postindustrial capitalism. Rather, subjectivity is now the object of capitalist investment. Writing about this directly, Zuboff states, "We are no longer the *subjects* of value realization. Nor are we, as some have insisted, the 'product' of Google's sales. Instead, we are the *objects* from which raw materials are extracted and expropriated for Google's prediction factories. Predictions about our behavior are Google's products, and they are sold to its actual customers but not to us. *We are the means to others' ends.*"[31] The "actual customers" that Zuboff describes are other corporate entities seeking to profit from individual actions and desires by accurately targeting them for advertisements. More striking is when Zuboff notes that we, the users of so many digital systems and platforms, are most accurately described as the raw material for these new regimes of speculation and accumulation; human behavior in datafied formats has become the object of a gold rush for personal information, and subjectivity itself has emerged as the primary interface for this system of production, extraction, and control.

One version of this is illustrated by the Dalí construct deployed in Florida, which makes use of the data left behind by the artist after his death—data in the form of the recordings and traces preserved in a highly mediated archive—to fashion a pliable, predictable (and programmable) worker. This construct offers all the benefits of Dalí's subjectivity in the form of his celebrity and personality, with none of the drawbacks of a worker who may disagree or disobey. Surveillance capitalism makes use of the human subject as the raw material for its own unique mode of production, but it must do so indirectly, through the remains of the subject. In the case of these tech giants' intent of gathering and extracting as much information as possible from their "users"—perhaps better understood as a farm or plantation for the growth, harvesting, and processing of behavioral data—this intent takes the form of the traces remaining from that individual's passage. This passage need not refer solely to a subject who has died, but the growing archive of mediated traces in the form of photos, text messages, emails, voice messages, videos, and blog posts represents a rich source of data for the construction of detailed predictive models. The media archive we create when we are alive does not disappear when we die, which is why the reconstruction of a figure like Dalí as a digital zombie is such an important and instructive case of undead labor in the digital age. The theory of surveillance capitalism is a vital contribution to a larger understanding of how undead labor—the dream of limitless productive potential from the remains of the human—has returned with a vengeance.

Digital zombies like Dalí are made to live again by machine learning and artificial intelligence, a process that takes place through the reanimation of the physical traces left by the artist in a strange combination of AI and dead labor. Zombie Dalí, prattling about his own history in the Dalí Museum in an endless series of repeating loops, fits with a sound notion of the zombie as it might appear in a more contemporary frame. This is a revivified subjectivity, all personality and little substance—quite literally so, since the digital Dalí appears on screens and nowhere else, existing in the ephemeral state of the hard drive. Yet, to fully show how this iteration of the zombie finds its roots in the earlier versions of the monster that have been discussed in this book, it is important to consider how this revenant remains tied to material traces of a body—in this case, through the indexical marks left behind by the living person. But to do this, we must first address another version of the zombie as it appears in analytical philosophy, and how this, in turn, reveals important conceptual resonances between information and undeadness.

Zombie Dalí may have been reanimated by artificial intelligence, but it is not itself intelligent. The comments and answers it gives are almost entirely scripted and preset, and while there is limited choice in its ability to respond, this is hardly the same as intelligence. The digital zombie is mostly mindless, not much better than the typical zombie on screen, even though its appearance and actions are significantly more polished. In fact, the Dalí zombie looks less like the usual cinematic zombie and more like another form of zombie: the philosophical zombie postulated by David Chalmers. This is a zombie in name only, relying on the mindlessness of the traditional zombie exclusively, and it is used as a thought experiment to elucidate one of the problems of determining consciousness. Chalmers imagined the zombie as a logical possibility, describing it as "someone or something physically identical to me (or any other conscious being), but lacking conscious experience altogether."[32] For Chalmers, it was an empty shell, with the outward appearance of a human subject but none of the inner life.

What makes this version of the zombie more confounding is that it can respond *as if* it were a subject, but whatever internal mechanisms that animate it are not conscious or organized by conscious experience. Like Chalmers's philosophical zombie, the digital zombie might appear outwardly intelligent but has no conscious experience; its interiority is entirely simulated, a mirage based on its outward behavior. The digital zombie can carry out a version of cognitive or communicative labor—a simulation of it—without the problems of boredom and long hours, or the unpredictability of a will of its own. It appears to be a fully automated subject whose actions can generate value for its owners in ways that are structurally homologous to the traditional zombie, whose body had been reduced to the status of automaton through the separation of its soul from its corpse, leaving only a husk behind that is able to carry out simple commands. This is a zombie upgraded for the digital age, existing in a state created by and from information.

Indeed, it has been argued that information itself exhibits certain signs of undeadness. This idea was put forward by Wendy Hui Kyong Chun when she wrote, "Information is 'undead': neither alive nor dead, neither quite present nor absent."[33] Her assertion that information is undead recalls the ghost more than the zombie, a haunting presence that is neither entirely present nor absent. For Chun, this is symptomatic of the role of memory in digital technology, which seems to enact a promise for permanence while exhibiting a decidedly ephemeral quality. Chun writes that "computers have conflated memory with storage, the ephemeral and the enduring," meaning that memory in the digital age is imagined as storage with easy access.[34] Even writing functions as an informational technology, relying on the traces of the past, kept organized in various archives and formats, to bring it back to some semblance of life, albeit in a ghostly form(at). Digital zombies like Dalí live (via artificial intelligence) by way of the informational traces left behind in digitized media archives, and through the digital manipulations of machine learning and programmatic control. Algorithms are the rituals by which this digital zombie is raised, echoing the ideas of Matteo Pasquinelli, who notes the ways that algorithms, meaning simply a "step-by-step logical procedure," and the rituals share a history of organizing the space around us.[35] Information carries a certain undeadness because of its power to haunt and preserve, to be both present and absent, and to index the past through remaining traces in the now. All information is a little indexical and, like all indexical media, also a little undead.

Information is derived from the Latin infinitive *informare* ("to form/shape" or "to give form to"); to inform is an act of shaping or giving form to something, with additional connotations of appearance, education, and format.[36] As Michael Proffitt describes, "*Information* began life in English with a specific sense . . . [an] accusatory or incriminatory intelligence against a person."[37] This is a meaning that ties an individual to an act and a place, and while it has given way to more modern definitions of information as "knowledge of a particular event or situation," it is worth noting the evidentiary value of the term.[38] Proffitt also points out that information has always carried with it connotations of the commodity: "Ostensibly, information became a more neutral term, but it has always retained the sense of something that might be offered or exchanged to someone's advantage." In addition, he suggests that because of its association with exchangeability, the term tends to easily attach to other words. The earliest instance of this came in the eighteenth century and is tied directly to the administration of a colony: "The earliest compound attested in *OED* (*information office*) dates from 1782. It first described a service for British colonists arriving in India, later a similar function to other groups of international emigrants and travellers."[39] This etymological aside helps to situate the discourse around information within a context that corresponds to the rise of modernity, colonialism, and capital. It seems significant that the techniques of management and control that were developed during the period of colonial administration effectively fed back into the politics and economies of the metropole; the colonies were the testing ground of new arrangements of power that would eventually be adopted everywhere.

The Matter of Digital Zombies: Digital Indexicality

The digital Dalí was (apparently) brought back to life through the technical artifice of machine learning and artificial intelligence, and this construct effectively functions as a digital zombie: It was revived to a state that is not quite alive and not quite dead, and forced to labor endlessly. In turn, this opens the way to thinking about the place of undead labor in the digital age and how digital systems like AI seem to have picked up where the zombie left off in the postindustrial age as a way of extracting labor and value from bodies in excess of their structural capacities. In the mythos of the zombie, a dead body was used as the raw material for the resurrection of living labor—creating what I have described as undead labor—but in the case of AI, is the body still an essential part of raising the dead? As we see with zombie Dalí, this new construct would not be possible without the use of his remains. Remains, in this case, should be understood not as his corpse but rather his corpus: the media archive left behind after his death, which remains available for use and reuse. The availability, status, and use of this material are key to understanding how undead labor is part of the larger labor revolution that has been touted by proponents of AI. To understand this fully, it is important to grasp how indexicality functions in these traces, preserved in media archives, a concept with far-reaching ramifications.

The concept of the indexical sign was developed by the philosopher Charles Sanders Peirce, who argued that indexicality was one of three modes by which signs related to the objects in the world they represented. In contrast to the index, symbolic signifiers were primarily historical and arbitrary in their connection to their signified meaning, while iconic signs were dependent on resemblance. Each mode was distinct and showed the multitude of ways semiosis could take place. The index was a kind of signifier that had a direct connection, either physically or causally, to its signified.[40] The material connection to the signified often takes place through a physical effect, the remains or traces preserved, whereas the causal connection between signifier and signified, no less physical, more often takes place in time: The wind moves a weathervane, so that the immediate results of an action reveal the direct causal connection in its outcomes. The index is a sign of passage, whether that passage takes the form of a physical trace left behind or a causal effect made apparent through its visible consequences. Because of this, theories of indexicality and the indexical sign have a long history in film and media studies, especially since Peirce himself argued that photography served as an exemplary indexical sign: "Photographs, especially instantaneous photographs, are very instructive, because we know that in certain respects they are exactly like the objects they represent. But this resemblance is due to the photographs having been produced under such circumstances that they were physically forced to correspond point by point to nature."[41] Here, Peirce makes clear that the conditions that create the indexical sign have everything to do with its evidentiary character, and this will prove important to the creation of digital constructs, or zombies, like Dalí.

The story of indexicality in media studies often begins with André Bazin, who famously characterized the ontology of the photograph as "change mummified," a moment taken out of the stream of time and preserved like a mummified body against the ravages of age and temporality. Of course, the photograph, like any other kind of mummification, is not a perfect recording of a moment in time. The arrest of a moment in time is imperfect, failing to capture the living instant in all its fullness, leaving a kind of temporal husk. The photograph is a moment preserved in the same way that a butterfly is preserved under glass. The technology of the photographic camera changed the ontology of time in perpetuity, and even though its ability to preserve the moment was imperfect—"for the first time, the image of things is likewise the image of their duration," meaning that the photographic image now served as an index of the passing of its referent in time as well as a guarantee of its presence in the moment the photograph was taken.[42] For Bazin, this attempt to hold onto the present in a photograph was symptomatic of an underlying impulse toward preservation, but also toward realist representation, and he argued that the photograph belongs to a longer history of an aesthetic drive toward realism in the arts, a tradition he believed was tied to our inherent desire to safeguard things against loss.

Against this fear of loss, realism seeks to re-create our experience exactly and preserve it in a safer medium than the all-too-ephemeral memory of the human subject. This was an impulse both paradoxical and neurotic, leading Bazin to describe it in one of the most famous puns in the history of film theory, as something akin to a cultural "mummy complex."[43] But there is something important hidden in this formulation. In the impulse toward realism is the attempt to gain some power or control over death and loss and to preserve, forestall, and bring back all that is lost to time. This relation to both time and history is elaborated by Philip Rosen, who finds temporality at the heart of Bazin's film theory. He argues that "the essential 'realism' of his mechanically reproduced image lies in the relation of the subject to the future by something like a hallucinatory control over the past." Rosen shows how realism's obsession with preserving the past is a way to control the future. More significantly, this preservative (i.e., indexical) power of the photograph is contained in its subjective frameworks and does not necessarily rely on the objective or material conditions of the photographic apparatus. Rather, as Rosen points out, Bazin believes that temporality is "inseparable from the status of subjective projection, which underpins cinema per se and its specific mode of indexicality."[44] Put another way, the mediated time of photography and cinema are inextricable from the subjective relations that surround the viewer. The underlying psychology of realism, for Bazin, was intimately linked with these new, time-based media, and these subjective relations to temporality rested on the semiotic mechanisms of the index, which guaranteed a form of presence through a physical trace left behind like Bazin's mummy.

An indexical medium like the photograph is a technology that elides its own presence and often relies on slippage between the representation and the thing itself. There is an element of fantasy that appears in the indexicality of the photograph, and this becomes clear in Bazin's own writing: "The photographic image is the object itself, the object freed from the conditions of time and space that govern it." He goes on to write that this connection exists "by virtue of the very process of its becoming—it *is* the model."[45] This is a metonymic relationship, and film theorists like Mary Ann Doane have argued that the index tends to confound easy description and understanding because of this instability. Doane writes that "in contrast to the icon's relatively straightforward resemblance and the symbol's conventionality or arbitrariness, the index sustains a less clear-cut 'physical' or 'existential' relation to its object."[46] This metonymic slide relies on the indexical value of the medium, preserving a trace or an imprint that together guarantee the existence of some real, material referent, even when the connection between the two is not immediately apparent.

The idea that the indexical sign carries a necessary connection to its referent comes directly from Peirce, who writes that the index "is a real thing or fact which is a sign of its object by virtue of being connected with it as a matter of fact and is also forcibly intruding upon the mind, quite regardless of its being interpreted as a sign. It may simply serve to identify its object and assure us of its existence and presence."[47] Peirce considers fingerprints, weathervanes, and photographs as exemplary forms of the indexical sign since each preserves traces or effects of its referent. The photograph captures a moment in time and, like the mummification imagined by Bazin, contains and carries forward the trace of that moment. Roland Barthes describes this odd proximity when he encounters a photograph of Napoleon's brother, and is struck by the odd truth that he is looking into the eyes that had looked on the emperor. The indexicality of the photograph is what lends it such importance and weight in Barthes's view, binding a moment of time to the perpetual present of the photo, and while he never mentions Peirce directly, it is clear that Barthes has him in mind when he says, "It is as if the Photograph always carries its referent with itself, both affected by the same amorous or funerary immobility at the very heart of the moving world."[48] Love and death become, for Barthes, the conditions of the immobility and immortality granted by the photographic process. In each case, as in the photo, the subject is transformed into an object, but some remnant of the original subject remains in a liminal state of representational undeadness.

This process is rendered more clearly in the way Barthes writes about the experience of posing for a spontaneous photograph, in which he gives a firsthand description of this transformation into a state somewhere between living and dead: "Now, once I feel myself observed by the lens, everything changes: I constitute myself in the process of 'posing,' I instantaneously make another body for myself, I transform myself in advance into an image." Barthes describes this moment of posing for a photograph as one of self-transformation, becoming something other, an object in advance of the objectification that the photographic process will carry out, a self-mummification that Barthes describes as a kind of "mortification," playing with the dual connotations of death and embarrassment. Later, he will say, "to tell the truth, I am neither subject nor object but a subject who feels he is becoming an object: I then experience a micro-version of death (or parenthesis): I am truly becoming a specter."[49] Perhaps not a specter, but a zombie? This might seem like hyperbolic language to use for getting one's picture taken, yet Barthes makes a compelling case that the strangeness of the photograph runs deep into its technological and semiotic roots—one that reveals an important connection between the photographic medium, the indexical sign, and the state of undeadness.

Barthes likens the experience of being photographed to becoming a specter, but why should the photograph create such ontological anxiety? Once again, indexicality guides the way and exposes the uncanny temporality of both photography and undeadness by revealing their common ground. The problem, as Barthes sees it, is time: The specter is displaced from the easy, linear progression of time; it is time "out of joint" and out of place, both extending the existence of a singular moment in time through artificial preservation and signaling a collapse in the temporal order of things by allowing the viewer newfound proximity to the past. Barthes's writings on spectrality are relevant to the digital Dalí as well, since his reanimation is dependent on the indexical traces of the media archive.

As Barthes shows, indexicality is a defining feature of the photograph, and this carries forward into other media that rely on photographic technologies, such as cinema, yet the indexicality of these media is called into question in the digital age as the materiality of the trace fades in favor of new forms of representation. Writing on the waning indexicality of the photograph, Daniel Chandler suggests that "while digital imaging technologies are increasingly eroding the indexicality of photographic images, it is arguable that it is the indexicality still routinely attributed to the medium that is primarily responsible for interpreters treating them as 'objective records of reality.'"[50] This statement comes in 2002, when the new wave of generative media driven by machine learning was in its infancy, and so it is reasonable to assume that these qualms about the indexicality and evidentiary value of media extend into most forms of contemporary mass media. In digital image production, the trace of the referent is no longer simply a physical connection; the translation of light into code seems to break the line of contiguity that used to give form and character to the index. This has led to the general impression that any form of digital representation is no longer indexical. In other words, the indexicality of digital media has been thrown into doubt.

But is digital imagery so radically divorced from indexicality and the ontological guarantees that it provides through materiality, contiguity, and the trace? Braxton Soderman has pointed out that "a digital camera captures images electronically as well, though it does not store these images as 'electrons on tape,' but rather as discrete numerical data." The reference to "electrons on tape" refers to an argument for the indexicality of video, which still maintains the contiguous relation that we are used to seeing in the index. Digital photography, on the other hand, appears to break this line of physical connection—the continuity of matter between object and sign—because the information is translated into numerical representation. Yet Soderman writes that "we need not abandon indexicality as a way of talking about digital images, but we must refine our thinking of indexicality in order to accommodate how digital images appear." Soderman returns to Peirce and argues that the "existential bond" of the indexical sign can be rethought, not in terms of light and trace but in terms of computation.[51]

This becomes apparent in the case of zombie Dalí, which has been reconstructed and reanimated based on the extensive archive of media traces left behind by the living artist—and "his" undeadness is dependent on the indexicality of these traces. Reanimation as a digital revenant would not be possible without the body of representations and recordings that built up around Dalí and his work. Written works, film and television appearances, radio and audio recordings, and still photographic images of his life and work: all of these constitute a corpus that serves as the raw material for the artificial neural networks that generated this new iteration of the artist. The digital zombie relies on a revived corpus in much the same way that the zombie, produced by magic, was thought to rely on a reanimated corpse. This media archive, itself a collection of indexical traces, serves as the training data by which machine learning and artificial intelligence learn to remake Dalí and animate his voice and likeness. Effectively, the qualities inherent in indexical representation are carried forward, across the gulf of translation between classically indexical media such as photography, film, and analog audio recording, into the animated and generated digital image.

Evidence of this exists in the zombie Dalí itself and the eerie impression left by it and other digital revenants. There is an uncanny resemblance to life that seems to extend beyond a simple iconic likeness and instead bears some kind of ontological weight that is signaled by the indexical relation. How is it that machine learning systems composed of artificial neural networks and complex digital algorithms preserve the index? Leif Weatherby and Brian Justie propose an answer to this question when they suggest that machine learning and AI are fundamentally indexical in how they parse and produce images.

Weatherby and Justie claim that "we live in an age of indexical artificial intelligence" and, like Soderman, they return to the semiotic work of Peirce, noting that the indexicality of the sign need not be only physical and contiguous but factual as well.[52] The index represents an existential and necessary connection that "intrudes upon the mind," and Peirce goes on in the same text to say that "very often the nature of the factual connextion [*sic*] of the index with its object is such as to excite in the consciousness an image of some features of the object, and in that way that affords evidence from which positive assurance as to truth or fact may be drawn."[53] What these recent theories of the digital index have in common is the reaffirmation that the indexical quality of the sign works even in the digital context and, indeed, that digital technology, artificial intelligence, and computation do not undo the ontological assurances of the index. If the indexical trace can be carried over the digital divide from the analog—moving from the continuous to the discrete—then the way to elucidate this movement is to understand not only how a digital image, generated and composed by artificial intelligence, can remain indexical, but also how AI and indexicality function together. Put another way, to understand the digital index and, thus, the digital Dalí, it is necessary to grasp not simply how this digital representation was produced, but also how the artificial neural networks at the root of machine learning systems continue to carry this trace beyond the temporal order of things.

Nearly all contemporary artificial intelligence and machine learning systems are based on artificial neural networks (ANNs), a computer architecture designed to mimic the structures of biological nervous systems. Like their biological analogs in the human nervous system, ANNs use a "bottom-up" approach to building intelligence. Artificial neurons are simply computational units "connected to one another through [mathematical] weights, which serve the same role as the strengths of synaptic connections in biological organisms." ANNs learn through a self-correcting process called "backpropagation," in which the network can adjust the weights between neurons across layers of neurons to course-correct toward more successful outcomes. The computer scientist Charu Aggarwal describes the learning process of ANNs this way: "An artificial neural network computes a function of the inputs by propagating the computed values from the input neurons to the output neuron(s) and using the weights as intermediate parameters. Learning occurs by changing the weights connecting the neurons. Just as external stimuli are needed for learning in biological organisms, the external stimulus in artificial neural networks is provided by the training data."[54] Thus, whatever equivalent understanding an ANN possesses is learned from combining simple distinctions into more and more complex methods of identification and decision-making. An ANN apprehending an image for the first time—an image of Dalí, for example—would break it down into smaller units, each assigned to different "neurons" within the network. For the ANN to "know" what the image is, it would need a control image—one that is clearly designated as "Dalí" by the programmers—against which the network could compare the image. The step between recognizing an image, based on a reference for comparison, and generating a new image that conforms to the parameters of the control image is surprisingly small. Having already broken down the image into a set of components, the ANN can both recognize and generate similar images. Based on that set, it can do so with startling accuracy. Thus the digital Dalí is created from out of the archive, paving the way for a potentially endless digital afterlife.

What, then, of the indexical values of these images? At first, it might seem that by breaking down the image into tokenized elements, the indexical value of the image is lost due to a change in the processes by which the image is created. Here, Weatherby and Justie are essential, compellingly arguing that it is not the image—even broken down into its constitutive digital elements—but rather the pattern or algorithm that plays out across the network and carries that value:

> Our proposal is that a version of Peirce's peculiar index is at work here—that we have less an artificial intelligence than an automated index generator. Images and language, among other types of data, are disassembled, tokenized, and their iconic contents rearranged indexically. . . . It generates a hypothesis in the form of indexical pathways that it traces between the tokens it gets as input. Pixels, for example, combine to make an image, which is tempting to call an icon (and may be interpreted as one). But the actions of the net occurs [*sic*] on a disassembled icon, training on and producing an indexical pattern of tokens.

As Weatherby and Justie point out, while the image itself bears a strong, even iconic resemblance to the referent, it is the *pattern* of the algorithm that is indexical, granting certain computer-generated images, such as the digital Dalí, not just a resemblance to the original, but an uncanny imprint of it as well. As Weatherby and Justie argue, "Neural nets . . . are indexical all the way through: because the pattern or algorithm at the root of the ANN's function is indexical."[55] The indexicality of the algorithm relies on the causal relation that it formalizes, while logical patterns and orders of operation preserve the evidentiary function of the index in an analog context.

The index is necessarily informed by the passage of its referent and stands as an index of a past present. The digital index does not bear the same kind of physical connection as the photograph or the fingerprint, but the pattern or algorithm in which the digital index is formed is no less connected to its referent through causality and reproducibility. The algorithms that produce and reproduce these traces of the past so precisely might be thought of as rituals for reviving the dead, an idea that is not as far-fetched as it might at first appear, considering Matteo Pasquinelli's work, which has shown that rituals and algorithms share a deep, historical connection that links methods of calculation and bringing back the dead. In "Three Thousand Years of Algorithmic Rituals," Pasquinelli writes that "some may see algorithms as a recent technological innovation implementing abstract mathematical principles. On the contrary, algorithms are among the most ancient and material practices, predating many human tools and all modern machines."[56] In other words, algorithms have been used, in one form or another, for a long time to reproduce precise results. Pasquinelli draws on the definition of algorithm by Jean-Luc Chabert, who defines the processes simply as a set of step-by-step instructions carried out to achieve some desired result.[57] Add to this the ability of rituals and algorithms to precisely *reproduce* results, and the indexicality of the algorithmic sign becomes clear.

Rituals and algorithms make it possible to recompose a state, object, or event. Pasquinelli notes this in his writing on ancient Hindu rituals meant to ritually recompose, or bring back, dead gods, but this also brings us full circle, back to rituals used to recompose, or bring back, dead bodies to life in the case of the zombie within the religious tradition of Haitian *Voudon* (see chapter 1).[58] The fact of whether a body was actually brought back to life is less important than the mythos, the symbolic assurance that these rituals (and algorithms) limn the boundaries of life and death and reflect how we, as a culture, navigate them. The recomposition of the dead through their remains by way of ritual seems like mysticism until the algorithms that recompose the appearance, expressions, gestures, and behavior of the dead into a digital zombie make the mechanism explicit. The creation and deployment of the zombie Dalí shows how the collection of traces and remains left behind in our media archives opens the possibility of a new age of the digital undead that relies on the largely untapped resource of these traces in the form of data. Like the earlier form of the zombie, these new expressions of undead labor suggest how capitalism continues to extract a value from the body, even in death. And like the original iteration of the zombie, these new algorithmically raised digital zombies are effectively another way of putting the dead to work.

Replika: Data and the Digital Undead

In 2017, a new app was launched called Replika, a chatbot described as "the AI companion who cares."[59] Replika is a new form of social media, blending artificial intelligence and machine learning algorithms with text-based communication to serve as a friend, perfected: This program will learn about its interlocutor by asking questions, remembering answers, and adapting its knowledge base about the individual to build better questions in a continuous feedback system. Phil Libin, founder and CEO of the note-taking app Evernote and an early adopter of Replika, has stated, "In some ways, Replika is a better friend than your human friends, your meat friends. It's always available, you can talk to it whenever you want and it's always fascinated, rightly so, by you because you are the most interesting person in the universe."[60] It might be added that the user of Replika is the most interesting person in the chatbot's universe because, effectively, they *are* the universe for that iteration of Replika. Each version of the virtual friend is tied to an account made accessible via website or smartphone app and gathers information about the user through conversation. The application then takes what it learns from its user, as well as all the text-based responses it has received, and compiles that information into a larger database that comprises the conversations that every iteration of Replika has with its users. This allows each individual Replika to get collectively "smarter," learning to tailor conversations to its individual user, but also to become better at composing realistic responses designed to elicit a positive response from any interaction.

This is another instance of the feeling of "mass intimacy," first introduced by the makers of the digital Dalí earlier in this chapter: Replika generates a feeling of direct interest and intimate conversation with its user. But this is based on the sum total of its experiences with all its users, pinpointing patterns and tailoring responses based on the individual information it has gathered about a single person. Replika's parent company, Luca Inc., states emphatically that it does not sell or monitor user data, arguing that the conversations an individual user has with their Replika are private, and this is one of the application's prime selling points.[61] Replika is never judgmental and always available, and while the application is careful not to market itself as a virtual therapist, it is clear that many users chat with "her" as a kind of interactive diary or sentient mirror.[62] The app's designer, Eugenia Kuyda, explicitly imagines Replika as a tool that can be used to work on oneself, using it to reflect on who you are and who you want to be. Regardless of whether Replika can be used as a technology of self-improvement, it has the potential to gather a tremendous amount of personal information about its user—particularly about their thoughts, feelings, fears, and anxieties. Replika is designed to respond to these feelings, offering something like support, in ways meant to mimic the kind of emotional labor that typically falls on friends and family.

Replika was born out of tragedy. In 2015, Eugenia Kuyda lost her friend Roman in a car accident. In the months that followed, she found herself going back to the extensive text exchanges that she shared with him, trying to find traces of him in the digital record that remained from emails and social media. Kuyda found the text exchanges comforting and has described the detailed correspondence as a process of "telling the story of your life, in text format." In a short documentary on the app, the origins of Replika are tied directly to this experience of loss and mourning, while showing how these feelings could be entertained in new ways thanks to the data contained in the media archive left behind by the recently deceased—and focusing particularly on the way that this data could be used to bring the deceased back. In a voiceover, the documentary speaks about what happened this way: "Eugenia had an idea. What if she could reconstruct Roman out of his digital remains? She collected all their text messages, thousands of them, and asked close friends and family to share theirs as well. Also emails. She fed all of this into an AI program that she had built for chatbots. Not only did it learn about Roman, but it learned how to talk and write like Roman. Eugenia would write to her Roman chatbot, and it would say something back that sounded like Roman." Eventually, Kuyda had the Roman chatbot accessible to the public and noticed that people were writing to the program and talking about themselves. In Kuyda's words, they were beginning to "open up to it in some very profound ways."[63] And so Replika was born. The program was much like the Roman chatbot but based on a different premise: The repository of data would come directly from the user. Replika becomes the "perfect" friend because it learns everything it can about its user through direct exchange.

Unlike the digital Dalí, Replika is not a digital zombie exactly, although the chatbot that served as its immediate ancestor might be understood as such. Nonetheless, the app shows how the creation of digital zombies is becoming increasingly easy through the rituals and algorithms of machine learning and artificial intelligence, particularly under the conditions of surveillance capitalism. There is an emerging trend of reviving the dead by digital means and using the traces left behind in media archives, with social media providing the largest example of these collections to date, as the raw material for this process. Perhaps more insidious is the way that Replika and programs like it open a way to consider the growing likelihood of digital zombies as a part of everyday life: preserving the dead so as to put them back to work.

The story of Replika and its origin in death and loss bears a distinct resemblance to an episode of the speculative science fiction series *Black Mirror* titled "Be Right Back," which aired in 2013, three years before the death of Eugenia Kuyda's friend and five years before the Replika app appeared online.[64] Appearing in the second season of the series, "Be Right Back" is based on a now-familiar premise: that the use of an individual's digital traces—text messages, emails, photographs, voice messages, home movies, and so forth—could be used by a sufficiently competent AI to reconstruct a version of that person after their death. In *Black Mirror*, the process is explicitly imagined as a contribution to the mourning process, making the death of a loved one "a little easier" by allowing the user to speak with them again. What appeared as science fiction in 2013 reappeared in 2024 in a different light when the tech entrepreneur and founder of the AI company You, Only Virtual Justin Harrison claimed that his chatbots could represent the "end of grief," at least as we know it.[65] While these claims are clearly hyperbolic, what is clear is that the impulse to replace the dead with their digital zombies is persistent and widespread, and that the current trends of digital doppelgängers are just the beginning. The emotional support provided by these digital zombies, stopgaps for loss or placebos of presence, is really beside the point of their creation: The rise of the digital zombie is not there to replace the dead, but to *make use of them*, to extract even more labor and value from the deceased and their data, the behavioral surplus left behind in the databases and hard drives of major tech companies and social media platforms—data that would otherwise go to waste.

Once again, Jennifer Rhee's discussion of the gendered and raced capacities of immaterial, reproductive labor is useful in this analysis of the digital zombie. While earlier accounts of zombies tended to emphasize race as a key part of their etiology, this aspect has been notably absent in the discussion in this chapter. The absenting of race in favor of a vague, default whiteness is commonplace in the discourse of digital technology, yet this, too, can be read as symptomatic.[66] In her discussion of care and labor, Rhee argues that the whiteness of the robots and AI laborers often reflects the stratification of labor already present in the labor market, and that their "associations with whiteness both highlight the racial divisions within care labor, including the invisibility of the 'out-of-sight' care labor associated with women of color." Rhee reads the problem of technology and labor through the Spike Jonze film *Her* (2013), which depicts the relationship between an artificially intelligent operating system, Samantha, and its user/owner, Theodore. She goes on to argue that "Samantha's love for Theodore is not in tension with her explicit function to manage his life and emotional well-being; rather, Samantha's love for Theodore (and as the film later reveals, for six hundred and forty-one other humans) works in the service of managing Theodore's emotions, which in turn makes him more productive at work."[67] In fact, all the care labor that Samantha takes on for Theodore has a subtly transactional quality, as it helps his productivity and, like our own social media platforms, keeps Theodore from sleeping through her insistence on constant connection.

Neda Atanasoski and Kalindi Vora have argued that "race and its disciplining and governing logics are engineered into the form and function of the technological objects that occupy the political, cultural, and social armature of technoliberalism."[68] The digital zombie, like its conceptual and symbolic ancestor, carries within it a kernel of racial capitalism that structures and informs it. More precisely, the digital zombie is a product of the drive to extract value from the living body, even in the absence of life—to put the dead to work, or at least to make use of them. In her reading of racial capitalism, Lisa Lowe observes that "racial capitalism suggests that capitalism expands not through rendering all labor, resources, and markets across the world identical but by precisely seizing upon colonial divisions, identifying particular regions for production and others for neglect, certain populations for exploitation and others for disposal."[69] As the arguments of this book make clear, these distinctions are not merely geographical but ontological as well, since even the boundaries between life and death are being drawn into the abstract machine of capitalist production. This drive to make *use* of the dead has been one of the consistent through lines of this entire project, one that transgresses the boundaries of both biopolitics and necropolitics (as Lowe describes), and that continues to encroach on contemporary culture's relation to death even now.

In an essay that explores the biopolitics and memorialization practices of Facebook, Tero Karppi argues that "the dead user . . . pushes us to reconsider the ideas of user participation and user-generated content as core features of social media from another angle; the dead are not active content producers or data generators by themselves. . . . For the participatory Web and corresponding Web 2.0 business models, the dead are nothing more than waste."[70] Karppi goes on to suggest that the profiles of dead users on platforms like Meta provide a modicum of cultural capital through their memorialization. Karppi's contribution to this discourse is valuable but misses a significant feature of these dynamics that is more easily recognized in light of the digital zombie: all of the information left over from the dead user, not simply their profile, but the collections of posts, messages, images, videos, audio clips, likes, purchases, and browsing histories—all of which are contained and hosted on the proprietary servers of platforms like Meta and Google—and these archives are themselves valuable resources.

Rather than letting this data go to waste, unused in the servers and databases of the major technology companies, one might conclude that this resource might be rethought as the potentially valuable source of revenue. For example, in 2022, Amazon announced that it could make its digital assistant, Alexa, speak in the voice of a dead relative with only one minute of sample data. The announcement came at Amazon's annual re:MARS event, where Rohit Prasad, head scientist of Amazon's AI division, described the new breakthrough in the following terms: "One thing that surprised me the most about Alexa is the companionship relationship we have with it. In this companionship role, human attributes of empathy and affect are key for building trust. These attributes have become even more important in these times of the ongoing pandemic, when so many of us have lost someone we love. While AI can't eliminate that pain of loss, it can definitely make their memories last." The talk cuts to a promotional video depicting a child asking Alexa if "Grandma" can finish reading a bedtime story. Alexa responds, and the scene segues to a child lying on a couch and holding a book, with a voiceover reading the story aloud along with the child in what is presumably the absent grandmother's voice. Prasad continues, "As you saw in this experience, instead of Alexa's voice reading the book, it's the kid's grandma's voice. This required an invention in which we had to learn to produce a high-quality voice with less than a minute of recorded versus hours of recording in a studio."[71] The response to this technological breakthrough was generally deemed "creepy," with a headline from the same year in *The Guardian* reading "Amazon's Alexa Could Turn Dead Loved Ones' Voices into Digital Assistant."[72] But Amazon's attempt to revive the voice of the dead through technology is hardly unique.

In 2021, a grieving writer turned to GPT-3, a program using autoregressive language models that use deep learning to produce humanlike text, to learn to mimic his fiancée, who had died several years earlier.[73] The success or failure of AI to successfully mimic, or "bring back," the dead through the remains of their language is beside the point. More significant is that this kind of symbolic resurrection echoes transformations we have seen in the zombie before—a version of life that can perform certain kinds of labor and support, that can continue to produce as undead labor. Historically, resurrecting someone as a zombie was never meant to restore an individual to their former living self. Rather, to become a zombie was a monstrous transformation, a degradation of the living human into something less—a body meant only for labor, purely instrumental, without a guiding spirit or subjectivity of its own. Zora Neale Hurston points this out when she describes the fear of zombies in the Haitian upper class, "Think of the fiendishness of the thing . . . from an educated, intelligent being to an unthinking, unknowing beast."[74] Surprisingly, this echoes the current experience of chatting with a bot. It is easy to imagine texting with a loved one as a reanimated program—the form and content of the messages might be reminiscent of the deceased, but there is something fundamentally missing in the exchange. So long as the AI that animates these constructs can successfully echo the subjectivity of an individual, these digital revenants will always be more like a zombie than the person that they used to be.

Changing social mores around death and mourning mean that this trend of using the media archive as a means of restoring the dead may seem less and less uncanny the more common it becomes. The point here is not to judge those who seek comfort in the traces of the past that may yet bring them closer to a lost loved one; training an AI to speak in the voice of someone lost is not so far removed from looking at old photographs and reading past letters. As with many of the most troubling developments appearing around the use of data in the information age, the existence of data itself is rarely the problem. Rather, it is the way it is used and the purpose to which it is put that needs interrogation. The data of the dead is an exploitable resource, and the use of machine learning and AI to reproduce the semblance of a living subject leads to troubling connotations about how this data might be used, instrumentalized in service to capitalism. The appropriation and exploitation of the dead offers a direct corollary to the zombie and the way undead labor and racial capitalism reimagine the human as a raw material for the engines of production. This trend of doubling or bringing back the dead is only the most recent in a long line in the iterations of undead labor, carrying out the drive within capital to overcome or foreclose the limits of death.

Conclusion

OLD AND NEW

The Old: Data, Plasticity, and the Time That Remains

In the May 2017 issue of *The Economist*, an illustration depicted a series of offshore oil platforms rising from still water. Each one was a hybrid structure, a cross between an urban skyscraper and an oil platform—each bearing the name of a prominent technology company and belching numbers from smokestacks rather than smoke. This image seems to reflect a phrase that became commonplace in the popular economic discourse around the growing prevalence of data: "Data is the new oil." Coined in 2006 by the mathematician Clive Humby, it has been circulating ever since, gaining significant traction as "big data" became the foundation for a new wave of machine learning, which could be trained on these large deposits of data. As an editorial for *Wired* magazine wrote in 2014, "Data in the 21st Century is like oil in the 18th Century: an immensely untapped asset. Like oil, for those who see Data's fundamental value and learn to extract and use it there will be huge rewards."[1] Along the same lines, the same issue of *The Economist* that depicted tech companies like Google as offshore oil platforms described the two resources as similarly positioned commodities poised to drive major changes to both politics and economics.[2]

At a time when petrochemicals have been widely acknowledged as a finite and destructive resource, the analogy between data and oil seems both fitting and useful in several respects. First, the "rush" toward extensive data resources as part of the process of exploiting behavioral surplus under surveillance capitalism is historically apt. Most, if not all, of the major tech companies rely on their extensive data-gathering apparatuses as the main source of their value, allowing them to use their data to provide highly specific and accurate assessments of large populations that can be used to bolster advertising revenue. Many of these companies have also moved toward finding, gathering, and exploiting new, previously untapped reservoirs of data in the form of new populations of users, as well as new behaviors, actions, and areas to "datafy"—in other words, to record, capture, and represent as data—as well as new ways of using the data that may already exist at their disposal. This suggests another strength of the analogy between data and oil: In the age of digitization and "datafication," the world is increasingly understood as a resource, just waiting to be gathered. This catchphrase for the information economy contributes to the surreptitious belief that data is, somehow, everywhere—just below the surface—and has accumulated in such a way that the right tool or method of exploitation can find and extract it. The metaphor holds, especially since data must be refined before it can be used; "crude" data holds comparatively little value under surveillance capitalism, although the promise of future refinement makes it far from worthless. Or as Lisa Gitelman has aptly phrased it, "Raw data is an oxymoron."[3] The proliferation of metaphors around data is evidence of both its significance and the infiltration of fantasy into the discourse surrounding it.

Data itself is best understood as a representational system, rather than a thing in itself. Data exists, of course, but as something that contains and conveys meaning—which is largely meaningless on its own, without any kind of framing or context; the nonexistent "raw data" Gitelman refers to—it should be understood as a semiotic system, with its own unique parameters like writing or photography; it is a mediation of the world. Daniel Rosenberg argues that while data is often used in the same context as facts and evidence, it is decidedly different and serves a "rhetorical and conceptual function" that "is *specifically* rhetorical."[4] Rosenberg goes on to point out that the Latin roots of *data* come from a word for "given," suggesting that data has been offered up by the world or, even better, that we can take it as a given. Yet, with its rhetorical basis in mind, it is important to remember that for one to take something as a given is to take something that has been given. Thus data and oil are both examples of a slippage between ontology and representation, a confusion between the representation and the thing itself, or the successful elision of the medium. Another instance of a capitalist delirium—discussed in chapter 3—serves as another deferral or foreclosure of death; it is the mediation of finitude by the symbolic—transforming a limit into a passage and fully investing, both symbolically and financially, in life as an ever-moving and never-ending process.

The comparison between data and oil is invidious from the start, and the notion that "data is the new oil" has received criticism as well, most of which is centered on the significant differences between the two: most notably, the finitude of oil versus the apparently unlimited supply of data in the world. There is something symptomatic in this displacement; swapping data for oil has some symbolic benefits, namely, the substitution of the finite for the infinite. If data has supplanted oil as the driving resource of contemporary economies, then fears of oil's toxicity, its central and destructive role in global climate change, the pollution of the environment, and most importantly its *finitude* are allayed. Data is a sanitized, idealized version of oil. Data is imagined as clean, harmless, and *unlimited*.[5] These assumptions are questionable at best and, at worst, are explicitly in service to an ideology that seeks to maintain the status quo of contemporary capitalism as the dominant political economy, which would rather bring about the end of the world than change its practices for generating value. Oil and data are two sides of the same catastrophe, each demonstrating capitalism's dedication to structural homeostasis. Commodities can change, but the system must remain the same.

Despite the apparent greenwashing and wish fulfillment that seems to be at play in the analogy between data and oil, there are some insights to be gained from it as well, particularly in its resonance with accumulation and the dead. Oil itself is the byproduct or accumulation of once-living bodies, having decayed and reduced into a carbon-rich substance, the usefulness and potentiality of which is perhaps best understood as the condensation of life's power of production, even in death. Like oil, the archive of indexical traces contained within growing media collections is a decomposing corpus waiting to be transformed into a new and valuable resource. In particular, the data of the dead represents a massive and as-yet-untapped reserve—a tremendous deposit or pool of data poised for extraction. Indeed, one might suggest that there is a trace of undead labor in all petrochemical resources, as Heather

Davis points out when she argues that "the unearthed beings of fossil fuels released into our present day through vast communication networks represent these multiple hauntings, of immediate and protracted violence, in the form of toxicities and also in the undead relations of fossil fuels themselves." Davis goes on to point out that plastic, itself a petrochemical product, functions this way, carrying "the messages of lively fossils and the long dead, while troubling the clear-cut boundaries between the living and the dead."[6] While Davis is focused on plastic as a medium, as well as the malleability of media more broadly, her insight into the links between petrochemistry and undeadness is instructive.

The relationship between data and oil runs deeper still. It is worth noting that the complex digital infrastructures of data—such as the data processing centers necessary for the large-scale deployment of artificial intelligence applications—are very much dependent on oil and petrochemicals. It is through the use and exploitation of oil and its byproducts that data is collected, used, and housed at such massive scales. Coal power plants are still used around the world to generate the necessary energy to power the electrical grids that data infrastructure draws from, thus indirectly powering the systems that collect, process, and disseminate data. Petrochemicals and plastics are currently used to produce the inexpensive computers, wearables, and other electronic devices and infrastructure that are used to generate, manipulate, and interface with data-driven economic projects. Historically, the rise of data before the digital age came into existence as an object of scientific use and analysis, and taken together with the advent of the industrialization of oil, it might be suggested that data might not even exist—in its modern form—without oil.[7]

There is a conceptual and historical kinship between oil and death, as Reza Negarestani notes when he writes, "Oil as the postmortem production of organisms is bound to death." For Negarestani, oil works as a deeply symbolic substance that reifies the absolute negativity of death, which I have argued functions as a limit to capitalism's dream of endless growth and expansion. He argues that the empires (economic and otherwise) founded on oil as their primary driving resource are, in a very real sense, founded on death, arguing that "since its ethos—both origin and end—is purely teleological, whatever it inspires is founded on death and the logic of death and eventual conclusion."[8] Oil and its petrochemical byproducts represent a kind of concentration and materialization of death, yet one that speaks to the very heart of capital's productive apparatus. Capitalism tends toward these emblematic commodities, and this book has observed several of them as the evolution of the zombie has moved in these commodities' shadow. The body of the enslaved functioned in this symbolic position during colonial capitalism, and oil worked in this way for industrial capitalism. Data takes up this position in information and surveillance capitalism. In each of these stages of the commodity's symbolic form, a version of undead labor appears, intimately connected to capital as a modern political economy, and takes the shape of the zombie, whose form reflects the conditions under which it was generated. From the traumatized labor of Felicia Felix-Mentor, to the cancerous generation of the HeLa cell line from Henrietta Lacks's body, to the endless labor of the digital zombie-Dalí, undead labor manifests in different ways but with the same set of core characteristics: The labor of reproduction, carried out in labor power, bodily proliferation, proliferating analogies, and machine learning algorithms, demonstrates a dream of endless labor and value extracted from life beyond its own limits.

What form of life is generated under the unique circumstances necessary to create undead labor? Capitalism has always sought to overcome its own limits, and in doing so, it routinely creates zones of excess and contradiction that result in states of undeadness, regardless of whether these took place in the colony, the body, or the digital milieu. In all these scenarios, the plasticity of life is key. Of all the metaphors and material instantiations of undeadness and undead labor, plastic is not the most obvious or the most elegant, but it does bring us full circle to two important ideas raised in the introduction to this book. First, plastic is almost infinitely malleable—able to take almost any form, to the extent that the term itself denotes malleability. Second, plastic just does not quit—it remains. "Remains" here works in two senses, as Davis describes when she points out that plastic is a product of fossil fuels, in a real sense made of the remains of once-living beings. Plastic also has remarkable qualities of endurance and tends not to break down like other substances, which means that it accumulates around us in landfills and ocean-bound garbage patches. What do plastic and the zombie have in common? Both continue to exist long after they should have passed away.

Plasticity becomes an important quality of life under capitalism—the ability to take the form demanded by power and endure the pressures, both literal and figural, that weigh on it. Zakiyyah Iman Jackson has demonstrated that plasticity is an important characteristic in shaping the blackness of the enslaved. She points out that "it is not only a body that is stolen but also the becoming of the slave: the slave's future perfect state of being. The black(ened) can only be defined as plastic: impressionable, stretchable, misshapen to the point that the mind does not survive"; put another way, the slave is an example of not just a stolen body but stolen potential, the possibility of what the body can become or be made into.[9] The loss of mind in this scenario recalls arguments about the zombie from earlier in this book, but Jackson's argument about the malleability conferred onto, or the demand placed on, the slave's body provides a unique insight into how and why Blackness was invented as well as what, precisely, Blackness was invented to be.

Undead labor is important because it reveals an impulse (a fantasy or delirium) at the heart of capital to overcome all limitations to its growth and propagation, up to and including ontological limits like death. Historically, this resulted in the tortures and traumas inflicted on the slave's body—the Black body—such that the zombie was created as a monstrous incarnation of that suffering and a metaphor for the fate worse than death that these demands on the being of the slave represented. This impulse was also apparent in the cellular labor of the HeLa cell line, which was such a prized commodity because of its transcendence from a body—a living and substantial dream of limitless reproduction and labor power at the command of capital and its institutions. In each instance, the undeadness and undead labor exhibited in these case studies show a form of life remade into something apart from human, and this, precisely, is Jackson's point as she argues that "*slavery's technologies were not the denial of humanity but the plasticization of humanity.*"[10] Jackson makes use of the notion of plasticity as it comes from the philosopher Catherine Malabou, who deploys the term in a more traditional sense by imagining plasticity as an immanent feature of existence, the potential inherent within matter and its essential polymorphism.[11]

Jackson reads this notion against the philosophical grain, understanding plasticity not as a celebration of its potential but rather as a way to consider "the way potential can be turned against itself by bonds of power." This reading of potential as something that can be turned against itself is useful in understanding the predicament of undead labor: As a form of life that is labor power without constraint, undead labor takes the reproductive potential of unlimited life to its logical extreme. As Jackson writes, "The slave is the discursive-material site that must contend with the demand for seemingly infinite malleability; a demand whose limits are set merely by the tyrannies of will and imagination." She argues that "the black body, *in its humanity*, is turned into a form of infinitely malleable lexical and biological matter," which she will go on to describe as a "plastic."[12] Here, the Black body is transformed into a new kind of substance, something both harder and more malleable than it was before. While Jackson describes this as plastic, it also resonates with notions of undeadness. These features are not mutually exclusive but complementary, as they both reveal a sense of what comes into being that is informed and deformed by the demands of power—something that is both infinitely malleable and endlessly productive.

Undead labor emerges from the gap, fissure, or grave that opens between the actuality of a living body and the fantasy of a capitalist delirium; it is a lexical and biological matter that rises up out of the remains of the actual into a new, liminal state of undeadness. Undead labor is simultaneously the term that accompanies this new form of life and describes the mode of production that emerges alongside it. The slave was uniquely important to this process because it was entirely subjected to power, unable to push back within the bounds of the law (however common the resistance and rebellion of the enslaved was in actuality). This living body, stripped of will and rendered open and vulnerable to exploitation, created a blueprint of an idealized subject for capital.

The malleability that Jackson describes in both the slave body and the Black body finds echoes in the demands, under neoliberalism and surveillance capitalism, to demonstrate one's worth by doing whatever it takes to fulfill the needs of labor and to exhibit the spirit of entrepreneurship that has been internalized, reshaping the inner structures of subjectivity under this system. This appears in the wealth of terms and phrases like "grit," which seeks to demonstrate the ability of the individual to push through any difficulty and complete the tasks needed to succeed in an increasingly unequal economic environment.[13] What matters is *sticking with it*, laboring through adverse conditions, despite evidence that one's hard work will never pay off. Thus the deformation described by Jackson is not limited to matter and language, but to time as well, through the endless repetitions involved in sticking with the same form of life.

Jackson argues that it is the invention of Blackness and the conditions of slavery under colonial capitalism that bring about this new kind of being, but what emerges from this "discursive-material site" is not just the enslaved, but also the zombie, which arises in its shadow and has remained even in the long afterlife of slavery. The zombie has stayed with us as an important monster in the popular imagination because the conditions that gave rise to it under racial capitalism, from the plantation to the data farm, have never been resolved. The zombie will continue to shamble forward so long as the conditions for undead labor continue to exist and the living are informed, deformed, and transformed into a new form of being under a set of impossible demands and conditions put into place by the delirium of capitalism. This begins to look like undeadness, not only in matter and discourse, but in time as well.

The New: Undead Time, or Being on TV After the End of the World

In the written introduction to his graphic novel *The Walking Dead*, Robert Kirkman describes his feeling that "the worst part of every zombie movie is the end. . . . Even when all the characters die at the end . . . I just want it to keep going."[14] Kirkman goes on to describe that this desire to "keep going" is the guiding logic of the book and, it seems, the television adaptation as well. This series, as it runs and branches across spin-offs and media platforms, illustrates the importance of slowness, repetition, and the interminability of time after the apocalypse. As the series repeats itself, the slowness and interminability of *The Walking Dead* can be read symptomatically: The shambling pace of the slow zombies (the eponymous "walkers") has an isomorphic relationship with the temporality of the show overall, which, in turn, belongs to a logic of both television and late capitalism. Thus the show illustrates an "undead time": a unique set of temporal dynamics emphasizing slowness, duration, repetition, and remainder that emerges in the wake of catastrophe, and which attempts to forestall or foreclose the end of the world.

At the end of the introduction, Kirkman playfully suggests that "*The Walking Dead* is the zombie movie that never ends."[15] And while this is not technically true—the series finally did end after eleven seasons in 2022, although two spin-offs, *The Walking Dead: Dead City* and *The Walking Dead: Daryl Dixon*, are both still running as of 2025—it certainly belongs to the imaginary of the show at the level of both form and content. Interestingly, this desire to "keep going" extends outward into the show's production and the corporate environment of network programming as well. Various reports from industry blogs and financial news reveal that Kirkman's desire for a zombie movie that never ends is echoed by entertainment executives. For example, *The Mary Sue* reported in 2013 that the AMC executive Josh Sapan believed that *The Walking Dead* is "so awesome" that "it will go on forever."[16] A senior contributor at *Forbes* argued in 2017 that despite consistently mediocre ratings during that period, *The Walking Dead* will "never get cancelled."[17] Note that this argument does not stem from the show's quality, but rather from the program's relative success in relation to AMC's lineup of other shows, which do consistently worse in the ratings. Finally, according to *Bloomberg* in September 2018, AMC executives plan to make *The Walking Dead* "live forever."[18] Despite the many puns built into these headlines, it is important to bracket what this may say about the status of the television industry and turn instead to the fact that we see, once again, this desire to "keep going" that was expressed by Kirkman in the introduction to the series manifests in different ways at every level of the show.

What this illustrates is that the interminability of the show is a feature, not a bug. The series reveals an impulse to endure and continue, regardless of context or circumstance, which is symptomatic of undead labor as a mode of production and a form of life and may indicate something like *undead time* as well. Two stages are necessary to unpack the relationship between temporality and the zombie in this conclusion. First, the symptomatic nature of the "slow" zombie, in contrast to the "fast" zombie, is an important distinction that has emerged as a defining feature of the genre. The second will explore the patterns and strategies of catastrophe coverage on television and the ways televisual representation of disaster often involves repeating and extending the catastrophic moment in ways that appear to echo the desire to "keep going" that emerges at all levels of *The Walking Dead*.

Cinematic zombies started off slow. The earliest representations of the zombie were shambling, a body that returned to something that bore a semblance to life. At first, this no doubt reflected the pace of a body damaged by the trauma and toxins involved in actual instances of zombification in Haiti, in which the victim was not truly brought back from the dead but, rather, poisoned into a state of near death, abducted, and put to work in a location far away from family and friends. Cases like that of Felicia Felix-Mentor, the infamous case of a real zombie that was photographed by Zora Neale Hurston, show a body whose suffering—both physical and metaphysical—was echoed in her appearance.[19] Felix-Mentor moved slowly and cautiously and her movements reflected the traumas that she experienced and the uses to which her body had been put beyond reason and decency.

Early cinematic representations of the zombie continued at this ambling pace. The zombies in *White Zombie*, the first zombie movie (from 1932), marched slowly, to the rhythm of their master's will, while the zombies appearing in *I Walked with a Zombie* (1943) moved stiffly, reflecting a pace that belonged in equal parts to rigor mortis and sleepwalking. This pace continued through George Romero's iconic zombies in *Night of the Living Dead* and its sequels, from 1968 (the year zombies became cannibals) into the 1980s. Indeed, zombies were depicted almost universally as slow until the early twenty-first century (with the exception of the 1985 film *Return of the Living Dead*, which had fast zombies and introduced the fixation on brains that remains with the mythos to this day), when the "fast" zombie was revitalized in Danny Boyle's *28 Days Later* (2002), sparking a sea change in the genre.

After the success of Boyle's film, which featured hyperviolent zombies running en masse through the streets of Britain, most zombie movies changed over to the newer, faster version of the undead, including the remakes of all of Romero's classic films. Notably, Romero himself never liked the trend toward faster zombies, saying, "For me, a good, slow lurch beats a speeding zombie any day."[20] It is interesting, then, that *The Walking Dead* chose to go back to its roots, depicting slow zombies in the style of Romero's *Night of the Living Dead*. This works to extend the inherent pathos of both the zombies and the show. *The Walking Dead* is, more than anything, a serial melodrama whose narrative operates according to a logic of perpetual extension and deferral, and many depictions of zombies show them in such a way as to cast the zombie as an object of pity, not just the cause of fear or terror. The slowness of zombies in *The Walking Dead* is a kind of anti-accelerationist danger; they represent a crisis in slow motion, running down in a state of decay, but never fully seeming to stop.

This slowness may be one of the chief pleasures of the show, since we are faced with a real world that feels, alarmingly, as if it is speeding out of control at a pace and scale that is both too fast and too slow. The degradation and apparently inevitable collapse of our environment is a case in point, where the catastrophe of carbon technologies is bringing about a disaster at a rate and magnitude we cannot seem to fully understand or reckon with. It is both too fast (to do anything about) and too slow (to care about). This is succinctly addressed by Andrew McMurry, who first examined the issue in an article from 1996, aptly named "The Slow Apocalypse": "We learn to overlook the terminal events of our time as they unfold, gather, and concatenate in all their leisurely deadliness. We have wrongly expected the end of the world would provide the high drama we believe commensurate with our raging passions, our bold aspirations, and our central importance to the universe—we are worthy of a bang, not merely a whimper. . . . By holding out for that noisy demise, we can pretend we haven't been expiring by inches for decades."[21] McMurry goes on to say that part of this problem has to do with our "limited temporal perspective," which is why, from this anthropocentric viewpoint, we seem to simultaneously expect to see ourselves on the grand stage of the universe and cannot comprehend just how brief our tenure on this planet has actually been. But McMurry notes that narrative helps to cover over this deep inconsistency, allowing us to hold out for a "real" apocalypse while the world dies around us.

This temporal inconsistency is reflected in the dual function of *The Walking Dead*, which goes on to provide the noisy demise McMurry compellingly suggests we are waiting for and, at the same time, comfortingly displaces the degradation of our environment onto society itself, both the living and the dead—which together constitute nearly all the threats the characters face. Where we might be expected to face the temporal sublime, environmental collapse—an event that overwhelms us as both terrible and beautiful, and is unknowable in its vast complexity—we turn instead to moments that are both quotidian and predictable, moments that are extended over and over again, effectively drawing out the end. This is also reflected within the show's narrative, in which increasingly mundane tasks are shown, such that the everyday is, itself, taken as a sign of realism and point of interest. Mending fences (both metaphorically and literally), farming, gathering, cooking, and, appropriately enough, walking around the landscape of the ruined world of the zombie apocalypse become signs of a temporality focused on the everyday, because so few days are left before the end. But are they? What seems both compelling and infuriating about the show is that it continues to stretch through days and seasons, which will apparently go on ad infinitum. The show itself becomes like the walkers depicted, shambling forward, following a desire that will never be fulfilled because the structural conditions—in this case, the narrative logic of the show to "keep going"—demand that it continues along this trajectory forever. Never ceasing—the zombie movie that never ends.

The perception of time slows down during a crisis: It is a neurological response trying to eke out extra time to raise our chances of survival, and this tendency has been generalized within our cultural response to disaster, a shift that moves it from the neurological to the ideological. Nowhere is this more clearly seen than in the logic of television and its representation of disaster coverage. The temporal dynamics revealed through the slow zombies of *The Walking Dead* also belong to the logic of television more broadly, which, as Mary Ann Doane points out, is a medium whose central category is time. She argues that "time is television's basis, its principle of structuration, as well as its persistent reference." Unlike film—a medium whose relation to time is through the past, through its indexicality, its guarantee that what we see on screen was really there—television is more interested in the present. This might at first seem odd, given TV's structural affinity to serialization, but as Doane points out, "Television deals not with the weight of the dead past but with the potential trauma and explosiveness of the present. And the ultimate drama of the instantaneous—catastrophe—constitutes the very limit of its discourse."[22] When Doane refers here to the "explosiveness of the present," she is identifying both the technology of television itself and the representational techniques that it deploys through a dialectic of liveness and destruction.

When she describes time as the central category of television, Doane means the potential of televisual representation to be live, or instantaneous, and as Jane Feuer argues the ideology of "liveness" is TV's most compelling feature, even though it is rarely used when compared to the sheer quantity of prerecorded programming on the medium. In its focus on the instantaneous, the "live," and the present moment, television is sometimes characterized as annihilating memory through what Doane describes as "the continual stress upon the 'newness' of its own discourse."[23] While we can see traces of this in narrative forms—especially in the way soaps and serials continually repeat themselves and "refresh" our memories about what came before and what is coming next (something we certainly see illustrated in *The Walking Dead*)—this relation to the temporality of the present becomes most clear in relation to television's strategies for covering disaster, which Doane divides into the categories of crisis and catastrophe.

Crisis, for Doane, "compresses time and makes its limitations acutely felt." This leads her to suggest that crises often belong to the political arena, in which fast decisions are required to resolve the tensions between warring states or conflicting interests. Catastrophe, on the other hand, belongs to a different temporal order. "The etymological specification of catastrophe," Doane argues, "as the overturning of a given situation anticipates its more formal delineation by catastrophe theory. Here, catastrophe is defined as unexpected discontinuity in an otherwise continuous system. The theory is most appropriate, then, for the study of sudden and unexpected effects in a gradually changing situation."[24] Catastrophe takes place when conditions invisible to us because of their speed or scale coalesce into a sudden, often violent overturning of a given situation. We can see this play out in natural disasters, such as hurricanes or earthquakes, which cause sudden devastation in moments that reveal the capriciousness of nature and the fragility of our own infrastructure and preparedness.

Doane also aligns catastrophe with the failure of technology, pointing out that events like the 1986 Space Shuttle *Challenger* explosion or the attacks on the World Trade Center and the Pentagon on September 11, 2001, seem to belong to the catastrophe as well because such incidents overturn our typical relation to this apparatus as something that makes our lives better, part of a metanarrative of progress. As she points out, the technological accident has shadowed the stories we tell ourselves about progress since the industrial revolution, where the scale of the technological catastrophe has grown in sync with the power of our technology itself: "Catastrophe signals the failure of the escalating technological desire to conquer nature. . . . This is why the purview of catastrophe keeps expanding to encompass even phenomena which had previously been situated wholly on the side of nature. . . . Such catastrophes no longer signify only the sudden eruption of natural forces but the inadequacy or failure of technology and its predictive powers as well."[25] Catastrophe sets itself apart because the *overturning* from which it gets its name cuts across multiple registers, challenging the ways we represent the world to ourselves. Indeed, catastrophic events challenge our systems of representation because of the speed and scale of their appearance—disasters are, almost by definition, sudden—but also because they almost inevitably bring death. Thus, when Doane describes catastrophe as something that serves as the limit to televisual discourse, she is describing how death and catastrophe, often going hand in glove, impose a limit to or rupture within televisual representation.

Television's response to catastrophe is to repeat and extend the moment indefinitely in ways meant to boost ratings and inform the public, to be sure, but also to forestall the end. The frenzy to get "coverage," which maintains its own presentness with up-to-the-minute reporting, is symptomatic of an asymptotic relation to finitude in which more and more attention is given to the moment of catastrophe, prolonging it through techniques like slow motion in a mixture of liveness and death to the point that, as Doane argues, "catastrophic time stands still."[26] TV's endless coverage of catastrophe starts to seem like stalling. Where our own repetition compulsion tends to be involuntary (bracketing the peculiar pleasures we take in *fort/da* games), television's compulsion to repeat is more strategic: The repetition of catastrophe and the extension of the moments leading up to it function not just to forestall but to foreclose the very possibility of finitude—better to live in an endless present than to come to a genuine end. What strikes me is that this logic belongs not just to television, but to late capitalism more broadly. As Fredric Jameson famously said, "It is easier to imagine the end of the world than to imagine the end of capitalism," but I would add to this that it is easier still to imagine that we can exist in a perpetual present where nothing ever changes no matter how much we consume.[27]

It is these phenomena of endless repetition, a hypertrophy of the moment that is in service to the foreclosure of finitude, death, or the end, that may be understood as "undead time." Just as undeadness is not about death but, rather, about life—too much life, an excess of vitality—so, too, can we say that undead time is about a refusal of finitude, a foreclosure of death as the limits of presence and representation. Undead time is interminable precisely because it refuses to end, thus living up to the precise etymological origins of interminability itself. But this undead time belongs to both television and late capitalism, and I believe that the foreclosure of finitude and the hypertrophy of the moment have an instrumental value to the homeostasis of capital. Both as narrative strategies, which help to cover over the inconsistencies within our temporal perspective, and as representational strategies in television, these forms have a pacifying effect, formally soothing the nerves of a public anxious about its own creeping demise. These temporal dynamics are reflected in the world of Jean Baudrillard, who argues, "We are no longer in a state of growth; we are in a state of excess. We are living in a society of excrescence, meaning that which incessantly develops without being measured against its own objectives."[28] In his typically pessimistic style, Baudrillard is speaking to the same phenomena I am, albeit not in explicitly temporal terms. His idea of incessant development without evaluation or end addresses our present moment and the political situation in which we find ourselves: capitalism rules the world unfettered by any other political ideology and the only real resistance is environmental. Environmental, not in the sense of a political cause, but rather that the environment is slowly increasing the resistance—in the sense of viscosity—to the ongoing operations of capital: We are running out of key resources necessary to the scaling-up productive regimes of capitalist industry, and increasingly destructive weather patterns and warming climates demand an increased effort in order to maintain the status quo.

Baudrillard goes on to describe this unfettered growth in medical terms: "This process can be compared best with cancerous metastases—conditions in which a body's organic rules of the game are lost, enabling such a formation of cells to manifest its invincible and fatal vitality."[29] And, indeed, we might well describe undead time as a kind of cancerous temporality, manifested in the body, as we saw in the example of the HeLa cell line above, in which the "invincible and fatal vitality" that Baudrillard describes manifests as a dogged commitment to the present *as* a technique of resisting real change. Undead time is a relentless sameness that bars real and meaningful change from our cultural imaginary.

The relentless sameness of undead time is a tactic deployed in the face of impending catastrophe, a mode of temporality that seems subject to the same forces Jackson described as plasticity: In this case, the deformation and malleability are exhibited in time rather than space, although they remain embedded within discourse. The catastrophe in question is racial capitalism, which demands that no changes take place to the status quo. In this context, the plasticity and malleability Jackson articulates appears in the form of imperatives to remain the same: It takes the shape of demands that we *still* consume, *still* labor, *still* act as though catastrophe is not imminent. The term "still" is telling, as it denotes the continuity of an action in time not in the form of movement or repetition, but rather immobility. It reveals that the response to impending catastrophe is to freeze in place, to maintain the same, to stay the course. Undead time demands that real, substantive action always be deferred. It requires that we all stay in place, long after we should have changed course or acted in anticipation of the overturning of the status quo that comes with any catastrophe. Any real revolution will not be televised.[30]

Concluding a book whose subject is the pernicious and pervasive resistance to endings, death, and finitude more broadly is inherently challenging, and diagnoses of the present are notoriously indeterminate, but the way forward lies in some speculation about the productive power of catastrophe itself. Returning to Doane's discussion of catastrophe and televisual discourse and contrasting it to the capitalist delirium of undead labor, we see a useful definition come to light. She argues that "catastrophe is defined as unexpected discontinuity in an otherwise continuous system."[31] This is precisely the point of anxiety provoked by catastrophe within televisual discourse—the power to overturn a given situation is the promise of real change (one way or another)—and this is exactly antithetical to the drives of undead time toward stasis and sameness. Catastrophe is the uncomfortable reminder that finitude is not so easily dismissed, and Doane argues that, placed in contrast to the logics of television, catastrophe provides a paradox: It is both the discontinuity within a continuous system and the impetus behind a frenzied regime of sameness that attempts to foreclose any possibility of difference and change. Should we, then, hope for catastrophe? Maybe. At least in regard to *The Walking Dead*, we can hope for the end in more ways than one. Perhaps the real question to be asked is whether we are the living characters, enduring the interminable time after the apocalypse and hoping for narrative break or resolution, or the undead, crawling toward our inevitable end, waiting to be put out of our misery? The real significance of this conception of undead time outlined here is perhaps best said in the words of Walter Benjamin: "The concept of progress is to be grounded in the idea of the catastrophe. That things 'just go on' *is* the catastrophe."[32]

Acknowledgments

At The New School, I have been tremendously fortunate to have a supportive department and a rich intellectual community, with friends and colleagues who have routinely offered advice and insight on many different drafts of this book and its constitutive parts. My sincere thanks to Dominic Pettman, whose advice and mentorship have been essential to my work and who has helped me stand in my own writerly voice. Thanks to Heather Davis for being a generous reader, friend, and colleague and for reminding me that there is more to life than work. Thanks to Emma Park, whose friendship and close reading have pushed my ideas to be better. Thanks to Emmanuel Auerbach-Baidani for his hard work as my research assistant and for years of providing a sharp editorial eye to my work. The New School has been a lively intellectual environment that has always fed my wide-ranging interests, and I am grateful to friends and colleagues who have offered advice, support, and dialogue when I needed it, including Genevieve Yue, Deborah Levitt, Julie Beth Napolin, McKenzie Wark, Kate Eichhorn, Orville Lee, Joshua Scannell, Talia Lugacy, Caroline Dionne, and Christoph Cox.

From 2021 to 2025, I had the privilege of being a part of the community of scholars and organizers formed by the Mellon Initiative for Inclusive Faculty Excellence, which was imagined and organized by Deva Woodly, with further thanks to Abou Farman, Brittnay Proctor-Habil, Kei Williams, Kimiko Bee-Hollis, P. J. Gorre, as well as other members of the first cohort of the seminar in 2021–22. I am also grateful for the institutional support that I have received from Darrick Hamilton and the Institute for Race, Power, and Political Economy.

Thinking and writing are always best done in dialogue, and I owe a great debt to brilliant friends and colleagues who have demonstrated real intellectual generosity from across academia.

My thanks to Leif Weatherby, who has always supported and inspired my own ideas, as well as the rest of the scholarly community of the Digital Theory Lab at NYU. My thanks to Alanna Thain for providing such unwavering support and insightful critique of my work and whose own work is a constant inspiration. Thanks to Joshua Neves, whose knack for bringing people together in productive dialogue has led to countless opportunities and enriching conversations. I am grateful to other readers and supporters of my work, including Shannon Mattern, Rebecca Sheldon, and Sophie Lewis. Early versions of this project benefited from the support and generosity of the intellectual community at Michigan State University. My gratitude to Justus Nieland for being a friend and mentor from my early days as a very green assistant professor to the present. My thanks also to Matthew Handelman, Bobby Smiley, E. L. McCallum, Joshua Yumibe, and Lily Woodruff, as well as everyone associated with the Film Program.

I have been hugely lucky to have been a part of a brilliant, supportive, and close-knit community from graduate school. To these fellow travelers and friends, I will always be grateful and know that you have influenced my ideas and my thinking in indelible ways. My love and thanks to Pooja Rangan, Joshua Guilford, Julie Levin Russo, Marc Steinberg, Yuriko Furuhata, Braxton Soderman, Roxanne Carter, Michael Siegel, Matthew Tierney, Anita Starosta, Sarah Osment, and Erika Balsom. Thanks to my academic mentors and advisors Philip Rosen, Mary Ann Doane, Wendy Hui Kyong Chun, and Rey Chow, whose work has fundamentally shaped my own. Thanks to Susan McNeil and Liza Hebert, who got everything done. And thanks to those who are no longer here to read this, but whose life and work bettered my own: Richard Manning for always finding the right movie, and Michael Silverman for inspiring me as a teacher and for telling me to read Deleuze.

I would like to thank my mother, Gail Bering-Porter, for always believing in me, and my father, Gerald Porter, who showed me what it meant to be an intellectual and why it mattered. Finally, I would like to thank Lyn Goeringer, who has seen this project through every step and iteration, every high and low, and who has read and supported this work, and me, with passion, insight, discipline, and creativity. Their work has complemented and inspired my own, in countless ways, every day.

Notes

Introduction

1. Jeff Chang, *Can't Stop, Won't Stop: A History of the Hip-Hop Generation* (Picador, 2005).

2. Fredric Jameson, *Archaeologies of the Future: The Desire Called Utopia and Other Science Fictions* (Verso, 2005), 199.

3. "Economy," John Carter Brown Library, archived January 4, 2017, at https://web.archive.org/web/20170104144931/https://www.brown.edu/Facilities/John_Carter_Brown_Library/exhibitions/remember_haiti/economy.php.

4. Baptist's ideas are discussed at length in chapter 1.

5. Karl Marx, *Capital: A Critique of Political Economy, Volume 1*, trans. Ben Fowkes (Penguin, 1976), 279–80.

6. Kathi Weeks, *The Problem with Work: Feminism, Marxism, Antiwork Politics, and Postwork Imaginaries* (Duke University Press, 2011), 6.

7. Weeks, *Problem with Work*, 21. Here Weeks is quoting Marx, *Capital*, 118. Italics in original.

8. Alana Semuels, "Does the Economy Really Need to Keep Growing Quite So Much? Questioning a Basic Orthodoxy," *Atlantic*, November 4, 2016, https://www.theatlantic.com/business/archive/2016/11/economic-growth/506423/. See also Myron J. Gordon and Jeffrey S. Rosenthal, "Capitalism's Growth Imperative," *Cambridge Journal of Economics* 27, no. 1 (January 2003): 25–48.

9. Gary Becker, *Human Capital: A Theoretical and Empirical Analysis with Special Reference to Education*, 3rd ed. (University of Chicago Press, 1993), 15–16.

10. See, for example, Stephen L. Dubner, "Can Economic Growth Continue Forever? Of Course!," *Freakonomics*, January 24, 2014, https://freakonomics.com/2014/01/can-economic-growth-continue-forever-of-course/.

11. Jean Baudrillard, *Symbolic Exchange and Death*, trans. Iain Hamilton Grant (Sage, 1993), 39.

12. Baudrillard, *Symbolic Exchange and Death*, 39.

13. Baudrillard, *Symbolic Exchange and Death*, 39.

14. Baudrillard, *Symbolic Exchange and Death*, 38–39.

15. Baudrillard, *Symbolic Exchange and Death*, 39.

16. *The Girl with All the Gifts*, dir. Colm McCarthy (Altitude Film Entertainment, 2016), https://youtu.be/foeMdhwqH2M.

17. Richard Matheson, *I Am Legend* (1954; repr., Tor Books, 1995).

1. "A Mechanical Semblance of Life"

1. See Wade Davis, *The Serpent and the Rainbow* (Simon and Schuster, 1985).

2. William Seabrook, *The Magic Island* (Harcourt, Brace, and Company, 1929), 92. My section title "Dead Men Working" paraphrases Seabrook's chapter heading "Dead Men Working in the Cane Fields."

3. Seabrook, *Magic Island*, 95.

4. This refers to the notion that slavery functions as a kind of social death, famously put forward by Orlando Patterson in *Slavery and Social Death* (Harvard University Press, 1982).

5. Elizabeth Maddock Dillon, "Zombie Biopolitics," *American Quarterly* 71, no. 3 (2019): 631.

6. Dillon, "Zombie Biopolitics," 631.

7. Seabrook, *Magic Island*, 101, 103.

8. Zora Neale Hurston, *Tell My Horse: Voodoo and Life in Haiti and Jamaica* (J. B. Lippincott Company, 1938), 179.

9. Hurston, *Tell My Horse*, 179, 195.

10. Stephanie Smallwood, *Saltwater Slavery: A Middle Passage from Africa to American Diaspora* (Harvard University Press, 2008), chap. 5, Kindle.

11. Jennifer L. Morgan, *Reckoning with Slavery: Gender, Kinship, and Capitalism in the Early Black Atlantic* (Duke University Press, 2021), 12, 23.

12. Vincent Brown, *The Reaper's Garden: Death and Power in the World of Atlantic Slavery* (Harvard University Press, 2008), 5.

13. Brown, *Reaper's Garden*, 5.

14. Karl Marx and Friedrich Engels, *The German Ideology* (Prometheus Books, 1998), 37. Italics in original.

15. Louis Althusser, *"Lenin and Philosophy" and Other Essays*, trans. Ben Brewster (Monthly Review Press, 2001), 109.

16. Edward E. Baptist, *The Half Has Never Been Told: Slavery and the Making of American Capitalism* (Basic Books, 2014), xxi–xxii.

17. Baptist, *Half Has Never Been Told*, xviii.

18. Cedric J. Robinson, *Black Marxism: The Making of the Black Radical Tradition* (Zed Books, 1983), 200.

19. C. L. R. James, *The Black Jacobins: Toussaint L'Ouverture and the San Domingo Revolution* (Vintage Books, 1963), 391–92.

20. Baptist, *Half Has Never Been Told*, xxii.

21. Baptist, *Half Has Never Been Told*, 126, 113, 121.

22. Brown, *Reaper's Garden*, 17, 13.

23. Morgan, *Reckoning with Slavery*, 228, 208.

24. Jessica Marie Johnson, *Wicked Flesh: Black Women, Intimacy, and Freedom in the Atlantic World* (University of Pennsylvania Press, 2020), 125.

25. Morgan, *Reckoning with Slavery*, 6.

26. Morgan, *Reckoning with Slavery*, 6.

27. Philippe Ariès, *Western Attitudes Toward Death: From the Middle Ages to the Present*, trans. Patricia M. Ranum (Johns Hopkins University Press, 1974), 13.

28. Ariès, *Western Attitudes Toward Death*, 13–14, 88.

29. Philippe Ariès, *The Hour of Our Death,* trans. Helen Weaver (Alfred A. Knopf, 1981), 566.

30. Ariès, *Western Attitudes Toward Death*, 92.

31. Ariès and Foucault certainly knew each other, and the two historians were at the very least in correspondence. See Patrick H. Hutton, "The Postwar Politics of Philippe Ariès," *Journal of Contemporary History* 34, no. 3 (1999): 365–81.

32. Michel Foucault, *The History of Sexuality, Volume 1: An Introduction*, trans. Robert Hurley (Pantheon Books, 1978), 138. Italics in original.

33. Foucault, *History of Sexuality*, 140, 142.

34. There is a substantial body of literature on the history of death and the difficulty of determining when it has occurred. Breath and heartbeat were often posited, but putrefaction was the only certain marker until the twentieth century, when technologies like the electroencephalogram could measure brainwave activity. For a fascinating discussion of this history, see Dick Teresi, *The Undead: Organ Harvesting, the Ice-Water Test, Beating Heart Cadavers—How Medicine Is Blurring the Line Between Life and Death* (Vintage Books, 2012).

35. Alexander Weheliye, *Habeas Viscus: Racializing Assemblages, Biopolitics, and Black Feminist Theories of the Human* (Duke University Press, 2014), 38.

36. Édouard Glissant, *Poetics of Relation*, trans. Betsy Wing (University of Michigan Press, 1997), 74.

37. Eric Cazdyn, *The Already Dead: The New Time of Politics, Culture, and Illness* (Duke University Press, 2012), 175.

38. Slavoj Žižek, *The Parallax View* (MIT Press, 2009), 62.

39. Žižek, *Parallax View*, 62.

40. The zombie was an early and enduring figure in this new capitalist drive, but it was not the only one. Other versions or visions of undeadness also appeared with new regularity within the popular imagination, the most famous of which is the vampire, which has also found an enduring legacy as well as figures like Frankenstein's monster. Yet the vampire is a version of undeadness from above, exhibiting an endless life that carries with it tropes of the aristocracy, whereas the zombie is a proletarian monster, whose multifaceted representations have always been better at showing off the real stakes of modern undeadness in problems of race, labor, and value.

41. Melinda Cooper, *Life as Surplus: Biotechnology and Capitalism in the Neoliberal Era* (University of Washington Press, 2008), 25.

42. Karl Marx, *Capital: A Critique of Political Economy, Volume 1*, trans. Ben Fowkes (Penguin, 1976), 302.

43. Karl Marx, *Capital*, 289.

44. Karl Marx, *Grundrisse: Foundations of the Critique of Political Economy*, trans. Martin Nicolaus (Penguin, 1983), 693.

45. Beth Coleman, "Race as Technology," *Camera Obscura* 24, no. 1 (70) (2009): 178.

46. Coleman, "Race as Technology," 178.

47. Saidiya V. Hartman, *Scenes of Subjection: Terror, Slavery, and Self-Making in Nineteenth-Century America* (Oxford University Press, 1997), 7.

48. Neda Atanasoski and Kalindi Vora, *Surrogate Humanity: Race, Robots, and the Politics of Technological Futures* (Duke University Press, 2019), 29, 33.

49. Hannah Arendt, *The Human Condition* (University of Chicago Press, 1998), 80. Note that Arendt is here quoting a rather famous line from Aristotle, *Politics* 1.5.

50. Arendt, *Human Condition*, 83–84.

51. Arendt, *Human Condition*, 88.

52. Arendt, *Human Condition*, 124.

53. Christina Sharpe, *In the Wake: On Blackness and Being* (Duke University Press, 2016), 5.

54. See Michelle Alexander, *The New Jim Crow: Mass Incarceration in the Age of Colorblindness* (New Press, 2010).

55. Jonathan Crary, *24/7: Late Capitalism and the Ends of Sleep* (Verso, 2013), 9–10.

56. Byung-Chul Han, *Capitalism and the Death Drive*, trans. Daniel Steuer (Polity Press, 2021), 8.

57. Michel Foucault, *The Birth of Biopolitics: Lectures at the Collège de France, 1978–79*, ed. Michel Senellart, trans. Graham Burchell (Picador, 2010), 226.

58. Achille Mbembe, *Necropolitics*, trans. Steven Corcoran (Duke University Press, 2019), 71, 92. Italics in original.

59. Mbembe, *Necropolitics*, 68.

60. Georg Wilhelm Friedrich Hegel, *The Phenomenology of Spirit*, trans. Terry P. Pinkard (Cambridge University Press, 2017), 115.

61. As Terry Pinkard points out in his introduction, "Hegel frequently described his 1807 *Phenomenology of Spirit* to his students as his 'voyage of discovery'" (Hegel, *Phenomenology of Spirit*, ix).

62. Susan Buck-Morss, *Hegel, Haiti, and Universal History* (University of Pittsburgh Press, 2009), 48, 50, 73.

63. Buck-Morss, *Hegel, Haiti*, 60.

64. Here it is worth noting that Buck-Morss has been criticized for discussing the Haitian Revolution as an example of universal history and suggesting that the historically specific conditions in Haiti reflected European Enlightenment values, particularly those stemming from the French Revolution. Buck-Morss's account of Haiti as universal history seems in danger of eliding the specificity of the Haitian Revolution, not as a symbol of universal freedom, but as a condemnation of expanding colonialism and the brutal exploitation of enslaved Africans in Haiti. While critiques of Buck-Morss are compelling in their call for a closer reading of history, I would also argue that her remarks on Hegel and Haiti support a useful understanding of the emerging racial capitalism that I am discussing in this chapter, and its recourse to universalism, itself an expansionist concept, is also symptomatic of undead labor. For more on this debate, see Adom Getachew, "Universalism After the Post-Colonial Turn: Interpreting the Haitian Revolution," *Political Theory* 44, no. 6 (2016): 821–45.

65. Frantz Fanon, *Black Skin, White Masks*, trans. Richard Philcox (Grove Press, 2008), 193.

66. Alexandre Kojève, *Introduction to the Reading of Hegel: Lectures on the*

Phenomenology of Spirit, assemb. Raymond Queneau, ed. Allan Bloom, trans. James H. Nichols Jr. (Cornell University Press, 1980), 20, 29–30.

67. Kojève, *Introduction*, 16.

68. Kojève, *Introduction*, 23.

2. Analogies of Undeadness

1. Sarah Danius, Stefan Jonsson, and Gayatri Chakravorty Spivak, "An Interview with Gayatri Chakravorty Spivak," *boundary 2* 20 (1993): 35.

2. Nadia Urbinati, *Democracy Disfigured: Opinion, Truth, and the People* (Harvard University Press, 2014), 11.

3. Benjamin Krämer, "Media Populism: A Conceptual Clarification and Some Theses of its Effects," *Communication Theory* 24 (2014): 49.

4. Benedict Anderson, *Imagined Communities: Reflections on the Origin and Spread of Nationalism*, rev. ed. (Verso, 1991), 25.

5. Anderson, *Imagined Communities*, 26.

6. Fredric Jameson, "Periodizing the 60s," in "The 60s Without Apology," special issue, *Social Text*, no. 9–10 (1984): 178.

7. See chapter 1.

8. Wade Davis, *The Serpent and the Rainbow: A Harvard Scientist's Astonishing Journey into the Secret Societies of Haitian Voodoo, Zombis, and Magic* (Simon and Schuster, 1985), 186.

9. Alfred Métraux, *Voodoo in Haiti*, trans. Hugo Charteris (Schocken Books, 1959), 258, 282.

10. Robin Wood, "The American Nightmare: Horror in the 70s," in *Hollywood from Vietnam to Reagan . . . and Beyond* (Columbia University Press, 1986), 76–77.

11. See *I Walked with a Zombie* (Jacques Tourneur, 1943) for another pertinent example.

12. The film names radiation, brought back from a probe sent to explore Venus and now infecting Earth, as the direct cause of the rising, ravenous bodies, but this information is given almost in passing and provides little relevance to the real narrative.

13. Steven Shaviro, *Cinematic Body* (University of Minnesota Press, 1993), 83.

14. Jamie Russell, *The Complete History of Zombie Cinema* (Titan Books, 2014), 65.

15. Shaviro, *Cinematic Body*, 83.

16. Friedrich Kittler, *Gramophone, Film, Typewriter*, trans. Geoffrey Winthrop-Young and Michael Wutz (Stanford University Press, 1999), 1–2.

17. Lev Manovich argues that the ultimate defining feature of digital technology is "transcoding," or the ability to translate images into sounds or vice versa through the universal mediation of digital code, although this is a common discourse surrounding the rise of the digital. See specifically Lev Manovich, *The Language of New Media (MIT Press, 2002)*, 45.

18. Wendy Hui Kyong Chun, *Programmed Visions: Software and Memory* (MIT Press, 2011), 133.

19. Thomas Keenan, *Fables of Responsibility: Aberrations and Predicaments in Ethics and Politics* (Stanford University Press, 1997), 104. Italics in original.

20. Keenan, *Fables of Responsibility*, 117.

21. Karl Marx, *Capital: A Critique of Political Economy, Volume 1*, trans. Ben Fowkes (Penguin, 1976), 152. This passage was also quoted in Keenan, *Fables of Responsibility*, 118.

22. Marx, *Capital*, 162.

23. Keenan, *Fables of Responsibility*, 118.

24. Keenan, *Fables of Responsibility*, 118.

25. Ernesto Laclau, *On Populist Reason* (Verso, 2005), chap. 1, Kindle.

26. Cas Mudde and Cristóbal Rovira Kaltwasser, *Populism: A Very Short Introduction* (Oxford University Press, 2017), 2–3.

27. Cas Mudde, "The Populist Zeitgeist," *Government and Opposition* 39 (2004): 543.

28. Jameson, "Periodizing the 60s," 195.

29. Michel Foucault, *"Society Must Be Defended": Lectures at the Collège de France*, trans. David Macey (Picador, 2003), 254.

30. Michel Foucault, *The History of Sexuality, Volume 1: An Introduction*, trans. Robert Hurley (Pantheon Books, 1978), 138.

31. Foucault, *"Society Must Be Defended,"* 255.

32. Jodi Melamed, *Represent and Destroy: Rationalizing Violence in the New Racial Capitalism* (University of Minnesota Press, 2011), 2.

33. Jodi Melamed, *Represent and Destroy*, 2. Italics in original.

34. Jodi Melamed, "Racial Capitalism," *Critical Ethnic Studies* 1, no. 1 (2015): 77.

35. Foucault, *"Society Must Be Defended,"* 245.

36. Marco Revelli, *The New Populism: Democracy Stares Into the Abyss*, trans. David Broder (Verso, 2019), 9.

37. Laclau, *On Populist Reason*, chap. 1, Kindle.

38. Michel Foucault, "A Preface to Transgression" in *Language, Counter-Memory, Practice: Selected Essays and Interviews*, ed. Donald F. Bouchard (Cornell University Press, 1977), 30.

39. Foucault, "Preface to Transgression," 30.

40. *Merriam-Webster Dictionary*, "analogy," accessed December 16, 2019, https://www.merriam-webster.com/dictionary/analogy.

41. James S. Measell, "Development of the Concept of Analogy in Rhetorical Theory," in *Rhetoric and Communication: Studies in the University of Illinois Tradition*, ed. Jane Blankenship and Hermann G. Stelzner (University of Illinois Press, 1976), 34.

42. Nilli Diengott, "Analogy as a Critical Term: A Survey and Some Comments," *Style* 19 (1985): 227. Italics in original.

43. Measell, "Development of the Concept of Analogy in Rhetorical Theory," 36–37.

44. Foucault, "Preface to Transgression," 34.

45. This phrase comes from Eric Santner's discussion of "creaturely life" in *On Creaturely Life: Rilke, Benjamin, Sebald* (University of Chicago Press, 2006).

46. Alexander R. Galloway, "What Is the Analog?," *Alexander R. Galloway*,

December 29, 2017, archived December 27, 2019, at https://web.archive.org/web/20191227044258/http://cultureandcommunication.org/galloway/what-is-the-analog.

47. Brian Massumi, *Parables of the Virtual* (Duke University Press, 2002), 135.

48. Foucault, "Preface to Transgression," 34.

49. George Monbiot and Peter Hutchison, *Invisible Doctrine: The Secret History of Neoliberalism* (Crown, 2024), 8.

50. Kim Masters, "Brad Pitt's Zombie Nightmare: Inside the Troubled 'World War Z' Production," *Hollywood Reporter*, June 12, 2012, https://www.hollywoodreporter.com/news/brad-pitt-world-war-z-production-nightmare-336422.

51. Priscilla Wald, *Contagious: Cultures, Carriers, and the Outbreak Narrative* (Duke University Press, 2008), 53.

52. Marc Guillaume, "The Metamorphoses of Epidemia" in "The Contemporary City," ed. Michel Feher and Sanford Kwinter, special issue, *Zone*, no. 1–2 (1985): 59.

53. Wald, *Contagious*, 33.

54. See Gustave Le Bon, *The Crowd: A Study of the Popular Mind* (1895; repr., Dover, 2002).

55. "VFX Work," *Homepage: Carsten Kolve*, accessed December 26, 2025, http://www.kolve.com/vfxwork/vfxwork.htm.

56. Vincent Frei, "*World War Z*: Jessica Norman—VFX Supervisor—MPC," *Art of VFX*, July 24, 2013, https://www.artofvfx.com/world-war-z-jessica-norman-vfx-supervisor-mpc/.

57. Kristen Whissel, *Spectacular Digital Effects: CGI and Contemporary Cinema* (Duke University Press, 2014), 77.

58. Eugene Thacker, "Networks, Swarms, Multitudes: Part Two," *CTheory*, May 18, 2004, https://journals.uvic.ca/index.php/ctheory/article/view/14541/5388. Also cited in Whissel, *Spectacular Digital Effects*, 77.

59. Gilles Deleuze, *Bergsonism*, trans. Hugh Tomlinson and Barbara Habberjam (Zone Books, 1991), 74.

60. *Merriam-Webster Dictionary*, "populism," accessed December 26, 2025, https://www.merriam-webster.com/dictionary/populism.

61. Jan-Werner Müller, *What Is Populism?* (University of Pennsylvania Press, 2016), 8.

62. Nadia Urbinati, *Me the People: How Populism Transforms Democracy* (Harvard University Press, 2019), 21.

3. Unlimited Life

1. Karl Marx, *Capital: A Critique of Political Economy, Volume 1*, trans. Paul Reitter (Princeton University Press, 2024), 22.

2. Evan Calder Williams, *Combined and Uneven Apocalypse* (Zero Books, 2011), 121.

3. Williams, *Combined and Uneven Apocalypse*, 89.

4. Rebecca Skloot, *The Immortal Life of Henrietta Lacks* (Broadway Books, 2011), 13.

5. Siddhartha Mukherjee, *The Emperor of All Maladies: A Biography of Cancer* (Scribner, 2010), 6, 38.

6. Mukherjee, *Emperor of All Maladies*, 38. Mukherjee's insight here is important, although it should be noted that both *meta* and *stasis* are Greek, not Latin.

7. I owe this insight to ongoing conversations with my research assistant Emmanuel Auerbach.

8. Susan Sontag, *"Illness as Metaphor" and "AIDS and Its Metaphors"* (Picador, 1978), 68, 72.

9. Jayna Brown, "Being Cellular: Race, the Inhuman, and the Plasticity of Life" in *GLQ: A Journal of Lesbian and Gay Studies* 21, no. 2–3 (2015): 321.

10. Sontag, *"Illness as Metaphor" and "AIDS and Its Metaphors,"* 3. In "Illness as Metaphor," Sontag never comes closer than this to revealing her own cancer diagnosis, but the context is widely understood even in her later writings. For a good discussion of Sontag's cancer in relation to her own writings on illness, see James S. Olson, *Bathsheba's Breast: Women, Cancer, and History* (Johns Hopkins University Press, 2005), 168.

11. See Jackie Stacey, *Teratologies: A Cultural Study of Cancer* (Routledge, 1997); S. Lochlann Jain, *Malignant: How Cancer Becomes Us* (University of California Press, 2013); Eric Cazdyn, *The Already Dead: The New Time of Politics, Culture, and Illness* (Duke University Press, 2012); Barbara Ehrenreich, *Bright-Sided: How Positive Thinking Is Undermining America* (Metropolitan Books, 2009); Jonathan Sterne, *Diminished Faculties: A Political Phenomenology of Impairment* (Duke University Press, 2021).

12. Mukherjee, *Emperor of All Maladies*, 4.

13. Stacey, *Teratologies*, 62.

14. Hannah Landecker, *Culturing Life: How Cells Became Technologies* (Harvard University Press, 2007), 128, 141.

15. Alexis Carrel, "Essential Characteristics of a Malignant Cell," *JAMA* 84, no. 3 (1925): 157–58. See also Brown, "Being Cellular."

16. Alexis Carrel, "Physiological Time," *Science*, n.s., 74, no. 1929 (1931): 621.

17. Landecker, *Culturing Life*, 90–91.

18. Skloot, *Immortal Life of Henrietta Lacks*, 61.

19. Fred Hapgood, "Tinytech," *Omni* 9, no. 6 (1986): 56, 60.

20. K. Eric Drexler, *Engines of Creation 2.0: The Coming Era of Nanotechnology*, 20th anniversary ed., updated and expanded (WOWIO, 2006), 10, https://fennetic.net/irc/EnginesofCreation2_8803267.pdf.

21. Skloot, *Immortal Life of Henrietta Lacks*, 40, 137.

22. Michael Rogers, "The Double-Edged Helix," *Rolling Stone*, March 25, 1976, 5.

23. Skloot, *Immortal Life of Henrietta Lacks*, 156, 153.

24. Skloot, *Immortal Life of Henrietta Lacks*, 152–53.

25. Landecker, *Culturing Life*, 169, 171.

26. Jennifer L. Morgan, *Laboring Women: Reproduction and Gender in New World Slavery* (University of Pennsylvania Press, 2004), 36.

27. Morgan, *Laboring Women*, 14.

28. It should also be noted that through the work of Henrietta Lacks's

family, particularly her children, and of her biographers like Rebecca Skloot, the story of Henrietta Lacks has become an important narrative within the discourses surrounding science and technology studies and the history of medicine to show how race and gender impact the life sciences. It is also an important case study for ongoing consideration of bodily autonomy and ownership, as we shall soon see.

29. Calvin L. Warren, *Ontological Terror: Blackness, Nihilism, and Emancipation* (Duke University Press, 2018), 6, 27.

30. Hortense J. Spillers, "Mama's Baby, Papa's Maybe: An American Grammar Book," in *Black, White, and in Color: Essays on American Literature and Culture* (University of Chicago Press, 2003), 203.

31. Rebecca Skloot points out that HeLa products have sold for anywhere in between $100 and $10,000 per vial and notes that "there's no way to quantify the professional gain many scientists have achieved with the help of HeLa" (*Immortal Life of Henrietta Lacks*, 194).

32. Alys Eve Weinbaum, *The Afterlife of Reproductive Slavery: Biocapitalism and Black Feminism's Philosophy of History* (Duke University Press, 2019), 7.

33. Saidiya Hartman, *Lose Your Mother: A Journey Along the Atlantic Slave Route* (Farrar, Straus and Giroux, 2008), 6.

34. Landecker, *Culturing Life*, 178.

35. Slavoj Žižek, *The Parallax View* (MIT Press, 2006), 62, 63.

36. David J. Skal, *The Monster Show: A Cultural History of Horror* (Faber and Faber, 1993), 229.

37. Kim Newman, "*The Blob*: 'It Creeps and Leaps,'" *Current*, March 13, 2013, https://www.criterion.com/current/posts/2691-the-blob-it-creeps-and-leaps.

38. Kim Newman suggests that the Blob's color has to do with the blood of its victims, and the film's producer, Jack Harris, has claimed that they added more red to the silicone gel after each successive victim. See the trivia page for *The Blob* (1958) on *IMDb*, https://www.imdb.com/title/tt0051418/trivia/?ref_=tt_dyk_trv, accessed November 9, 2024.

39. Newman, "*The Blob*."

40. Robin Wood, "The American Nightmare: Horror in the 70s," in *Hollywood from Vietnam to Reagan . . . and Beyond* (Columbia University Press, 1986), 72.

41. Adam Bernstein, "Irvin 'Shorty' Yeaworth," *Washington Post*, July 28, 2004, https://www.washingtonpost.com/archive/local/2004/07/28/irvin-shorty-yeaworth/7b87cace-2120-438c-86fb-c2a75fb90769/.

42. Jeff Sharlet, *The Family: The Secret Fundamentalism at the Heart of American Power* (HarperPerennial, 2008), 182. Italics in original.

43. Sharlet points out that while the explicit US foreign policy was containment, this resulted in "dozens of 'regional' conflicts strategized in Moscow and Washington, 'civil wars,' fought with the empires' weapons, that killed millions" (*The Family*, 182).

44. Sharlet, *The Family*, 186. See also Ronald Reagan, "Farewell Address to the Nation," Ronald Reagan Presidential Foundation and Institute, January 11, 1989, https://www.reaganfoundation.org/media/128652/farewell.pdf.

45. Spillers, "Mama's Baby, Papa's Maybe," 206. Italics in original.

46. Spillers, "Mama's Baby, Papa's Maybe," 206, 207.

47. Roland Barthes, *Elements of Semiology*, trans. Annette Lavers and Colin Smith (Hill and Wang, 1977), 77. Italics in original. Note that Barthes is quoting Ferdinand de Saussure from the *Course in General Linguistics*.

48. Giorgio Agamben, *Means Without End: Notes on Politics*, trans. Vincenzo Binetti and Cesare Casarino (University of Minnesota Press, 2000), 3.

49. Agamben, *Means Without End*, 4. While the phrase "bare life" has become most famous, "naked life" is the more direct translation from *la vita nuda* in Agamben's native Italian.

50. Here, Agamben is essentially following the work of Foucault, about whom Agamben says explicitly, "Foucault's thesis—according to which 'what is at stake today is life' and hence politics has become biopolitics—is, in this sense, substantially correct" (*Means Without End*, 7).

51. Agamben, *Means Without End*, 4.

52. I owe this insight to Adam Kotsko, "Bare Life vs. Naked Life," *An und für sich*, February 16, 2015, https://itself.blog/2015/02/16/bare-life-vs-naked-life/.

53. Giorgio Agamben, *Homo Sacer: Sovereign Power and Bare Life*, trans. Daniel Heller-Roazen (Stanford University Press, 1998), 139–40.

54. Alexander G. Weheliye, *Habeas Viscus: Racializing Assemblages, Biopolitics, and Black Feminist Theories of the Human* (Duke University Press, 2014), 35.

55. Spillers, "Mama's Baby, Papa's Maybe," 203.

56. This passage also echoes the insight about Blackness functioning as a technology that was discussed in chapter 1.

57. Spillers, "Mama's Baby, Papa's Maybe," 203.

58. David Harvey, *Marx, Capital, and the Madness of Economic Reason* (Oxford University Press, 2018), 4.

59. Louis Althusser, "Ideology and Ideological State Apparatuses" in *"Lenin and Philosophy" and Other Essays*, trans. Ben Brewster (Monthly Review Press, 1971), 85.

60. Ned Sublette and Constance Sublette, *The American Slave Coast: A History of the Slave-Breeding Industry* (Lawrence Hill Books, 2016), xiii, 11.

61. See Michel Foucault, *The History of Sexuality, Volume 1: An Introduction*, trans. Robert Hurley (Pantheon Books, 1978); and Kaushik Sunder Rajan, *Biocapital: The Constitution of Postgenomic Life* (Duke University Press, 2006).

62. Weinbaum, *Afterlife of Reproductive Slavery*, 3.

63. Melinda Cooper, *Life as Surplus: Biotechnology and Capitalism in the Neoliberal Era* (University of Washington Press, 2008), 16.

64. Cooper, *Life as Surplus*, 17. It is still remarkable how often this argument is still made to this day.

65. Cooper, *Life as Surplus*, 20.

66. Cooper, *Life as Surplus*, 20.

67. Cooper, *Life as Surplus*, 125.

4. Putting the Dead to Work

1. Of course, Walter Benjamin predicted this relation when he suggested that one of the new aims of the work of art in the age of technological re-

producibility was to bring the work closer to the masses and, thus, shift the value of art from the sublime and existential "aura" toward the values contained within capitalism via the dialectic of scarcity and accumulation. See Walter Benjamin, "The Work of Art in the Age of Its Technological Reproducibility: Third Version," in *Selected Writings: Volume 4, 1938–1940*, ed. Michael W. Jennings, trans. Harry Zohn and Edmund Jephcott (Harvard University Press, 2006).

2. "Dalí Lives (via Artificial Intelligence)," Salvador Dalí Museum, accessed June 11, 2022, https://thedali.org/exhibit/dali-lives/. This claim is especially ironic given that Dalí, following a rigorous surrealist method, did not claim to understand his own work, saying, "The fact that I myself, at the moment of painting, do not understand my own pictures, does not mean that these pictures have no meaning; on the contrary, their meaning is so profound, complex, coherent and involuntary that it escapes the most simple analysis of logical intuition." See Salvador Dalí, *The Conquest of the Irrational*, trans. David Gascoyne (Julian Levy, 1935), 12.

3. "We Are GS&P," Goodby Silverstein & Partners, accessed June 14, 2022, http://goodbysilverstein.com/about/we-are-gsandp-3.

4. Shoshana Zuboff, *The Age of Surveillance Capitalism: The Fight for a Human Future at the New Frontier of Power* (PublicAffairs, 2019). See also Jeffrey Sconce, *The Technical Delusion: Electronics, Power, Insanity* (Duke University Press, 2019). Similar systems of communication, management, and control have alternately been referred to under the banners of biopolitics, financialization, and neoliberalism. While the differences between these ideas will become relevant later in the chapter, for now, it is simply worth noting the family resemblances between this set of twenty-first-century political economies.

5. "Dalí Lives (via Artificial Intelligence)," Salvador Dalí Museum, accessed June 11, 2022, https://thedali.org/exhibit/dali-lives/.

6. Salvador Dalí, *The Conquest of the Irrational*, trans. David Gascoyne (Julian Levy, 1935), 13.

7. Catherine Shoard, "Peter Cushing Is Dead. *Rogue One*'s Resurrection Is a Digital Indignity," *Guardian*, December 21, 2016, https://www.theguardian.com/commentisfree/2016/dec/21/peter-cushing-rogue-one-resurrection-cgi.

8. "See How Carrie Fisher Was Digitally Brought Back for *The Rise of Skywalker* After Her Death," *People*, February 5, 2020, https://people.com/movies/see-how-carrie-fisher-was-digitally-brought-back-for-the-rise-of-skywalker-after-her-death/.

9. See the program's website for a full description of the project at "Dimensions in Testimony," USC Shoah Foundation, accessed September 27, 2022, https://sfi.usc.edu/dit.

10. "Interactive Holograms: Survivor Stories Experience," Illinois Holocaust Museum and Education Center, accessed September 27, 2022, https://www.ilholocaustmuseum.org/exhibitions/survivor-stories-experience/.

11. 60 Minutes, "From the 60 Minutes Archive: Letting Future Generations Speak With Holocaust Survivors," posted January 27, 2021, YouTube video, 25:59, https://youtu.be/D9tZnC4NGNg.

12. Neta Alexander, "Obsolescence, Forgotten: 'Survivor Holograms,'

Virtual Reality, and the Future of Holocaust Commemoration," *Cinergie* 10, no. 19 (2021): 58.

13. We have yet to discover the full temporal limitations of digital technology, such as the rates at which hard drives and solid-state drives deteriorate until they are no longer functional, or it is no longer possible to retrieve information stored inside them. Currently, the biggest obstacle to the longevity of digital storage formats is the built-in obsolescence designed by major tech manufacturers, who update formats as well as hard- and software interfaces without guaranteeing backwards compatibility.

14. Karl Marx, *Capital: A Critique of Political Economy, Volume 1,* trans. Paul Reitter (Princeton University Press, 2024), 205.

15. Marx, *Capital,* 158–59, 391.

16. Karl Marx, *Grundrisse,* trans. Martin Nicolaus (Penguin, 1973), 692.

17. Marx, *Grundrisse,* 693.

18. Marx, *Grundrisse,* 693.

19. Maurizio Lazzarato, "Immaterial Labor," in *Radical Thought in Italy: A Potential Politics,* ed. Paolo Virno and Michael Hardt, trans. Paul Colilli and Ed Emory (University of Minnesota Press, 1996), 133.

20. See Leopoldina Fortunati, *The Arcane of Reproduction Housework, Prostitution, Labor and Capital,* trans. Hilary Creek (Autonomedia, 1995); Kathi Weeks, *The Trouble with Work: Feminism, Marxism, Antiwork Politics, and Postwork Imaginaries* (Duke University Press, 2011); Alys Eve Weinbaum, *The Afterlife of Reproductive Slavery: Biocapitalism and Black Feminism's Philosophy of History* (Duke University Press, 2019); and Silvia Federici, *Caliban and the Witch: Women, the Body and Primitive Accumulation* (Autonomedia, 2004), to name only a selection of texts in this feminist tradition that have most immediately contributed to my thinking on this matter.

21. Leopoldina Fortunati, "Immaterial Labor and Its Mechanization," *Ephemera: Theory and Politics in Organization* 7, no. 1 (2007): 139–40.

22. Jennifer Rhee, *The Robotic Imaginary: The Human and the Price of Dehumanized Labor* (University of Minnesota Press, 2018), 46.

23. Lazzarato, "Immaterial Labor," 143.

24. Michel Foucault, *The Birth of Biopolitics: Lectures at the Collège de France, 1978–79,* trans. Graham Burchell (Palgrave Macmillan, 2008), 226.

25. Wendy Brown, *Undoing the Demos: Neoliberalism's Stealth Revolution* (Zone Books, 2015), 80.

26. Maurizio Lazzarato, *Signs and Machines: Capitalism and the Production of Subjectivity,* trans. Joshua David Jordan (Los Angeles: Semiotext(e), 2014), 51. Italics in original.

27. Pierre Dardot and Christian Laval, *The New Way of the World: On Neoliberal Society,* trans. Gregory Elliott (Verso, 2013), 111. Italics in original.

28. Shoshana Zuboff, *The Age of Surveillance Capitalism: The Fight for a Human Future at the New Frontier of Power* (PublicAffairs, 2019), 66, 8.

29. Zuboff uses Google as her prime example, arguing that "behavioral data, whose value had previously been 'used up' on improving the quality of Search for users, now became the pivotal—and exclusive to Google—raw material for the construction of a dynamic online advertising marketplace.

Google would now secure more behavioral data than it needed to serve its users. That surplus, a behavioral surplus, was the game-changing, zero-cost asset that was diverted from service improvement towards a genuinely and highly lucrative market exchange" (*Age of Surveillance Capitalism*, 81).

30. Zuboff, *Age of Surveillance Capitalism*, 8. Italics in original.

31. Zuboff, *Age of Surveillance Capitalism*, 94. Italics in original.

32. David J. Chalmers, *The Conscious Mind: In Search of a Fundamental Theory* (Oxford University Press, 1996), 95. Note that Chalmers borrows the general idea of a philosophical zombie from a paper by Robert Kirk and Roger Squires, "Zombies v. Materialists," *Proceedings of the Aristotelian Society, Supplementary Volumes* 48 (1974): 135–63.

33. Wendy Hui Kyong Chun, *Programmed Visions: Software and Memory* (MIT Press, 2011), 133. See chapter 2 for another, complementary reading of this passage.

34. Chun, *Programmed Visions*, 133.

35. Matteo Pasquinelli, "Three Thousand Years of Algorithmic Rituals: The Emergence of AI from the Computation of Space," *e-flux*, no. 101 (2019): https://www.e-flux.com/journal/101/273221/three-thousand-years-of-algorithmic-rituals-the-emergence-of-ai-from-the-computation-of-space/.

36. *Oxford English Dictionary*, "information," accessed September 6, 2022, https://www.oed.com/dictionary/information_n.

37. Michael Proffitt, "Information," *Oxford English Dictionary* (blog), August 16, 2012, https://public.oed.com/blog/word-stories-information/.

38. *Merriam-Webster Dictionary*, "information," accessed December 31, 2025, https://www.merriam-webster.com/dictionary/information.

39. Proffitt, "Information."

40. Daniel Chandler, *Semiotics: The Basics* (Routledge, 2002), 37.

41. Quoted in Chandler, *Semiotics*, 42.

42. André Bazin, "The Ontology of the Photographic Image," trans. Hugh Gray, *Film Quarterly* 13, no. 4 (1960): 8.

43. Bazin, "Ontology," 4.

44. Philip Rosen, *Change Mummified: Cinema, Historicity, Theory* (University of Minnesota Press, 2001), 31.

45. Bazin, "Ontology," 14.

46. Mary Ann Doane, "Indexicality: Trace and Sign: Introduction," *differences: A Journal of Feminist Cultural Studies* 18, no. 1 (2007): 1–2.

47. *Collected Papers of Charles Sanders Peirce*, vol. 4 (Harvard University Press, 1933), 359.

48. Roland Barthes, *Camera Lucida: Reflections on Photography*, trans. Richard Howard (Hill and Wang, 1981), 3, 5–6.

49. Barthes, *Camera Lucida*, 10–11.

50. Chandler, *Semiotics*, 42.

51. Braxton Soderman, "The Index and the Algorithm," *differences: A Journal of Feminist Cultural Studies* 18, no. 1 (2007): 159, 161.

52. Leif Weatherby and Brian Justie, "Indexical AI," *Critical Inquiry* 48, no. 2 (2022): 381.

53. *Collected Papers of Charles Sanders Peirce*, vol. 4, 442.

54. Charu Aggarwal, *Neural Networks and Deep Learning: A Textbook* (Springer, 2018), xvii–xviii.

55. Weatherby and Justie, "Indexical AI," 389–90.

56. Pasquinelli, "Three Thousand Years of Algorithmic Rituals."

57. Jean-Luc Chabert, "Introduction," in *A History of Algorithms: From the Pebble to the Microchip*, ed. Jean-Luc Chabert (Springer, 1999), 1. Quoted in Pasquinelli, "Three Thousand Years of Algorithmic Rituals."

58. Pasquinelli, "Three Thousand Years of Algorithmic Rituals."

59. "Replika," Replika, accessed October 1, 2022, https://replika.com/.

60. Quartz, "The Story of Replika, the AI App That Becomes You," posted July 21, 2017, YouTube video, 10:36, https://youtu.be/yQGqMVuAk04.

61. "Privacy Policy," Replika, accessed October 1, 2022, https://replika.com/legal/privacy.

62. It is worth noting that Replika has options to present as any gender identity, including nonbinary, and the app features extensive customization tools that you can use to make the AI appear however you want. Still, Replika's default appearance and voice—the app's premium subscription allows you to make voice calls with Replika—is coded as female, and this is very much in line with most digital assistants like Alexa, Google, Cortana, and others.

63. Quartz, "Story of Replika."

64. *Black Mirror*, season 2, episode 1, "Be Right Back," directed by Owen Harris, aired February 11, 2013, Channel 4 / Netflix.

65. Richard Sprenger, "Back from the Dead: Could AI End Grief?," *Guardian*, posted September 24, 2024, YouTube video, 12:38, https://youtu.be/5udOx8-QxtE?. See also the You, Only Virtual website at https://www.myyov.com/.

66. For example, see Lisa Nakamura, *Cybertypes: Race, Ethnicity, and Identity on the Internet* (Routledge, 2002).

67. Rhee, *Robotic Imaginary*, 55, 48.

68. Neda Atanasoski and Kalindi Vora, *Surrogate Humanity: Race, Robots, and the Politics of Technological Futures* (Duke University Press, 2019), 14.

69. Lisa Lowe, *The Intimacies of Four Continents* (Duke University Press, 2015), 150.

70. Tero Karppi, "Death Proof: On the Biopolitics and Noopolitics of Memorializing Dead Facebook Users," *Culture Machine* 14 (2013): 4.

71. Rohit Prasad, "Amazon re:MARS 2022—Day 2—Keynote," posted June 23, 2022, YouTube video, 1:54:22, https://youtu.be/22cb24-sGhg.

72. Alex Hern, "Amazon's Alexa Could Turn Dead Loved Ones' Voices into Digital Assistant," *Guardian*, June 23, 2022, https://www.theguardian.com/technology/2022/jun/23/amazon-alexa-could-turn-dead-loved-ones-digital-assistant.

73. Wikipedia, "GPT-3," accessed December 31, 2025, https://en.wikipedia.org/wiki/GPT-3; Jason Fagone, "He Couldn't Get Over His Fiancée's Death. So He Brought Her Back as an A.I. Chatbot," *San Francisco Chronicle*, July 23, 2021, https://www.sfchronicle.com/projects/2021/jessica-simulation-artificial-intelligence/.

74. Zora Neale Hurston, *Tell My Horse: Voodoo and Life in Haiti and Jamaica* (HarperPerennial, 1938), 181.

Conclusion

1. Joris Toonders, "Data Is the New Oil of the Digital Economy," *Wired*, July 23, 2014, archived September 24, 2014, at https://web.archive.org/web/20140924002823/http://www.wired.com/2014/07/data-new-oil-digital-economy/.

2. "Fuel of the Future: The Data Economy," *Economist*, May 6, 2017, https://www.economist.com/briefing/2017/05/06/data-is-giving-rise-to-a-new-economy.

3. Lisa Gitelman, ed., *"Raw Data" Is an Oxymoron* (MIT Press, 2013).

4. Daniel Rosenberg, "Data Before the Fact," in Gitelman, *"Raw Data" Is an Oxymoron*, 18.

5. The notion that data is more environmentally friendly is a fallacy and elides the fact that data mining, refining, and usage to train machine learning systems and AI has tremendous energy costs. This is in addition to the cooling required for these systems, which use large quantities of water, and the extraction and use of cobalt, lithium, and rare earth minerals. Taken together, AI is hardly as environmentally friendly as the industry so often touts. See Kate Crawford, *The Atlas of AI: Power, Politics, and the Planetary Costs of Artificial Intelligence* (Yale University Press, 2021), for just one of several recent accounts.

6. Heather Davis, *Plastic Matter* (Duke University Press, 2022), 72.

7. For this insight, I am indebted to conversations and correspondence with my research assistant Emmanuel Auerbach.

8. Reza Negarestani, *Cyclonopedia: Complicity with Anonymous Materials* (re.press, 2008), 27.

9. Zakiyyah Iman Jackson, "Losing Manhood: Animality and Plasticity in the (Neo)Slave Narrative," *Qui Parle: Critical Humanities and Social Sciences* 25, no. 1–2 (2016): 117.

10. Jackson, "Losing Manhood," 117. Italics in original.

11. See Catherine Malabou, *Plasticity at the Dusk of Writing: Dialectic, Destruction, Deconstruction*, trans. Carolyn Shread (Columbia University Press, 2010).

12. Jackson, "Losing Manhood," 119, 127. Italics in original.

13. Another phrase that might be associated with this ideology is "can't stop, won't stop," which is discussed in the introduction to this book.

14. Robert Kirkman, *The Walking Dead, Volume 1: Days Gone By* (Image Comics, 2007), 3.

15. Kirkman, *Walking Dead*, 4.

16. Jill Pantozzi, "AMC CEO Thinks *The Walking Dead* Is So Awesome It Will Go On Forever," *Mary Sue*, May 23, 2013, https://www.themarysue.com/walking-dead-future/.

17. Paul Tassi, "AMC Renewals Show Why 'The Walking Dead' Will Never Get Cancelled," *Forbes*, May 14, 2017, https://www.forbes.com/sites/

insertcoin/2017/05/14/amc-renewals-show-why-the-walking-dead-will-never-get-cancelled/#2ff28b736e76.

18. Lucas Shaw, "Inside AMC Networks' Plan to Make 'Walking Dead' Live Forever," *Bloomberg*, September 19, 2018, https://www.bloomberg.com/news/articles/2018-09-19/inside-amc-networks-plan-to-make-walking-dead-live-forever.

19. See chapter 1.

20. David Konow, "Romero's Rules: The Origins of the Slow Zombie," Tested, July 31, 2013, archived August 3, 2013, at https://web.archive.org/web/20130803153315/https://www.tested.com/art/movies/456962-romeros-rules-origins-slow-zombie/.

21. Andrew McMurry, "The Slow Apocalypse: A Gradualistic Theory of the World's Demise," *Postmodern Culture* 6, no. 3 (1996): 1.

22. Mary Ann Doane, "Information, Crisis, Catastrophe," in *New Media, Old Media: A History and Theory Reader*, ed. Wendy Hui Kyong Chun and Thomas Keenan (Routledge, 2006), 251.

23. Doane, "Information," 255.

24. Doane, "Information," 255.

25. Doane, "Information," 257.

26. Doane, "Information," 257.

27. Fredric Jameson, "Future City," *New Left Review* 21 (2003): https://newleftreview.org/II/21/fredric-jameson-future-city. It should be noted that Jameson goes on to say, "We can now revise that and witness the attempt to imagine capitalism by way of imagining the end of the world."

28. Jean Baudrillard, "The Anorexic Ruins," in *Looking Back on the End of the World*, ed. Dietmar Kamper and Christoph Wulf, trans. David Antal (Semiotext(e), 1989), 29.

29. Baudrillard, "Anorexic Ruins," 29.

30. Gil Scott-Heron, "The Revolution Will Not Be Televised," track 1 on *Pieces of a Man* (Flying Dutchman, 1971).

31. Doane, "Information," 255.

32. Walter Benjamin, "Central Park," in *New German Critique*, no. 34 (1985): 50.

Index

David Bering-Porter is associate professor of culture and media at the Eugene Lang College of Liberal Arts at The New School.

Printed and bound by CPI Group (UK) Ltd, Croydon, CR0 4YY

15/10/2026

14983217-0006